Cary F. Goulson is a member of the Faculty of Education at the University of Victoria.

This is a comprehensive primary reference to a rich and often neglected storehouse of information on Canada's educational background.

As the boundary between full-fledged royal commissions and other official governmental inquiries is not always clear - and many legislative committee inquiries and special department of education investigations have been as significant in educational development as regular commissions - Goulson has included all major ministerial-level governmental inquiries in Canadian education between 1787 and 1978.

More than 300 inquiries are included, among them general, special interest, judicial, legislative, parliamentary, and other governmental committees. The information provided for each includes the type of commission or committee, its size, chairman, purpose, dates of appointment and reporting, and primary source references, as well as a selection of its major conclusions and/or recommendations.

Official governmental records and documents including the Reports themselves, Legislative Journals, House Debates and Hansard, Sessional Papers, Statutes, and Department of Education records were used as the resource base.

This volume will be of specific interest to teachers and students of the history of education, and most educators, no matter what their fields, will find it useful.

A Source Book of
Royal Commissions
and Other Major
Governmental Inquiries
in Canadian Education
1787-1978

CARY F. GOULSON

University of Toronto Press
Toronto Buffalo London

© University of Toronto Press   1981
Toronto   Buffalo   London
Printed in Canada
ISBN 0-8020-2408-4

Goulson, Carlyn Floyd.
  A source book of Royal Commissions and other
  major governmental inquiries in Canadian education
  1787-1978

  Includes bibliographical references and index.
  ISBN 0-8020-2408-4
  1. Governmental investigations – Canada – History.
  2. Education – Canada – History. 3. Education and
  state – Canada – History. I. Title.
  LA411.G68   379.71   C81-094660-2

This book has been published with the help of a grant from
the Social Science Federation of Canada, using funds
provided by the Social Sciences and Humanities Research
Council of Canada.

To Jean

Contents

Preface

The present study began as an examination of the use of
royal commissions in Canadian education. However, as my
research progressed, I found that the boundary between
full-fledged royal commissions and other official governmental inquiries was not always clear. Moreover, many of
the more important legislative committee inquiries and
special department of education investigations have played
as significant a role in educational development as have
the regular commissions. Therefore, my topic was broadened
to include other major (that is, ministerial level)
governmental inquiries in Canadian education. A very few
non-governmental inquiries have been added to the
'special committee' category because of their particular
relevance.

   I have included an introductory chapter, but the heart
of the publication is the sequence of 367 inquiries.
These are presented chronologically by province, beginning
on the eastern seaboard as did Canada's story.

   The type of 'commission' or 'committee' is shown for
each inquiry, and also the dates of appointing and reporting, the size of the commission/committee, the chairman
(and his or her position), the purpose, and the primary
reference sources. In addition major conclusions/recommen-
dations have been given. These of course represent
editorial choice, sometimes from very long formal listings.
I have tried always to include those items that have
seemed of major educational importance up through the
years, and I have endeavoured to reflect all findings as
accurately as possible. In every case I have conformed
closely to the wording of the original.

   For the most part my sources have been official government records and documents - the Reports themselves,

Legislative Journals, House Debates and Hansard, Sessional
Papers, Statutes, Department of Education records. Contem-
porary newspapers have also proven very useful. I have
been in correspondence with each province's Department of
Education and each Attorney General's Department, and I
have visited the Legislative Libraries in all eleven
capital cities. For the invaluable assistance everywhere
rendered, I am most grateful.

Cary F. Goulson

Victoria, British Columbia
December, 1980

Introduction

Inquiries are well-fitted for overloading every question with ten or fifteen times the quantity of matter necessary for its consideration. (W. E. Gladstone)

Inquiries are pregnant with prudent and sagacious suggestions for the improvement of the administration of affairs. (B. Disraeli) [1]

The use of official fact-finding commissions goes back a long way in English governmental history. Some authorities cite the Domesday survey as the first royal commission, having a similar intent and function but differing in form from those of modern times. Others, perhaps more precisely, name the Commission on Enclosures in 1517 as the first real royal commission.

In the days of crown control, the king's commissioners were often given blanket authority with powers that were at once investigative, judicial, and administrative. Under the Tudors and the early Stuarts especially, such practices led to notorious abuses, and the seventeenth century was one long constitutional struggle against such extraordinary powers and courts. Sir Edward Coke, the outstanding jurist of those centuries, pronounced strongly against the legality of government by commission. An ascendant Parliament strengthened by such judgments, stifled commission procedures throughout the eighteenth century. Not until well into the nineteenth century when the misery and corruption of industrial England made it absolutely necessary once again to make use of governmental investigative techniques did the royal commission overcome its stigma of disrepute and gain recognition as a legitimate function of modern democratic government.

Harried governments discovered that 'royal' commissions had many inherent advantages not possessed by parliamentary committees. Select committees were always sorely pressed for time. Their background investigation, their travel, their study of evidence, their report writing, all of these had to be rushed to meet sessional deadlines. The appointees were often inexpert in the area of investigation and were further hampered by party representation and loyalties. Furthermore, because they were a part of government, it was difficult to escape completely the suspicion of prejudice and puppetry.

By comparison, royal commissions had the prestige of monarchical appointment neatly coupled with the efficacy of government choice from nonpartisan ranks. Outstanding scholars, recognized experts, men above reproach could be named, and often such were found who, for altruistic rewards alone, were willing to serve until the job was done.[2] Their conscientious and unhurried reports, often the result of extensive travel, provided members of parliament and the public with documented facts and informed opinions so badly needed in the crusade against social wrong.

Paving the way for the humanitarian reform acts of the 1800s were the ever-multiplying commissions of inquiry. Professor Redlich in his study of the British House of Commons stated in 1908, 'Almost all the great reforms of the nineteenth century in internal administration, taxation, education, labour protection and other social questions, have been based on the full investigations made by royal commissions, often continued over a space of many years, and on their reports which, with the evidence collected, are laid before Parliament.'[3]

This latter-day revival of commissionism was not without opposition. Critics viewed with alarm the encroachment of commissioners into every cranny of everyday life. 'They would, in fact, put the whole earth in commission, and delivery over the whole human race saved from the flood....' Thus wrote Toulmin Smith, Barrister-at-Law in 1849.[4] Smith saw the spreading use of government by commission as an illegal device to dodge responsibility, to parcel out patronage and to whitewash Whigs.

Probably the most devestating and certainly the most entertaining criticism of royal commissions came from the pages of *Punch*. Sir Alan P. Herbert's poem 'Pageant

of Parliament' appeared in 1934 and read in part as
follows:

> *The necessity for action was clear to everyone,*
> *But the view was very general that nothing could*
> *be done,*
> *And the Government courageously decided that the*
> *Crown*
> *Should appoint a score of gentlemen to track the*
> *trouble down --*
> <u>*Which always takes a long, long time.*</u>
>
> *I am the Royal Commission on Kissing,*
> *Appointed by Gladstone in '74;*
> *The rest of my colleagues are buried or missing;*
> *Our Minutes were lost in the last Great War.*
> *But still I'm a Royal Commission,*
> *My task I intend to see through*
> *Though I know, as an old politician,*
> *Not much will be done if I do.*[5]

In spite of good natured or venomous barbs such as
these the golden age of British royal commissions
flourished well into the twentieth century. And when the
practice seemed somewhat on the wane in the Mother Country
the British Dominions were making extravagant use of this
investigative technique. Royal commissions of inquiry
were passed on to the British colonies and later dominions
as part of their constitutional heritage. In the early
years Britain appointed colonial commissions autocratically
as befitted a worthy imperialistic power, but after the
evolution of self-governing colonies and dominions, no
British commission was sent out except by consent or
invitation.

Interestingly, though the commission technique was
enthusiastically adopted by Canada, there appeared
distinctive differences in formation and use. The
federal government and each of the provinces passed a
Public Inquiries Act in some form, giving much more
sweeping powers to Canadian commissioners than had their
British counterparts.[6] The right to demand papers, to
summon witnesses, to hear evidence under oath with the
potential threat of legal penalties, all these have become
automatic in Canada. Britain, perhaps because of a
centuries-old conscience nagged by memories of autocratic

misuse, gives such powers only by special statute for
exceptional circumstances.

There are other differences as well. Canada has tended
to appoint fewer persons to each commission. Three has
been a common number, and one also has been very popular;
the latter, of course, having the built-in advantage of
no minority report. Smaller commissions may be a studied
attempt to get closer agreement (leaving the widely diverse
views to the witness chair), or it may be the realization
that group representation in Canada would become a hopeless
process, or it may be that there is a dearth of available
experts, or it might simply be that Canadian commissioners
expect recompense for their services. In the words of
J. E. Hodgetts, '...The British tradition of unpaid
commissioners and a chairman who is prepared to settle for
the Queen's gift of a silver inkstand has obviously not
caught on in Canada.'[7]

The purposes for which commissions are appointed are
many and varied. A royal commission may be formed to pave
the way for legislative action already decided upon by the
government. This sets the public mind into positive,
sympathetic motion. Or the government may be considering
an important line of action but it wishes to test and
gauge public opinion. A royal commission here acts as a
sort of trial balloon, an indication as to whether policy
in this direction would flush out unknown and perhaps
overwhelming opposition. Or a commission of inquiry may
be just *that* -- a painstaking investigation to get a
wealth of facts and knowledge which might lead to eventual
solution of some important public problem.

The afore-mentioned purposes are all examples of the
party in power having a relatively free choice as to
whether or not to institute a royal commission. Often,
however, the government is under pressure by the opposition, by the press, by the public, or by influential
factions to take investigative action. Not infrequently
the hint of maladministration or scandal is the catalyst.
In such instances the role of a commission of inquiry
might be to clear the name of an individual or department
-- or to 'whitewash', depending upon the viewpoint. The
government of course might move early to forestall
potential criticism or it might move late to stall hostile
developments purposely and to gain time, the great healer
of political maladies.

Education, because of the division of powers in 1867, is a provincial right, and so nearly all of the post-confederation governmental inquiries into education have emanated from provincial capitals. The 1910 Royal Commission on Industrial Training and Technical Education is an exception. In addition there have been federal commissions such as the Royal Commission on National Development in the Arts, Letters and Sciences (1949-1951) and the Royal Commission on Bilingualism and Biculturalism (1963-1970) that have important educational overtones.

For this study, 367 major inquiries into Canadian education have been considered. These have included investigations into education generally, into certain aspects of education in particular, and into other matters that were of significance to education in some way. Nearly all have been governmental investigations of some form or another, but a very few special inquiries sponsored from without government ranks have been noted. Even these have entailed indirect governmental involvement, whether through initial instigation, or interest and encouragement, or obvious repercussions.

Of the 367 inquiries, 127 can be considered 'royal commissions' since they were issued in the name of the Crown under a Great Seal and carried with them powers authorized by 'public inquiries' acts or by special acts. This group can be further divided into royal commissions having general educational significance, royal commissions in other areas but having special educational significance, and royal commissions of a judicial nature that were appointed to investigate a person or incident. These three divisions have been designated 'R1', 'R2', and 'R3', respectively, for the 'Bibliography-Index' in the Appendix and for the tabulation which follows. The decision as between R1 and R3 (that is, general and judicial) was not always clearcut, and the writer had to use editorial discretion. For instance, the 1861 Royal Commission on Affairs and Financial Conditions of Toronto University and University College; the 1893 Commission of Inquiry into Charges Relating to the Bathurst Schools and Other Schools in Gloucester County; and the 1924 Commission of Inquiry into the Extension of the Powers of the Board of Roman Catholic School Commissioners of Montreal, the Education of Jewish Children in Protestant Schools or in Others, and the Financial Situation of the Protestant Schools of Verdun, were included in the first broad grouping because it was felt that the findings and ramifications of commissions such as these were of wide interest rather than narrow. There were, then, 47 general royal commissions, 48 related commissions, and 32 judicial commissions.

The remaining 240 inquiries were also divided into three groups: legislative or parliamentary committees of various kinds (designated 'L'); departmental and other governmental committees ('D'); and special committees ('S'). In these divisions, 44 legislative committees were considered, 158 departmental committees, and 38 special committees. An index listing all 367 commissions and committees is provided in the Appendix, but a tabulation summary is presented at this point for clarification.

TABULATION OF INQUIRIES IN CANADIAN EDUCATION

	R1	R2	R3	L	D	S	TOTAL
Nfld.	3	6	1	1	3	2	16
N.S.	5	1	2	4	10	3	25
P.E.I.	4	–	2	8	1	2	17
N.B.	6	2	1	3	13	6	31
Que.	4	6	1	2	21	1	35
Ont.	7	9	14	8	38	3	79
Man.	6	2	2	3	9	4	26
Sask.	2	5	1	1	21	3	33
Alta.	4	3	2	4	15	3	31
B.C.	5	4	6	7	19	5	46
Canada	1	10	–	3	8	6	28
	47	48	32	44	158	38	367

Obviously all provinces (and the federal government as well) have made much use of fact finding techniques in the field of education. Outside of Ontario, which has been much the busiest, the inquiries are spread rather evenly among the other provinces.

Although legislative committees on education were much more widely used in pre-confederation days, it would be wrong to discount the importance of such in later periods. The 1934 Legislative Committee appointed to make a comprehensive survey and study of education in the rural districts of Alberta faced a formidable task (see Item 269). Ten years later, the 1944 Special Select Committee on Education in Manitoba undertook an inquiry as comprehensive as any royal commission -- and with 'powers of 'Commissioners' under Part V of the Manitoba Evidence Act' as well (Item 215). Ontario in 1962 appointed a Select Committee on Manpower Training, and two years later, a Select Committee on Youth. And there were many others.

The large group of 158 departmental and other governmental committees showed wide variance in manner of appointment. Some were very similar in power and scope to royal commissions, and indeed some were appointed under authority of a sub-section of a public inquiries act. However, if a Minister of Education (or other departmental minister) did the appointing rather than a Lieutenant Governor in Council, and if the resultant report was returned to the Minister, then it was adjudged a departmental committee or 'commission' rather than a royal commission. Examples of this type include the 1881 Ontario Commission of Inquiry 'to investigate certain charges against Dr. Samuel May of the Education Department', and the 1919 Manitoba Commission on Status and Salaries of Teachers.

Also within this broad category fell such significant inquiries as the Putman-Weir Survey of the School System in British Columbia in 1924, and the 1934 Commission on School Finance in the same province. Still another type of investigation was placed here -- that of the department official touring other provinces and other lands in search of new educational ideas. Ryerson's journeys in the mid 1800s and the technical education surveys of John Seath and Dr. Merchant in the early 1900s are examples. Not included at all in this study are the regular departmental reports representing ordinary departmental procedures. It should be noted that departmental committees have been very widely used as an investigative technique in recent years -- over one hundred of the 158 total dating from the mid 1960s.

Of particular interest are the 18 inquiries classified as 'special'. For some of these, international educators of high repute were brought in to view dispassionately the Canadian scene. In 1917, Harold W. Foght, Specialist on Rural School Practice from Washington, D.C., made a survey of education in the Province of Saskatchewan (Item 234). In 1933, C.A. Richardson, Inspector of His Majesty's schools in London, prepared a report on 'certain aspects of the educational system of Newfoundland' (Item 3). And in 1937, W.A.F. Hepburn, Director of Education from

Ayrshire, Scotland, headed the Quebec Protestant Education Survey Committee (Item 99).

In some instances philanthropic organizations have made their resources available. In 1921 (Nova Scotia) and again in 1923 (Manitoba), the Carnegie Foundation for the Advancement of Teaching sent personnel to assess higher education (see Items 20 and 210). The Ford Foundation rendered financial assistance to two 'commissions' investigating university affairs in the mid 1960s. These were the Duff-Berdahl Commission on university government and administration and the Bladen Commission on university finance (Items 352 and 353). There was also the Royal Institute of International Affairs which sponsored a Supervisory Committee on Newfoundland Studies from 1941 to 1946 (Item 5).

A very few non-governmental inquiries have been added to the 'special committee' category because of their particular relevance. Examples are the 1968 British Columbia Teachers' Federation Commission on Education (Item 317) and the 1975 Study of Northern People and Higher Education (Item 363).

Quite understandably the 32 judicial royal commissions were involved in investigations of a more personal and specific nature than were met with elsewhere in education. These inquiries resulted almost always from incidents and situations that deteriorated into sweeping accusations and wild charges played up usually by a grateful press. Since public officials or public institutions were involved, the Government eventually was forced to take action, and an objective commission of inquiry was an acceptable disinterested means. It is not surprising that by far the greatest number of these investigations were placed in the hands of legal experts -- usually a sole commissioner. Charges under consideration ranged from the obviously serious to the seemingly insignificant. Among them were depletion of funds, examination irregularities, mismanagement, excessively severe discipline, improper textbook contracts, mishandling of construction, and unacceptable art drawing books.

It is in the area of general royal commissions (R1) that particular attention should be paid, for it is here that the findings of widest interest and the recommendations of most lasting consequence are to be found. As can be seen in the previously presented tabulation, these 47 commissions have been spread fairly evenly across the

land. Saskatchewan shows only two, but the 1952-57 Royal
Commission on Agriculture and Rural Life in that province
included an important survey of education.

These 'general' commissions have tended to come in
waves. Depression lack-of-wherewithal was no doubt one
reason for the few commissions in the 'Thirties , because
there were most certainly educational woes in this period.
No such commission was appointed in World War I, and
during World War II only two were launched, and these in
the closing months of the struggle. Obviously the
nation's energy in these times of stress was being
directed to other fronts.

Through the years, twelve of the 47 commissions have
been directed to look at education generally. Twelve have
dealt with university affairs and higher education; six
with school taxes and educational finance;[8] three with
agricultural, technical and industrial education; two with
teachers' salaries; two with textbooks; and the remaining
nine with other miscellaneous matters.

The number of members appointed to these several
commissions shows wide divergence. Most popular have
been 3, 5, 1, and 7 in that order. Here is the tabulation
for the 47 noted.

Number of Commissioners	Number of Commissions	Number of Commissioners	Number of Commissions
1	5	8	2
2	1	9	2
3	14	10	1
4	1	12	1
5	9	21	1
6	3	22	1
7	5	25	1

Again, men of legal background have been popular choices
for chairman -- seventeen such being named. Eighteen
chairmen were from college or university life of some kind
(governors, administrators, deans, professors); four of
these being university presidents. Five of the chairmen
were department of education officials (three superintendents, a secretary of education, and a former deputy
minister). Also heading commissions were an industrialist,
an engineer, a newspaper editor, a minister of the church,
an assistant-deputy attorney general, and two senators.

Widely representative have been the remaining personnel. The Prairie Provinces in particular have appointed office-holders of influential citizen groups such as 'home and school', farm leagues, and women's organizations. Rarely have practising school teachers been made members. Illustrative of the breadth of background are the senator, past-president of the Federation of Home and School Associations, past-president of the Farm Women's Union, lawyer, department store manager, and university professor who made up the 1957 Alberta Royal Commission on Education.

As the writer read through the reports represented in this study he was impressed in general by the aspirations of the Commissioners, the eloquence of their presentations, and the intrinsic value of their findings. Here was a valuable source of reference material for the educational researcher, yet it lay largely unused. Report after report included historical summaries and statements of philosophies in clear, untechnical prose -- for these represented public commissions of inquiry. Tables of statistics, facts and figures, thoughtful suggestions, major recommendations were advanced. Taken in sequence they provide a thread of educational development in each province, and taken together they produce a comparative or composite picture, nationwide.

Trends and patterns are discernible in retrospect. From the first there has been conspicuous effort on the part of every province to lift up its own standards -- to look at the systems of education elsewhere and to endeavour not to be found too far wanting. Since the turn of the century, large district consolidation has been an ever recurring issue. In the early years of the 1900s, agricultural and technical education were stressed, and at mid-century, studies were suggesting ways and means of providing more diverse programmes to meet the age of automation and individual differences.

Through the years, teacher training, teacher supply, teachers' salaries have been high in problem priority. The raising of teaching standards and teacher status has been regarded as a hopeful solution. After World War II many general commissions favoured university degree programmes for all teachers, which meant an advance towards professional parity for elementary and secondary levels. More and more attention has been paid to higher education and to continuing education -- and in the 'Seventies , cultural fulfilment, minority group needs,

and declining enrolments have been recurring topics. Undoubtedly the one matter of greatest urgency in all periods
and at all levels has been educational finance. Equalization of assessment and equalization of opportunity has been
the cry -- a widespread desire, apparent in all the
provinces, to provide a maximum opportunity for all
children. And the costs have spiralled ever upwards.

Now, to assess in general, and in brief, the place of
royal commissions in the development of Canadian education!
Assignment of direct cause and effect can rarely be done
with certainty. Inferences, however, can be drawn, and
these show wide divergence in practice. There have been
major commissions shelved with little thanks. There have
been successive studies finding the same facts and
recommending the same remedies to the same province with
few apparent results. By contrast there have been many
instances of governments working with remarkable speed to
institute commission proposals. British Columbia put
into effect in a matter of months the main features of the
1945 Cameron Report, and the ink was hardly dry on the
Chant Report of 1960, before a full scale educational
overhaul was begun by the same province.

Subsequent implementation of ideas is not the only
contribution of commissions, however. Whether there is
immediate action, later action, or no action, the
accumulation of information and the directing of public
attention are of very real value. Conscientious scrutiny
and objective reassessment are good things to do on
occasion. 'Education is everybody's business' is an over-
worked maxim which nonetheless points up an inescapable
truth. Royal commissions and formal governmental inquiries
permit individuals and groups to have their say. A
commission is an excuse and a reason for channelling
extraordinary attention to education.

Reference Notes

[1] Cited in Hugh McDowall Clodie and J. William Robinson.
*Royal Commissions of Inquiry: The Significance of
Investigations in British Politics.* Palo Alto,
Stanford University Press, 1937, p. 80.

[2] The letter of commission setting up the 1919 Royal
Commission on Oxford and Cambridge Universities is a

good example of the calibre of person appointed in Britain. See Appendix, p. 377.

[3] Josef Redlich. *The Procedure of the House of Commons: A Study of Its History and Present Form.* (Translated from German by A. Ernest Steinthal) London, Archibald Constable, 1908, vol. II, p. 193.

[4] J. Toulmin Smith. *Government by Commissions: Illegal and Pernicious.* London, S. Sweet, 1849, p. 13.

[5] A.P.H., 'Pageant of Parliament', *Punch,* vol. 186, June 27, 1934, p. 708.

[6] See Appendix, p. 379 for listing of Canadian Public Inquiries Acts.

[7] John Edwin Hodgetts, 'Should Canada be De-Commissioned? A Commoner's View of Royal Commissions', *Queen's Quarterly,* vol. LXX, no. 4, Winter 1964, p. 477.

[8] To these six should be added several related 'R2' commissions on assessment and taxes.

Checklist

NEWFOUNDLAND

1 SELECT COMMITTEE ON THE PRESENT SCHOOL SYSTEM
(Legislative Committee)

Appointed   May 8, 1890

Reported   February 12, 1891

Committee   Nine members; James Murray (Member for Burgeo
             and LaPoile) chairman

Purpose   To take evidence upon the subject of the
             present school system and its operation.

Conclusions/Recommendations

That no change be made at present in the basis of the
educational system as a whole;

That no alteration be made in the number or personality of
the school inspectors;

That the education committee do all in their power to
promote uniformity in the management and practice of the
schools;

That the whole subject of placing the teachers' salaries
on a reasonable and satisfactory basis be considered;

That a metropolitan college or normal school for the
examination and grading of teachers be established as soon
as possible;

That future appointments of school inspectors whenever practicable be made from the ranks of school teachers in the colony.

References

Newfoundland, *Journals of Newfoundland House of Assembly,* 1890 & 1891.

2 BRITISH ROYAL COMMISSION ON THE FUTURE OF NEWFOUNDLAND
(Related Commission)

Appointed   February 17, 1933

Reported   October 4, 1933

Commission   Three members; William Warrender Mackenzie
             (Baron Amulree, King's Counsel) chairman

Purpose   To examine into the future of Newfoundland and
             in particular to report on the financial
             situation and prospects therein.

Conclusions/Recommendations

That existing forms of government be suspended until such time as the Island may become self-supporting again;

That a special Commission of Government take the place of the existing Legislature and Executive Council;

That the Commission of Government be composed of six members (exclusive of the Governor) -- three from Newfoundland and three from the United Kingdom;

That the United Kingdom assume general responsibility for the finances of the Island until it may become self-supporting again;

That as soon as the Island's difficulties are overcome, responsible government, on request from the people of Newfoundland, would be restored;

That the hope that any new educational curriculum, while giving an equal opportunity to all school children and meeting the requirements of students of exceptional promise, will better equip the average boy and girl for the only avenues of employment likely to be available to them in the Island.

References

British House of Commons, *Sessional Papers,* 14, 1933-34.

3 REPORT ON CERTAIN ASPECTS OF THE EDUCATIONAL SYSTEM OF NEWFOUNDLAND
(Special Committee)

Appointed   1933

Reported   October 18, 1933

Committee   One member; C.A. Richardson (H.M. Inspector of Schools)

Purpose   To study the subject of the curriculum in Newfoundland schools.

Conclusions/Recommendations

That the educational curriculum is very largely artificial and divorced from the actual experience and needs of the child;

That the freedom of the teacher is severely restricted making it difficult to use any special talent or ability;

That practically nothing is done, or can be done, to foster self-reliance and independent activity on the part of children.

References

Newfoundland, *Certain Aspects of the Educational System of Newfoundland,* 1933.

4 COMMISSION OF ENQUIRY INTO THE PRESENT CURRICULUM OF THE
COLLEGES AND SCHOOLS IN NEWFOUNDLAND
(General Commission)

Appointed   October 18, 1933

Reported   May 19, 1934

Commission   Ten members; Vincent P. Burke (Secretary for
              Education) chairman

Purpose   To reconsider the present curriculum of the
              public schools in Newfoundland, and to make
              suggestions or recommendations.

Conclusions/Recommendations

That it is unsound to give a utilitarian emphasis to the
work of the elementary school which must be informative and
cultural without much regard to future vocational
tendencies;

That local school boards be required to test popular
feeling on the matter of compulsory education;

That one-teacher schools be restrained from preparing
candidates for Grade XI examinations;

That an advisory body be appointed to draw up scales of
salaries that would be equitable and attract to the
teaching profession a sufficient number of qualified men
and women;

That the length of the teacher training course be at
least one year, preferably two;

That all women teachers who expect to teach in elementary
schools be qualified to teach needlework and knitting.

References

Newfoundland, *Report of the Commission of Enquiry into the
Present Curriculum of the Colleges and Schools in
Newfoundland,* 1934.

5 SUPERVISORY COMMITTEE ON NEWFOUNDLAND STUDIES
  (Special Committee)

Appointed   June, 1941

Reported   1946

Committee   Nine members; Sir Campbell Stuart (Chairman
                 Imperial Committee, Royal Institute of
                 International Affairs) chairman

Purpose   To supervise a research study of the economy
                 and external relations of the Island.

Conclusions/Recommendations

That it is clear that the basic difficulties facing
Newfoundland in the educational field in the past, as in
other fields of public welfare are economic, and that if
Newfoundland is to carry itself in the future the total
funds available for public services are likely to be
severely limited.

References

*Newfoundland: Economic, Diplomatic, and Strategic
Studies,* 1946. [Sponsored by the Royal Institute of
International Affairs]

6 NATIONAL CONVENTION EDUCATION COMMITTEE
  (Departmental Committee)

Appointed   1946

Reported   1946

Committee   Ten members; Malcolm Hollett (Magistrate)
                 chairman

Purpose   To survey the status of education with
                 particular attention to economic questions.

Conclusions/Recommendations

That education is no longer regarded as a luxury for those who can afford it, but a necessity for all, whether they can afford it or not;

That none of the existing services should be abolished or reduced and that the trend towards extension and improvement should be continued.

References

Newfoundland, 'Report of Committee on Education', 1946.

7 ROYAL COMMISSION FOR THE PREPARATION OF THE CASE OF THE GOVERNMENT OF NEWFOUNDLAND FOR THE REVISION OF THE FINANCIAL TERMS OF UNION
(Related Commission)

Appointed   December 3, 1953

Reported   May 13, 1957

Commission   Five members; Philip Joseph Lewis (Queen's Counsel) chairman

Purpose   To review the financial position of the Province of Newfoundland since Union.

Conclusions/Recommendations

That in the case of Newfoundland the isolation of the outports, the lack of communications and the want of means of the people, combine to deprive many an able child of his fundamental human right to develop his mind and his skills to the full extent of his capacities.

References

Newfoundland, *Report of the Newfoundland Royal Commission for the Preparation of the Case of the Government of Newfoundland for the Revision of the Financial Terms of Union*, 1957.

8 COMMISSION OF INQUIRY INTO THE QUESTIONS RELATING TO THE
  IMPOSITION OF THE SCHOOL TAX AT CORNER BROOK
  (General Commission)

  Appointed   March 5, 1956

  Reported   April 11, 1956

  Commission   Three members; Beaton J. Abbott (District
                 Magistrate, Grand Falls) chairman

  Purpose   To enquire into the questions relating to the
                 imposition of the school tax at Corner Brook.

  Conclusions/Recommendations

  That after long and close study of the evidence submitted
  there is no doubt whatever that the School Tax is quite
  justified;

  That the heartbreak, the disappointments in trying to
  build classrooms to meet an influx of children amounting
  to sometimes alarming propositions will not be swept
  aside and forgotten by the continuance of the School Tax.

  References

  Newfoundland, 'Report of the Commission of Enquiry into
  the Questions Relating to the Imposition of the School
  Tax at Corner Brook', 1956.

9 ROYAL COMMISSION OF NEWFOUNDLAND FINANCES UNDER THE TERMS
  OF UNION OF NEWFOUNDLAND WITH CANADA
  (Related Commission)

  Appointed   February 21, 1957

  Reported   May 31, 1958

  Commission   Three members; John Babbit McNair (Chief
                 Justice of New Brunswick) chairman

Purpose   To review the financial position of the
              Province of Newfoundland and to recommend the
              form and scale of additional financial assis-
              tance, if any.

Conclusions/Recommendations

That without voluntary contributions by the public and
financing by religious denominations, a system of local
taxation or higher provincial government expenditure would
be necessary in Newfoundland.

References

Newfoundland, *Royal Commission on Newfoundland Finances
Under the Terms of Union of Newfoundland with Canada,* 1958.

10 ROYAL COMMISSION ON EDUCATION AND YOUTH
   (General Commission)

Appointed   December 11, 1964

Reported   Volume One, January 15, 1967; Volume Two,
              October 23, 1967

Commission   Twelve members; P.J. Warren (Faculty of
              Education, Memorial University) chairman

Purpose ·   Generally to enquire into all aspects of
              education in the province.

Conclusions/Recommendations

That the Department of Education be reorganized on a
functional rather than a denominational basis;

That consolidation be undertaken to reduce the number of
school districts from 230 to approximately 35;

That long-range plans be undertaken for the upgrading of
teachers qualifications;

That immediate efforts be made to improve and diversify

the school curriculum;

That a systematic effort be made to improve the validity and reliability of public examinations;

That a province-wide 'Foundation Programme' be established with the entire cost to be borne by the Provincial Government.

References

Newfoundland, *Department of Education News Letter*, Dec., 1964, Vol. 16, No. 4.

Newfoundland, *Report of the Royal Commission on Education and Youth*, 1967.

11 ROYAL COMMISSION ON MUNICIPAL GOVERNMENT IN NEWFOUNDLAND AND LABRADOR
(Related Commission)

Appointed   August 23, 1972

Reported   September 18, 1974

Commission   Four members; Hugh J. Whalen (Political Science Department, Memorial University) chairman

Purpose   To enquire into and to make recommendations with respect to:

       a) the legislation presently in effect relating to local government and the policies of financial assistance to municipalities by the Province;

       b) the improvement of the structure and administration of local government;

       c) the establishment of criteria and procedures for the creation of new municipalities;

    d) the sources of revenue available to
       municipalities with particular reference to
       taxation;

    e) the levels of service that should be provided
       in municipalities;

    f) the establishment of adequate financial
       controls over municipal expenditures.

Conclusions/Recommendations

That school finance in Newfoundland is the responsibility
of the denominational school boards and of the Province,
and unlike New Brunswick and Prince Edward Island, and to
a lesser extent British Columbia, the Province does not
levy a real property tax generally for school purposes;

That due to the substantial provincial fiscal responsibility for education in Newfoundland, local ratepayers
contribute toward education at levels far below those
prevailing in most Canadian provinces; but Newfoundland's
school boards not only receive substantial funds from
government, school tax authorities and direct assessment
levies, they also receive a substantial benefit from
municipal services supplied to their tax-exempt schools
by local ratepayers;

That, upon the establishment of regional municipal
authorities, these units should become the tax billing
and tax collection agencies for all school boards within
their boundaries.

References

Newfoundland, *Royal Commission on Municipal Government in
Newfoundland and Labrador,* 1974.

12 ROYAL COMMISSION ON LABRADOR
(Related Commission)

Appointed   October 23, 1972

Reported   February, 1974

Commission   Four members; Donald Snowden (Director of
              Extension Services, Memorial University)
              chairman

Purpose   To inquire into the economic and sociological
              conditions of life in Labrador; including all
              phases of education in Labrador (including
              pre-school, primary, secondary and high
              school, adult education, vocational and
              technical training, arts and crafts
              programmes and life skills) and all matters
              related to teaching and teachers.

Conclusions/Recommendations

That supervisory personnel with school boards whose jurisdiction is in part or wholly in Labrador be required to
visit district schools at least three times a year;

That the Department of Education begin a thorough
examination of the present curriculum with a view to
developing courses with local relevance;

That immediate provision be made for employment of
bilingual teacher aides in schools with native populations;

That kindergartens be established in all schools with
native populations in Labrador;

That teacher training at Memorial University offer Indian
and Eskimo cross-cultural courses to teachers who are
considering teaching native children in Labrador schools;

That programmes which assist student travel and exchange
for educational purposes be extended to include travel
and exchange within Labrador.

References

Newfoundland, *Recommendations of the Royal Commission on
Labrador*, 1974.

13 COMMISSION OF ENQUIRY INTO THE ST. JOHN'S URBAN REGION
STUDY
(Related Commission)

Appointed   January 7, 1974

Reported   October 25, 1974

Commission   Three members; Alec G. Henley (St. John's
               businessman) chairman

Purpose   To make an enquiry into:

               a) the adoption of a Regional Plan for the St.
                  John's Urban Region;

               b) the precise boundaries of the Region;

               c) the standards and levels of municipal services
                  and policies required in the Region;

               d) the form of local government structure most
                  suitable for adoption in the Region;

               e) the possible future regional and municipal
                  tax base for the Region and proposals for
                  Federal and Provincial financial involve-
                  ment in this field.

Conclusions/Recommendations

That if the proposed policies were to be applied rigidly
over the Region, it is conceivable that there would be no
schools beyond junior grades in the local centres, and
there was fear that the acceptance of this particular
policy would mean that all major school facilities would
be located in the downtown St. John's central area;

That school facilities for the whole Region be examined by
the appropriate authorities so that all areas are provided
with adequate and proper school facilities in relation to
their needs and that regional school facilities should not
be substituted for a more decentralized system of schools
which could realistically be provided in local centres

within the Region.

References

Newfoundland, *Commission of Enquiry: St. John's Urban Region Study*, vol. 1, 1974.

14 COMMISSION OF INQUIRY INTO THE CLOSING OF UPPER GULLIES SCHOOL
(Judicial Commission)

Appointed   November 5, 1974

Reported   May 20, 1975

Commission   One member; Terrence J. Corbett (Placentia Magistrate)

Purpose   To make an enquiry into and concerning the events which led to the closing of the Upper Gullies Elementary School, and in particular the circumstances surrounding the installation, approval, inspection, operation and maintenance of the water and sewage systems.

Conclusions/Recommendations

That special consideration be given to the approval of plans and construction by the Department of Education, and that precise and detailed legislation be enacted which would ensure that school building projects would be carried out in conformity with approved plans and specifications;

That arrangements be made for the training of Board maintenance supervisors and of building caretakers;

That School Principals, Board Superintendents and Business Managers have sufficient appreciation of such material as to be aware of proper performance in care and maintenance of the school and its equipment;

That some form of routine checking or inspection be established to assure that reasonable standards of safety are maintained in school buildings.

References

Newfoundland, *Commission of Inquiry into the Closing of Upper Gullies School*, 1975.

15 MINISTER'S ADVISORY COMMITTEE ON GRADE XII
(Departmental Committee)

Appointed   1977

Reported   December, 1978

Committee   Nine members; C. Roebothan (Deputy Minister of Education) chairman

Purpose   To examine the question of introducing Grade XII in High Schools.

Conclusions/Recommendations

That an immediate decision be taken to add a twelfth grade to the Newfoundland secondary school system;

That planning for the implementation of that decision be commenced at once with a view to a phased introduction commencing with the Grade X class of 1980.

References

Newfoundland, *Report of Minister's Advisory Committee on Grade XII*, December 1978.

16 TASK FORCE ON DECLINING ENROLMENT IN EDUCATION
(Departmental Committee)

Appointed   May 1, 1978

Reported   June 30, 1978

Committee   Two members; R.K. Crocker (Director, Institute
             for Educational Research and Development,
             Memorial University) and F. Riggs (Department
             of Curriculum and Instruction, Memorial
             University) co-chairmen

Purpose   To conduct a survey of declining enrolments by
             School Districts and the impact of this
             decline on individual school programs, class
             size, teacher deployment and class and grade
             organization in each School District for the
             school year 1978-79; and to formulate recom-
             mendations concerning appropriate and
             realistic courses of action which Government
             and administrative groups in education should
             adopt in order to take advantage of declining
             enrolments to improve the quality of
             education.

Conclusions/Recommendations

That present teacher salary unit allocations be adjusted
to provide for additional full-time or specialist teachers.

References

Newfoundland, *Perspectives on Declining Enrolments in the Schools of Newfoundland and Labrador,* Interim Report, 1978.

NOVA SCOTIA

17 JOINT COMMITTEE OF COUNCIL AND ASSEMBLY ON EDUCATION
(Legislative Committee)

Appointed   1825 (?)

Reported   March 7, 1825

Committee   Eight members; Charles Fairbanks (Member for
              Halifax) chairman

Purpose   To review the whole system of common school
              education and to make recommendations for the
              future.

Conclusions/Recommendations

That education ought to be general throughout the Province
in order that none, even in the remotest and poorest
settlement, may be without some provision for the instruction of their youth;

That it should be compulsory in every place because too
many are found insensible of the just value of education;

That it should not be gratuitous because what costs
nothing is generally valued at nothing;

That it cannot be supported from the Provincial Treasury
because the expense would surpass the disposeable income
of the Colony;

That its funds should be raised by a general and equal

assessment on the whole population, according to each man's ability;

That the respectability and talents -- and consequent usefulness -- of the teachers should be secured by the adequateness and permanency of their salary.

References

Nova Scotia, *Journals of the House of Assembly of Nova Scotia,* 1825.

18 SELECT COMMITTEE ON EDUCATION
(Legislative Committee)

Appointed   January 31, 1848

Reported   March 23, 1848

Committee   Five members; George R. Young (Member for
               Pictou) chairman

Purpose   To enquire into the state of education of
               schools generally throughout the Province.

Conclusions/Recommendations

That Normal Schools for the training of a higher class of Masters be introduced, and that an Inspector or Superintendent be employed.

References

Nova Scotia, *Journals,* 1848, App. 77.

19 COMMISSION FOR THE PURPOSE OF INVESTIGATING THE BEST METHODS OF TEACHING ENGLISH IN THE SCHOOLS SITUATE IN THE FRENCH-SPEAKING DISTRICTS OF THE PROVINCE
(General Commission)

Appointed   April 18, 1902

Reported   April 28, 1902

Commission Eight members; W.E. MacLellan (Halifax
            Barrister, Editor of Morning Chronicle)
            chairman

Purpose   To investigate the best methods of teaching
            English in the schools situate in the French-
            speaking districts of the Province.

Conclusions/Recommendations

That the French-speaking sections of the Province have
been and continue to be at a very serious disadvantage in
the matter of education;

That English can be best and most effectively taught in the
French-speaking school sections of Nova Scotia by the
daily use in speaking and writing of that language,
taught according to the most approved methods, from the
pupils' first entrance into school;

That as long as necessary French-speaking pupils should,
while learning English, be taught the other subjects of
the curriculum in French, provided, however, that the use
or study of French shall be optional with every pupil;

That as far as practicable, in the French-speaking schools
of the Province, only bilingual teachers should be
employed.

References

Nova Scotia, 'The Acadian Commission', 1902.

20 REPORT ON EDUCATION IN THE MARITIME PROVINCES OF CANADA
   (Special Committee)

   Appointed   1921

   Reported   1922

Committee   William S. Learned (Carnegie Foundation) and
              Kenneth C.M. Sills (President, Bowdoin
              College)

Purpose   To consider a policy for aid to institutions
              of higher education in the Maritime provinces.

Conclusions/Recommendations

That there be a complete reconstruction and the use of
funds, not to strengthen one institution at the expense
of others, but to bring together into one new organization
at Halifax several institutions with their endowments and
equipment.

References

William S. Learned and Kenneth C.M. Sills, *Education in
the Maritime Provinces of Canada,* 1922.
[Sponsored by The Carnegie Foundation for the Advancement
of Teaching]

21 COMMITTEE ON SCHOOL STUDIES
   (Departmental Committee)

   Appointed   1930

   Reported   March, 1933

   Committee   Nine members; F.H. Sexton (Director of
                Technical Education) chairman

   Purpose   To examine fully into the subject of school
                studies as related to the present social,
                ecnomic and intellectual needs of this
                Province.

Conclusions/Recommendations

That new text books be recommended for use in the Common
and High School grades.

References

Nova Scotia, *Journals*, 1931 & 1934.

22 COMMISSION ON THE LARGER SCHOOL UNIT
(Departmental Committee)

Appointed   November 19, 1938

Reported   October 17, 1939

Committee   Six members; Henry P. Munro (Superintendent
               of Education) chairman

Purpose   To study the larger school unit.

Conclusions/Recommendations

That there be a provincial plan whereby district boards
would be replaced by municipal school boards, and property
and income would be properly reassessed;

That an immediately feasible transition plan be adopted
which would make the municipality a unit for school
finance and certain administrative functions.

References

Nova Scotia, *Report of the Committee on the Larger School
Unit*, 1939.

23 ROYAL COMMISSION ON PROVINCIAL DEVELOPMENT AND
REHABILITATION
(Related Commission)

Appointed   May 12, 1943

Reported   1944

Commission   One member; Robert MacGregor Dawson (Political
               Science Department, University of Toronto)

Purpose   To investigate problems of rehabilitation and
              development in Nova Scotia.

Conclusions/Recommendations

That in order to obtain the more thorough and intelligent
utilization of resources the province needs above everything else more and more knowledge of all kinds -- the
education in the common schools, the technical training of
the vocational institute, and the broader and more
advanced knowledge of the university;

That money was the most urgent need of education in Nova
Scotia, and the Dominion should give substantial assistance (based on need) to the poorer provinces for
educational purposes;

That salaries of teachers, which in Nova Scotia were
deplorably low, be raised so that a better calibre of
person would be drawn into and kept in the profession;

That teachers' qualifications and training be upgraded;

That without losing the necessary quota of traditional
studies there be a wider and more flexible offering of
courses to meet individual needs and abilities;

That the academic load in rural schools be lightened, and
consolidation be considered where feasible;

That at the university level some form of federation be
instituted.

References

Nova Scotia, *Royal Commission on Provincial Development
and Rehabilitation,* 1944.

24 COMMISSION TO INVESTIGATE AND REPORT ON ALL MATTERS
   AFFECTING TEACHERS SALARIES
   (Departmental Committee)

Appointed   [   ]

Reported   [1946]

Committee   Six members; John A. MacGregor (Mayor of Westville) chairman

Purpose   To investigate and report on all matters affecting teachers' salaries.

Conclusions/Recommendations

References

Nova Scotia, *Journals,* 1946.

25 COMMISSION ON TEACHER EDUCATION
   (Departmental Committee)

Appointed   May 1, 1950

Reported   November, 1950

Committee   Twelve members; Charles E. Phillips (Ontario College of Education) chairman

Purpose   To make recommendations for the training of elementary school teachers, high school teachers, and teachers of special subjects.

Conclusions/Recommendations

That support be given to three established trends in teacher education: first a movement towards parity of professional status for elementary school and high school teachers; second, a movement towards a longer minimum period of teacher education for the elementary school teacher; and third, a movement towards teacher preparation of a truly professional character at the university level.

References

Nova Scotia, *Report of the Commission on Teacher Education,* 1950.

26 SURVEY PROJECT OF THE JOINT COMMITTEE ON PUBLIC ATTITUDES
TOWARDS OUR SCHOOLS
(Special Committee)

Appointed   September, 1952

Reported   1954 (?)

Committee   Three members; Mortimer V. Marshall (Director,
               School of Education, Acadia University)
               chairman

Purpose   To survey public attitudes towards teachers,
               teacher-parent-pupil relationship, finance
               and administrative responsibility, physical
               facilities, and the school program.

Conclusions/Recommendations

(The 'General Conclusions' tabulated public opinion
regarding teachers, parent-teacher-pupil relationship,
finance and administration, and the program of the school.)

References

Nova Scotia, *A Survey Project of the Joint Committee on
Public Attitudes Toward Our Schools,* 1952.

27 ROYAL COMMISSION ON PUBLIC SCHOOL FINANCE IN NOVA SCOTIA
(General Commission)

Appointed   March 2, 1953

Reported   November 25, 1954

Commission   One member; V.J. Pottier, (Judge, Halifax
               County Court)

Purpose   To inquire into and report upon all matters
               relating to the financial support of schools
               established and operated under the Education
               Act, the Vocational Education Act, and special
               acts relating to the education of handicapped

children.

Conclusions/Recommendations

That every child in Nova Scotia be entitled to an
education in accordance with his abilities and needs;

That teachers should receive higher salaries, but they
must respond with an awakened interest, rekindled
enthusiasm and improved professional competence;

That every municipal unit should pay according to its
ability by equalized assessment.

References

Nova Scotia, *Report of the Royal Commission on Public
School Finance in Nova Scotia,* 1954.

28 ROYAL COMMISSION ON SCHOOL CONSTRUCTION IN NOVA SCOTIA
(General Commission)

Appointed   October 18, 1957

Reported   December 29, 1958

Commission   Three members; Ira P. Macnab (Civil Engineer)
               chairman

Purpose   To inquire into matters related to school
               construction.

Conclusions/Recommendations

That the prime purpose of a school building should be to
supply accommodation and facilities that will permit
adequate and proper education for children;

That schools must have all the facilities necessary, with
the minimum of non-essentials.

References

Nova Scotia, *Royal Commission on School Construction in Nova Scotia*, 1958.

29 SURVEY REPORT ON HIGHER EDUCATION IN NOVA SCOTIA
   (Special Committee)

Appointed   January 7, 1963

Reported   January 9, 1964

Committee   Three members; Norman A.M. MacKenzie, (former
             President, University of B.C.) chairman

Purpose   To enquire into and to advise the Government
             of the Province of Nova Scotia concerning
             aspects of higher education in the Province.

Conclusions/Recommendations

That grants totalling $1,500,000 be distributed to the
universities and colleges, as outlined in interim reports
of May 27, July 10 and December 5, 1963;

That to qualify for entrance to university in Nova Scotia
a candidate must meet the university entrance requirements
of his own province or country, provided that they are at
least equal to the Nova Scotia requirements;

That increases in tuition fees be seriously considered by
the universities, along with a system of bursaries;

That the ordinary requirement for admission to university
be set as Nova Scotia Grade 12 rather than Grade 11;

That serious consideration be given to the institution of
a year-round university calendar;

That some appropriate body, such as the Associated Atlantic
Universities or the Central Advisory Committee, assume
responsibility for ensuring the most effective cooperation
among universities and colleges in the Atlantic;

That teacher education in Nova Scotia be given thorough study.

References

Nova Scotia, *Higher Education in Nova Scotia,* 1964.

30 ROYAL COMMISSION ON THE SAFE TRANSPORTATION OF SCHOOL PUPILS
(General Commission)

Appointed   August 22, 1963

Reported   February 10, 1964

Commission   One member; C. Roger Rand (Queen's Counsel, Yarmouth)

Purpose   To enquire into measures designed to ensure the safety of pupils and other persons while being transported to and from schools.

Conclusions/Recommendations

That the value of any safety legislation is largely dependent upon its intelligent and sympathetic acceptance, understanding and use by school bus drivers, pupil passengers and the motoring public.

References

Nova Scotia, *Royal Commission on the Safe Transportation of School Pupils,* 1964.

31 TRIBUNAL ON BILINGUAL HIGHER EDUCATION IN NOVA SCOTIA
(Departmental Committee)

Appointed   March 25, 1969

Reported   November 13, 1969

Committee	Three members; David C. Munroe (Faculty of Education, McGill University) chairman
Purpose	To assess the needs, present and future, of higher education in western Nova Scotia, with special reference to those needs as related to the Acadian community of the Province, and others who may desire a bilingual education.

Conclusions/Recommendations

That a Bilingual Community College, to be known as the Community College of the Southwest — College Communautaire du sud-ouest — be established at Meteghan, in the District of Clare;

That the Community College, being situated in an Acadian community, give special consideration to the preservation and development of Acadian culture;

That immediate action be taken in providing training for teachers specialized in the teaching of French and English, so that the standards of language training may be improved.

References

Nova Scotia, *Tribunal on Bilingual Higher Education in Nova Scotia,* 1969.

32 ROYAL COMMISSION ON SECTION 3 OF THE EXPIRED COLLECTIVE AGREEMENT BETWEEN THE SYDNEY SCHOOL BOARD AND THE NOVA SCOTIA TEACHERS' UNION, SYDNEY LOCAL (Judicial Commission)

Appointed	October 14, 1969
Reported	December 11, 1969
Commission	One member; Arthur Moreira (Barrister)
Purpose	To deal with one residual question remaining unsettled after mediation.

Conclusions/Recommendations

That the $200.00 item in Section 3 of the expired collec-
tive agreement made between the Sydney School Board and
the Nova Scotia Teachers' Union, Sydney Local, is a
salary differential, and not a bonus.

References

Nova Scotia, *Report of Royal Commission on Section 3 of the
Expired Collective Agreement between the Sydney School
Board and the Nova Scotia Teachers' Union,* Sydney Local,
1969.

33 SURVEY OF DIGBY SCHOOL SYSTEM
   (Departmental Committee)

   Appointed   February, 1970

   Reported   March 26, 1970

   Committee   Three members; Maurice Keating (Superintendent
                 of Schools) chairman

   Purpose   To inquire into the administration and
                 operation of the public school system in the
                 District of Digby.

Conclusions/Recommendations

That the role of the Superintendent of Schools be primarily
that of an educator;

That the Digby School Boards study carefully their
functions as laid down in the Education Act;

That all sales and purchases of school buses, and all
other substantial sales and purchases be made by tender;

That the public have ready and easy access to School
Board records, financial statements, budgets, and minutes.

References

Nova Scotia, *Survey: Digby School System,* March 1970.

34 COMMUNITY COLLEGE PLANNING COMMISSION
   (Departmental Committee)

   Appointed   June 1, 1970

   Reported   March 31, 1971

   Committee   Three members; Alphonse B. Gaudet (Faculty of
                Education, University of Moncton) chairman

   Purpose   To make and carry out a plan for the estab-
                lishment in Southwestern Nova Scotia of a
                post-secondary bilingual community college.

Conclusions/Recommendations

That a Bilingual Community College be established at a
place in Southwestern Nova Scotia to meet the needs of both
Francophone and Anglophone students in the tri-county area:
Shelburne-Digby-Yarmouth;

That the Programs of the Bilingual Community College
include courses for both degree and non-degree requirements;

That the Administration and Personnel of the Bilingual
Community College be functionally bilingual;

That Anglophone and Francophone students integrate at
least one-third of their courses in the other official
language for degree or non-degree requirements;

That a strong French Department be established at the Nova
Scotia Bilingual Community College, in liaison with
department of education officials, with responsibilities
for curriculum revision in the teaching of French,
particularly in French Acadian schools;

That the establishment of the Bilingual Community College
in Southwest Nova Scotia in its Philosophy, Programs, and

Site Requirements be determined, once and for all, on the basis of Southwestern Nova Scotia community needs and not 'through, by and for' political expediency.

References

Nova Scotia, *Nova Scotia Bilingual Community College: Report of the Community College Planning Commission,* March 1971.

35 ROYAL COMMISSION ON EDUCATION, PUBLIC SERVICES AND PROVINCIAL-MUNICIPAL RELATIONS (General Commission)

Appointed   March 31, 1971

Reported   June 27, 1974

Commission   Three members; John F. Graham (former Head, Department of Economics, Dalhousie University) chairman

Purpose   To inquire generally into the provision of education and other public services in the Province of Nova Scotia.

Conclusions/Recommendations

That the Education Act define the general goals of education for the schools of Nova Scotia

1) to develop competence in effective communication, particularly through language, in accordance with standards established by the province;

2) to develop competence in basic arithmetic and under-standing of the basic principles of mathematics, in accordance with standards established by the province;

3) to develop the practice and methods of critical and disciplined thinking;

4) to provide in school programs and activities

opportunities for students:

a) to express and exercise originality and imagination;

b) to develop civic, social, and moral responsibility and judgement;

c) to have their curiosity encouraged and to develop knowledge and understanding of themselves, their fellowmen, their environment, and the relationship among the three;

d) to acquire habits, attitudes, and intellectual skills that will be helpful in employment and in training for employment.

References

Nova Scotia, *Royal Commission on Education, Public Services and Provincial-Municipal Relations; Volume I, Summary and Recommendations*, 1974.

36 COMMITTEE ON PRE-SCHOOL EDUCATION AND SOCIAL DEVELOPMENT PROGRAMS
(Departmental Committee)

Appointed   August 16, 1973

Reported   May, 1974

Committee   Seven members; G.W. MacKenzie (Director of Inspection Services) chairman

Purpose   To examine the training and teaching patterns being followed in the various pre-school programs; to determine whether or not common standards of practice should be developed in these pre-school programs; and to examine means by which the easy transfer of children from pre-school classes, Day-Care and Head Start Programs into the regular school situation could be facilitated.

Conclusions/Recommendations

That the age at which school boards in Nova Scotia are required to accept children in school be reduced by one year, from the present five years on October 1 of the school-year to four years on October 1 of the school-year;

That the lower age limit for compulsory attendance at school in Nova Scotia be reduced from six years to five years;

That the cost of educating the four-year old pupils be included in the Foundation Program of Education and thus be a shareable cost between school boards and the Department of Education under the Foundation Program cost-sharing formula.

References

Nova Scotia, *Report of the Committee on Pre-School Education and Social Development Programs,* May 1974.

37 FEDERAL-PROVINCIAL STUDY OF EDUCATIONAL TECHNOLOGY IN NOVA SCOTIA
(Departmental Committee)

Appointed   March 6, 1974

Reported   1975 [to Deputy Minister Responsible for Communications and to Department of Education]

Committee   Five members; Gaylen A. Duncan (Coordinator of Communications Policy, Province of Nova Scotia) chairman

Purpose   To examine educational technology to identify principles and procedures which could lead to enhancing the educational process in the Province of Nova Scotia through the cost-effective application of educational technology.

Conclusions/Recommendations

That the Minister of Education assert the principle of the
provision, by the Department of Education, of basic supportive services related to educational technology in order
to meet present and anticipated needs throughout the
province;

That the Minister of Education assert, as a principle, the
integration and coordination of existing departmental
programs and activities;

That by March 31, 1977, the Nova Scotia Minister of
Education implement minimum levels of materials, equipment
and facilities, and resolve issues related to copyright
and distribution;

That the Nova Scotia Minister of Education and the Nova
Scotia Minister Responsible for Communications agree,
subject to the development of an acceptable work plan, to
undertake Phase II of the Educational Technology Program
for Nova Scotia, until June 30, 1977.

References

Nova Scotia, *Educational Technology Program for Nova
Scotia: Initial Phase*, 1975.

38 SELECT COMMITTEE ON EDUCATION, PUBLIC SERVICES AND
PROVINCIAL-MUNICIPAL RELATIONS
(Legislative Committee)

Appointed   June 28, 1974

Reported   June, 1975

Committee   Eight members; Fraser Mooney (Minister of
              Municipal Affairs) chairman

Purpose   To consider and to report upon Education,
              Public Services and Provincial-Municipal
              Relations, with particular reference to the
              Report of the Royal Commission on Education,

Public Services and Provincial-Municipal
Relations tabled in the House on 27 June,
1974.

Conclusions/Recommendations

That the Royal Commission recommendation that Nova Scotia
be divided into 11 new municipalities called counties, each
covering both urban and rural areas, be considered
unacceptable;

That there is, understandably, widespread support for the
recommendation of the Royal Commission that the general
services of education, including libraries, health, social
services and housing, administration of justice and
certain transportation services should be provided and
financed entirely by the Province;

That there appears to be no consensus on the recommendations of the Royal Commission in regard to education.

References

Nova Scotia, *Report of the Select Committee of the House of
Assembly on Education, Public Services and Provincial-
Municipal Relations,* June, 1975.

39 SELECT COMMITTEE ON THE NOVA SCOTIA TECHNICAL COLLEGE ACT
   (Legislative Committee)

Appointed   November 26, 1974

Reported   1975

Committee   Seven members; Melinda MacLean (Member for
               Colchester) chairman

Purpose   To assess the Nova Scotia Technical College
               Act.

Conclusions/Recommendations

That the powers of the Board of Governors of Nova Scotia

Technical College be enlarged to authorize that Board,
subject to the approval of the Governor in Council, to
enter into and carry out agreements with any college or
university whereby the College may, for consideration or
otherwise, transfer to such college or university all or
any part of the undertaking, property, assets or
liabilities of the College, including the College's
contracts of employment with its staff and including any
assets held in trust by the College provided the college or
university agrees to assume such trust.

References

Nova Scotia, *Report to the House of Assembly of the Select
Committee on the Nova Scotia Technical College Act*, [1975].

40 COOPERATIVE EDUCATIONAL SURVEY
(Departmental Committee)

Appointed   1976

Reported   1977

Committee   Eleven members; Dorothy Walker (School Board
               Supervisor) coordinator

Purpose   To provide an in-depth assessment of
               facilities, staff and services in the Kings
               County System after five years of amalgamation;
               an assessment of testing and grading prac-
               tices compared provincially and/or nationally;
               and a comparison of results in standard
               projects between Kings County and the rest of
               Nova Scotia, or national norms over a period
               of at least three years.

Conclusions/Recommendations

That the Board assign or appoint a senior administrative
officer who would be primarily responsible for educational
programs and curriculum;

That the Board ensure that the unique needs of the junior

high student are met by providing a school program to meet the needs of *all* students at their identified ability level; providing the students with teachers who understand adolescents and respect them as individuals; and provide adequate guidance services;

That the Department of Education improve and increase its analytical research and reporting capacities;

That the Board initiate and continue as policy, meetings of teachers to discuss methodology, curricula, marking standards and pupil evaluation policies;

That the Board acquire the services of consultants in core subject areas to advise, monitor and supervise curricula and standards of academic achievement;

That the Board undertake a review of the attendance patterns and dropout rate of students;

That an official of supervisory status be appointed whose sole duties will be with continuing education for adults.

References

Nova Scotia, *Cooperative Educational Survey*, Kings County Amalgamated School Board and Department of Education, 1977.

41 ROYAL COMMISSION ON THE BOARD OF SCHOOL COMMISSIONERS FOR THE TOWN OF MULGRAVE
(Judicial Commission)

Appointed   May 25, 1976

Reported   November 15, 1976

Commission   One member; W.E. Moseley (former Deputy
                Minister of Municipal Affairs)

Purpose   To inquire into and concerning the manner in
                which the Board of School Commissioners of
                the Town of Mulgrave has carried out its
                duties and responsibilities.

Conclusions/Recommendations

That for a variety of fairly obvious reasons, no report can hope to solve the situation which the evidence has disclosed.

References

Nova Scotia, *Report of W.E. Moseley, Q.C., Commissioner, in the matter of The Board of School Commissioners for the Town of Mulgrave,* [November 1976].

PRINCE EDWARD ISLAND

42 SPECIAL COMMITTEE ON EDUCATION
   (Legislative Committee)

   Appointed   February 7, 1834

   Reported   February 20, 1834

   Committee   Six members; George Dalrymple (Member for
                Queen's County) chairman

   Purpose   To report their opinion as to the expediency
                of renewing or amending the Act of 11th Geo.
                4th, Cap. 3, for the Establishment and
                Support of Schools.

Conclusions/Recommendations

That an improved System of Education is the most
effectual means for preventing crimes and promoting the
welfare of the community;

That too much attention cannot be bestowed to insure the
selection of persons duly qualified to instruct the young
and form their morals as it has been invariably felt and
acknowledged that the expectations of the framers of the
present School Act have been in too many instances defeated
by the appointment of improper and incompetent persons to
the District Schools.

References

Prince Edward Island, *Journal of the House of Assembly of*

Prince Edward Island, 1834.

43 SPECIAL COMMITTEE ON EDUCATION
   (Legislative Committee)

   Appointed   March 28, 1839

   Reported   March 9, 1840

   Committee   Twelve members; A. Rae (Member for Prince
                 County) chairman

   Purpose   To acquire information during the Recess,
                 touching such amendments as it may be
                 expedient to make to the Act for the
                 encouragement and support of District and
                 other Schools.

Conclusions/Recommendations

That at all times the expense of instructing youth in the
higher branches must, in the counties, chiefly devolve on
the parents whose children are expected to be enabled
thereby to reap in after years emolument and honour -- and
that in the meantime the whole of the public money that
can be spared from the Treasury for educational purposes
should be devoted to the establishment of common schools.

References

Prince Edward Island, *Journals,* 1840, App. K.

44 JOINT COMMITTEE OF COUNCIL AND ASSEMBLY ON EDUCATION
   (Legislative Committee)

   Appointed   February 8 (Council) and February 10
                 (Assembly), 1842

   Reported   February 26, 1842

   Committee   Three members from Council, six from Assembly;

D. MacDonald, (Member for King's County) chairman

Purpose   To examine into and report upon the state of the Central Academy, and upon general education.

Conclusions/Recommendations

That the moneys arising from the sale of school land endowments be invested in the public Treasury of the Colony, and that the annual legal interest arising therefrom be applied to the gratuitous instructions in the District Schools of the children of the destitute poor, under the direction of the Legislature of the Colony.

References

Prince Edward Island, *Journals,* 1842.

45 SPECIAL COMMITTEE TO ENQUIRE INTO THE EXPEDIENCY OF MAKING EDUCATION FREE THROUGHOUT THE ISLAND (Legislative Committee)

Appointed   April 26, 1851

Reported   February 16, 1852

Committee   Twelve members; G. Coles (Member for Queen's County) chairman

Purpose   To enquire into the expediency of making education free throughout the Island.

Conclusions/Recommendations

That unless School Masters' salaries are wholly paid by the Government, and a system of Free Education established, many settlements will not be able to reap the benefits of Education for the rising generation under the present system.

References

Prince Edward Island, *Journals*, 1852.

46 COMMISSION TO INVESTIGATE THE CASES OF TEACHERS WHOSE
SALARIES WERE IN DISPUTE
(Judicial Commission)

Appointed   January 25, 1873

Reported   March 13, 1873

Commission   Three members; Peter Sinclair (Member of
Prince Edward Island Executive Council)
chairman

Purpose   To enquire into the cases of teachers whose
salaries have been intercepted by the late
Secretary of the Board of Education and to
report the facts connected with each case to
the Government.

Conclusions/Recommendations

That upon the Secretary of the Board of Education depends,
to a very great extent, the efficiency of the whole Free
System of Education;

That the present salary is a very inadequate one and the
services of a competent man are not likely to be had or
retained for such an insignificant sum.

References

Prince Edward Island, *Journals*, 1873, App. T.

47 SPECIAL LEGISLATIVE COMMITTEE TO INVESTIGATE THE WORKINGS
OF THE EDUCATION LAW
(Legislative Committee)

Appointed   April 24, 1876

Reported   April 29, 1876

Committee   Five members; Louis H. Davies (Member for King's County) chairman

Purpose   To investigate the workings of the Education Law.

Conclusions/Recommendations

That the Board of Education, as at present constituted, does not seem able, either to grapple with and remedy the evils or difficulties of the educational system of the Colony, or effectively to carry out the existing Law.

References

Prince Edward Island, *Journals*, 1876, App. AA.

48 ROYAL COMMISSION ON EDUCATION
(General Commission)

Appointed   October 15, 1908

Reported   February 14, 1910

Commission   Three members; Duncan C. McLeod (King's Counsel, Charlottetown) chairman

Purpose   Generally to deal with the whole matter of education in the Province.

Conclusions/Recommendations

That the schools of the Province be consolidated;

That Nature Study and Agriculture be given a considerable place in the school course;

That the new set of Readers published in Ontario be adopted;

That there be conscientious choosing and screening of

teachers;

That inspectors be of a very high calibre.

References

Prince Edward Island, *Report of the Committee on Education*, 1910.

49 ROYAL COMMISSION ON EDUCATION
   (General Commission)

   Appointed   July 25, 1929

   Reported   December 31, 1929

   Commission   Three members; Cyrus J. MacMillan (Chairman,
                 Department of English, McGill University)
                 chairman

   Purpose   To examine and report upon the subjects
                 relating to the consolidation of schools; the
                 condition under which licenses are to be
                 obtained; the question of promotion for long
                 and distinguished service of teachers;
                 pensions, salaries and proper means of pro-
                 viding for increase of same; the best text
                 books and their costs; the underlying cause
                 or causes of the large number of failures by
                 students at the entrance examinations to
                 Prince of Wales College and after admission
                 thereto; and other matters respecting
                 education.

Conclusions/Recommendations

That the administrative machinery of the Department of
Education be completely reorganized in order to provide
greater stability and continuity of policy, and to remove
it from the vicissitudes of party;

That consolidation be effected and that instruction in
grades nine and ten in one-roomed schools be discontinued

as soon as possible;

That in an attempt to stem the drift to towns the programme of studies in the upper grades of the rural schools
be reorganized to include optional courses in agriculture,
elementary mechanics and bookkeeping;

That school buildings be at least fit for children to live
and work in for a large part of the day;

That the role of the inspector be broadened to include
constructive supervision as well as critical inspection;

That certain teachers of experience and proved efficiency
act as travelling instructors or demonstrators to aid the
beginning teachers;

That the granting of teaching permits to academically
unqualified persons be wholly discontinued, and third-
class licenses be abolished;

That in the interests of contentment and stability,
teachers receive a living salary;

That the Board of Education and the Teachers Federation
should formulate a plan to provide pensions.

References

Prince Edward Island, 'Report of the Royal Commission on
Education', *Journals*, 1930, App. J.

50 COMMISSION ON SCHOOL DIVISION NO. 1
   (Judicial Commission)

   Appointed   April 7, 1955

   Reported   July 12, 1955

   Commission   Three members; Walter E. Darby (Judge of
                Prince County Court) chairman

   Purpose   To investigate the dissatisfaction felt by

some ratepayers in School District No. 1
regarding consolidation.

Conclusions/Recommendations

That whereas the larger unit of school administration is
providing much better educational facilities, a higher
standard of academic training, and a better qualified
teaching staff, School Division No. 1 should not be broken
up, nor should any school district within the Division be
permitted to withdraw;

That before any new Divisions are formed, considerable
study should be devoted to laying a proper foundation so
that an harmonious and working administration will result.

References

Prince Edward Island, 'Report of the Committee on School
Division No. 1', 1955.

51 SELECT STANDING COMMITTEE ON EDUCATION
(Legislative Committee)

Appointed   February 22, 1956

Reported   March 14, 1956

Committee   Five members; J. George MacKay (Member for
                 Prince County) chairman

Purpose   To consider problems in education generally,
                 and in particular to give careful considera-
                 tion to the problem of School District No. 1.

Conclusions/Recommendations

That School District Number 1 be broken up in conformity
with the wishes of the people as expressed in the
plebiscite.

References

Prince Edward Island, *Journals*, 1956.

52 SELECT STANDING COMMITTEE ON EDUCATION
(Legislative Committee)

Appointed   March 13, 1957

Reported   April 16, 1957

Committee   Nine members; Frederic A. Large (Member for
              Queen's County) chairman

Purpose   To hear representations from persons
              interested in presenting their ideas and
              opinions for educational change.

Conclusions/Recommendations

That a Government policy encouraging school districts to
unite voluntarily into larger administrative units be
undertaken;

That grades 9 and 10 be removed from one-room rural schools
and channelled to regional high schools which are desper-
ately needed;

That without losing sight of the fundamentals, a more
diversified curriculum be presented;

That standards for admission to teacher training be raised
with Grade 12 the minimum;

That a teachers' salary scale recognizing qualifications
and experience be put into operation;

That because of the enormous power wielded by the Minister
of Education, there be a return to the principle of a
Board of Education;

That federal aid be sought for financing, and that local
communities be expected to assume a fair share of the costs.

References

Prince Edward Island, 'Report of the Select Standing Committee on Education of the Legislative Assembly of Prince Edward Island', 1957.

53 SELECT STANDING COMMITTEE ON EDUCATION
(Legislative Committee)

Appointed   March 12, 1958

Reported   April 11, 1958

Committee   Seven members; Morley M. Bell (Member for Prince County) chairman

Purpose   To consider problems in education generally.

Conclusions/Recommendations

That satisfaction be expressed at the manner in which the recommendations of the Select Committee on Education of the 1957 Session of the Legislature have been implemented.

References

Prince Edward Island, *Journals*, 1958.

54 ROYAL COMMISSION ON EDUCATIONAL FINANCE AND RELATED PROBLEMS IN ADMINISTRATION
(General Commission)

Appointed   October 15, 1959

Reported   April, 1960

Commission   One member; Melton Ezra La Zerte (former Dean of Education, University of Alberta)

Purpose   To enquire into all matters relating to the administration and the financial support of

schools established and operated under The
Education Act and The School Act of the
Province, the relative tax paying ability of
the Province in comparison with that of the
other provinces of Canada, and the financial
problems in the training of teachers.

Conclusions/Recommendations

That Prince Edward Island adopt principles currently
shaping educational practice in most Canadian provinces;
including a foundation program, equal educational opportunity, and equality of responsibility for the support of
elementary and secondary education;

That a larger percentage of the net general expenditure of
the Province be spent annually on education;

That a foundation program supported by provincial grants
and uniform local taxation be prescribed for the Province;

That local school boards be urged to form consolidated
school districts;

That a minimum salary schedule be prescribed with incre-
ments based on qualifications and experience;

That diversified programs at secondary school level be
available in the five composite schools;

That minimum requirements for teacher training be senior
matriculation plus the completion of a two-year program of
academic and professional subjects.

References

Prince Edward Island, *Report of the Commissioner on
Educational Finance and Related Problems in Administration*,
1960.

55 ROYAL COMMISSION ON HIGHER EDUCATION
(General Commission)

Appointed   July 9, 1964

Reported   January 20, 1965

Commission   Three members; J. Sutherland Bonnell (Presby-
                 terian Minister) chairman

Purpose   To make full inquiry and to indicate how the
                 future requirements of the Province in the
                 field of higher education may best be met and
                 the available resources used in the most
                 efficient manner.

Conclusions/Recommendations

That the provincial allocation of funds at the university
level be increased;

That Prince of Wales College be made a degree granting
institution at once;

That Grade 12 be established as the standard university
entrance requirement;

That the Provincial Government cooperate in the federation
of St. Dunstan's and Prince of Wales by the establishment
of a University of Prince Edward Island with two colleges
as components.

References

Prince Edward Island, *Report of the Royal Commission on
Higher Education for Prince Edward Island,* 1965.

56 PROVINCE OF PRINCE EDWARD ISLAND: PROVINCIAL-MUNICIPAL
   FISCAL STUDY
   (Special Committee)

Appointed   September 12, 1968

Reported   August, 1969 [to Provincial Treasurer]

Committee   Touche, Ross, Bailey & Smart (Chartered

Accountants)

Purpose   To carry out a study of provincial and
             municipal taxation in Prince Edward Island.

Conclusions/Recommendations

That the major unit of local government in Prince Edward
Island has been the school board, not the municipality;

That outside of Charlottetown and Summerside the School Act
has provided not only for the levying of taxes but also for
their assessment;

That the province now introduce a foundations program of
public school education which would establish overall
standards for such items as teachers' salaries, maintenance
of school buildings, etc., for the entire Island (including
Charlottetown and Summerside);

That the province assume the full cost of the financing of
the public school foundation program;

That the province enter the real property tax field in
order to assist it in the financing of the public school
foundation program;

That the province continue its present policy of financing
two-thirds of the cost of public school education from
general revenues; the remaining one-third to come from a
new province-wide uniform education rate on real property.

References

Prince Edward Island, *Province of Prince Edward Island:
Provincial-Municipal Fiscal Study*, 1969.

57 COMMITTEE ON TEACHER EDUCATION IN PRINCE EDWARD ISLAND
   (Special Committee)

Appointed   April 16, 1970

Reported   April, 1971

Committee   Four members; Verner Smitheram (Department of
                 Philosophy, University of P.E.I.) chairman

Purpose   To consider the current development of teacher
                 education programs in Canada; the structure,
                 objectives, principles and graduate study for
                 teacher education at the University of P.E.I.;
                 the local needs of teachers and problems of
                 teacher training; the relation between the
                 Faculty of Education and other departments
                 in the University; the relationship between
                 the Faculty of Education and external bodies
                 such as the school system, the Atlantic
                 Institute of Education, the Provincial
                 Department of Education, the Teachers'
                 Federation and the Association of School
                 Trustees; and the professional status of
                 elementary and secondary school teachers.

Conclusions/Recommendations

[Among the 91 recommendations were the following:]

That all teachers now entering the profession undertake a
university program of studies leading to a baccalaureate
degree;

That procedures for the upgrading of practicing teachers
to degree level be established;

That Education students be required to meet the same or
higher academic standards as students in other Faculties;

That elementary and secondary school teachers be recognized
as peers, and that this be reflected in their preparatory
programs, responsibilities, and pay;

That affiliation with the Atlantic Institute of Education
be undertaken immediately so that graduate courses could
be offered in P.E.I., research in education relevant to
the Province could be coordinated, and U.P.E.I. have
access to educational specialists.

References

University of Prince Edward Island, *Teacher Education: Perseverance or Professionalism,* 1971.

58 EVALUATION OF ELEMENTARY AND SECONDARY EDUCATION IN PRINCE EDWARD ISLAND
(Departmental Committee)

Appointed   1973

Reported   1974   [to Department of Development]

Committee   Two members; Verner Smitheram (Department of Philosophy, University of P.E.I.) chairman

Purpose   To evaluate elementary and secondary education in Prince Edward Island from 1969 to 1973.

Conclusions/Recommendations

That the general policy of school consolidation be pursued to full implementation;

That special measures be established to ensure that the educational opportunities of disadvantaged children are improved to the same degree as those of other types of children;

That a decentralized organization for curriculum design and development engaging the collaboration of all school interested persons be instituted as soon as possible;

That wherever possible, learning opportunities be organized to permit each individual to progress at his own rate rather than at a group rate;

That evaluation be continuous rather than periodic and the use of self-evaluation procedures be maximized.

References

Prince Edward Island, *An Evaluation of Elementary and Secondary Education in Prince Edward Island,* vol. I & II, [1974].

59 COMMITTEE ON EDUCATION
   (Legislative Committee)

   Appointed   January 9, 1837

   Reported   February 14, 1837

   Committee   Five members; John A. Street (Member for
                Northumberland) chairman

   Purpose   To inquire into the Grammer School system in
                the Province.

   Conclusions/Recommendations

   That having taken the subject matter of these Petitions
   into their most serious consideration, the Committee cannot at present recommend the adoption of public assessments
   as a mode of supporting Grammar or other Schools.

   References

   New Brunswick, *Journal of the House of Assembly of New
   Brunswick*, 1837.

60 COMMITTEE ON EDUCATION
   (Legislative Committee)

   Appointed   January 31, 1842

<u>Reported</u>   March 31, 1842

<u>Committee</u>   Twelve members; L.A. Wilmot (Member for York)
            chairman

<u>Purpose</u>   To consider all matters brought before the
            House connected with the subject of Education
            throughout the Province.

Conclusions/Recommendations

That the present voluntary and therefore uncertain mode of
local contribution for the support of Teachers and the
erection of School Houses not be permitted to continue
longer;

That he who has property and no children should be compelled to contribute towards the education of the children
of those who may have no property.

References

New Brunswick, *Journals*, 1842.

61 GOVERNOR COLEBROOK'S ELABORATE INQUIRY INTO EDUCATION
   (Special Committee)

<u>Appointed</u>   1844

<u>Reported</u>   February, 1845

<u>Committee</u>   Three members; James Brown (Inspector of
            Schools) chairman

<u>Purpose</u>   To inquire into the present condition and
            future improvement of the Parish Schools.

Conclusions/Recommendations

That the most effectual remedy for the evils arising from
the apathy and backwardness of the people and the scanty
and irregular attendance of the children will be the
diffusion of information on the object and power of

education.

References

New Brunswick, *Journals*, 1845.

62 SELECT COMMITTEE ON EDUCATION
   (Legislative Committee)

   Appointed   February 3, 1845

   Reported   April 12, 1845

   Committee   Seven members; Lemuel Wilmot (Member for York)
                chairman

   Purpose   To report by Bill or otherwise on matters in
                His Excellency's Speech which relate to the
                Education of Youth.

Conclusions/Recommendations

That the Committee are deeply impressed with the importance
of this great subject and hope that the Legislature will be
prepared at the next Session to adopt such improvements in
the present system as will carry with them the approbation
and support of the country, and at the same time ensure
those Educational advantages which are in a great measure
denied by the present defective system.

References

New Brunswick, *Journals*, 1845.

63 ROYAL COMMISSION ON KING'S COLLEGE
   (General Commission)

   Appointed   May 1, 1854

   Reported   December 28, 1854

Commission   Five members; John Hamilton Gray (Queen's
               Counsel) chairman

Purpose   To inquire into the present state of King's
               College, its management and utility, with the
               view of improving the same and rendering that
               Institution more generally useful, and of
               suggesting the best mode of effecting that
               desirable object.

Conclusions/Recommendations

That the system of Collegiate Education be at once
comprehensive, special, and practical; that it ought to
embrace those branches of learning which are usually
taught in Colleges both in Great Britain and the United
States -- and special courses of instruction adapted to
the agricultural, mechanical, manufacturing, and commercial
pursuits and interests of New Brunswick; and that the
subjects and modes of instruction in science and the
modern languages (including English, French, and German)
should have practical reference to those pursuits and
interests;

That the idea of abolishing or suspending the Endowment of
King's College should not be entertained for a moment;

That a non-denominational plan with facilities for each
persuasion to give weekly religious instruction be
adopted;

That a provincial body under the style and title of 'The
University of New Brunswick' be established.

References

New Brunswick, *Journals,* 1854.

New Brunswick, *Report of the Commission appointed under the
Act of Assembly relating to King's College,* 1855.

64 COMMISSION OF INQUIRY INTO THE CONDUCT AND MANAGEMENT OF
   THE INSTITUTION FOR THE DEAF AND DUMB, FREDERICTON

(Judicial Commission)

Appointed   May 7, 1886

Reported   July 8, 1886

Commission   One member; James Mitchell (Surveyor General
               of New Brunswick)

Purpose   To inquire into the circumstances connected
               with the alleged misconduct and mismanagement
               at the Institution for the Deaf and Dumb,
               Fredericton.

Conclusions/Recommendations

That no grounds exist for the grave charges which have
been made.

References

New Brunswick, *Journals,* 1887, Supplementary Appendix.

65 COMMISSION OF INQUIRY INTO CHARGES RELATING TO THE
BATHURST SCHOOLS AND OTHER SCHOOLS IN GLOUCESTER COUNTY
(General Commission)

Appointed   April 18, 1893

Reported   November 23, 1893

Commission   One member; John James Fraser (Supreme Court
               Justice)

Purpose   To inquire into and fully and thoroughly
               investigate any alleged infractions of the
               Law or Regulations on the part of the Teachers
               or Trustees in the Bathurst schools and other
               schools in Gloucester County.

Conclusions/Recommendations

That all sorts and kinds of irregularities may occur in the

carrying on of the schools in any county, but unless they are brought to the notice of the Inspector of Schools for the county, and through him to the notice of the Board of Education itself, it would be manifestly unjust to charge the Board of Education with any dereliction of duty in regard to such irregularities.

References

New Brunswick, *Journals*, 1893.

New Brunswick, *Report upon Changes Relating to the Bathurst Schools and Other Schools in Gloucester County*, 1894.

66 COMMISSION IN RESPECT TO THE SALARIES OF TEACHERS IN THE PUBLIC SCHOOLS OF THE PROVINCE
(General Commission)

Appointed   April 17, 1919

Reported   March 19, 1920

Commission   Five members; W.S. Carter (Chief Superinten-
                dent of Education)

Purpose   To take into consideration and make recom-
                mendations as to the best means to provide
                increased salaries for teachers in the public
                schools of the Province.

Conclusions/Recommendations

That the County Fund tax be doubled and a sliding scale instituted to give needy districts more assistance;

That the minimum salary, including Government grants, to be paid in the poorest districts be $500 per year; in the middle districts, $600; and in the more prosperous districts, $700;

That the Board of Education withhold County and Provincial Grants from trustees who engaged teachers at lower than the proposed minimum salaries;

That teachers who accepted less than the minimum be suspended for a designated period.

References

New Brunswick, *Acts of the Legislative Assembly of New
Brunswick*, 9 George V., 1919, CAP. XXXIII.

New Brunswick, *Journals*, 1920, Supplementary Appendix.

67 ROYAL COMMISSION ON EDUCATION
(General Commission)

Appointed   May 15, 1931

Reported   March 1, 1932

Commission   Twenty-two members; A.S. McFarland (Chief
                Superintendent of Education) chairman

Purpose   To investigate the Educational system of the
                Province and particularly to consider: (a)
                the administration in co-operation of (i)
                common school, (ii) agricultural and (iii)
                vocational education; and (b) the method of
                raising money for the support of schools
                together with the area of school districts
                with a view to approximate equalization of
                school rates and especially to giving greater
                assistance to poor districts; (c) the relation
                of all branches of education in common,
                agricultural schools, vocational schools, to
                the universities in the Province, (d) such
                other subjects in relation thereto as the
                Council shall deem cognate to the inquiry.

Conclusions/Recommendations

That there be one central Board of Education to control all
branches of education, including academic, vocational,
agricultural education, and physical training if this
could be done without additional cost;

That Third Class temporary teaching licenses be abolished
and entrance requirements for Second Class training be
raised to Grade Eleven within three years;

That more professional training and practice teaching with
observation and criticism be given;

That entrance requirements for First Class be full High
School with good standing;

That since 140,000 of New Brunswick's 408,000 people are of
French origin, Normal Schools meet the increasing demand
for teachers who can teach both English and French;

That a system of Helping Teachers similar to that already
operating in Nova Scotia be introduced;

That a Provincial Tax Commission be appointed to insure
equalization of assessment and educational taxes;

That a minimum standard of school service and a suitable
schedule of minimum salaries be set up;

That the present County Grammar Schools and Parish
Superior Schools be replaced by a system of High Schools;

That the Grammar School Course be maintained for those
desiring matriculation but a modified programme be introduced;

That in order to improve the means of communication between
the English and French races and provide a more sympathetic
understanding of each other, book teachings in the first
two grades be exclusively in the native language of the
child, and special editions of text-books be made available
up to grade eight with the two-languages on opposite pages.

References

New Brunswick, *Report of the Committee on Education for the
Province of New Brunswick,* 1932.

(Special Committee)

Appointed   1937

Reported   1937

Committee   Three members; William A. Plenderleith
                 (British Columbia School Inspector) chairman

Purpose   To survey the methods of administering and
                 financing education in New Brunswick and to
                 make suggestions.

Conclusions/Recommendations

That an immediate improvement be made in rural school
conditions by following certain specific suggestions;

That greater financial responsibility for rural education
be undertaken by the Provincial Government;

That a re-organization of the administrative system be
undertaken.

References

New Brunswick, *The Plenderleith Report*, 1937.

69 COMMITTEE ON CURRICULUM AND TEXT BOOKS
   (Departmental Committee)

   Appointed   February 12, 1937

   Reported   [Created as a standing committee]

   Committee   Fourteen members; Fletcher Peacock (Director,
                    Educational Services) chairman

   Purpose   To make an exhaustive study of advances in
                    science and educational methods as well as
                    the requirements of a constantly changing
                    social order and to recommend a suitable
                    programme of studies.

Conclusions/Recommendations

References

New Brunswick, 'Report of the Director of Educational
Services', 1937.

70 ROYAL COMMISSION ON THE FINANCING OF SCHOOLS IN NEW
BRUNSWICK
(General Commission)

Appointed   September 11, 1953

Reported   January 26, 1955

Commission   Three members; William Havelock McKenzie
              (Superintendent of Schools) chairman

Purpose   To inquire into all matters proper to be
              considered for the disposition of government
              grants made available to and administered
              through the several school administrative
              units of the Province and the relative tax
              paying ability of the Province in comparison
              with that of the other provinces of Canada.

Conclusions/Recommendations

That the Federal Government participate, directly or
indirectly, in the financial support of the public schools
of New Brunswick, but in such manner, and only in such
manner, that the provincial government retains its full
control over the system; and further, that this participation be on the basis of fiscal need.

References

New Brunswick, *Report of the Royal Commission on the
Financing of Schools in New Brunswick*, 1955.

71 ROYAL COMMISSION ON HIGHER EDUCATION IN NEW BRUNSWICK
   (General Commission)

   Appointed   May 9, 1961

   Reported   June 21, 1962

   Commission   Three members; John J. Deutsch (Vice-Principal,
                  Queen's University) chairman

   Purpose   To make full inquiry and to make findings and
                  recommendations consistent with the public
                  interest and the general welfare of the
                  Province of New Brunswick respecting the
                  whole field of higher education, and to
                  indicate how the future requirements of the
                  Province may best be met by the various
                  institutions, and the role which the said
                  institutions should play in meeting those
                  requirements so that the available resources
                  of the Province can be used in the most
                  efficient manner.

Conclusions/Recommendations

That there be only two degree-granting institutions in the
province, one French-speaking and one English;

That the Legislative Assembly grant a charter to establish
the University of Moncton as the sole degree-granting
French-language institution of higher education in New
Brunswick;

That to this institution, St. Joseph's, Sacred Heart, and
St. Louis be affiliated for academic purposes but retain
their own administrative autonomy;

That St. Thomas University be federated with the University
of New Brunswick and transfer its operations to the
Fredericton campus;

That a permanent branch of the University of New Brunswick
be established in the Metropolitan Saint John area;

That Mount Allison continue its announced policy of
remaining a liberal arts college of limited enrolment;

That no new degree-granting institutions be established in
the province.

References

New Brunswick, *Report of the Royal Commission on Higher
Education in New Brunswick,* 1962.

72 ROYAL COMMISSION ON FINANCE AND MUNICIPAL TAXATION
(Related Commission)

Appointed   March 8, 1962

Reported   November 4, 1963

Commission   Five members; E.G. Byrne (Queen's Counsel,
               Bathurst) chairman

Purpose   To hold inquiry into and concerning the
               desirability and feasibility of maintaining
               or increasing the present revenues of muni-
               cipal bodies, and relieving individuals and
               industry of some part of municipal tax
               burdens by the sbustitution or creation of
               new or other sources of revenue or bases of
               taxation.

Conclusions/Recommendations

That the Provincial Government assume full responsibility
for administering and financing a uniform programme of
elementary and secondary education, both academic and
vocational;

That the province be reorganized into about sixty school
districts, each with at least one central high school and
with a number of feeder elementary and junior high schools;

That part of the costs be raised by a uniform provincially

imposed tax on an equally-assessed real property tax;

That a uniform salary scale be established for teachers, based at first on the high Saint John scale; and there be no more negotiation of salaries at the local level;

That adequate account be taken of the two main linguistic and cultural groups in New Brunswick, recognizing at the same time the essential unity of the educational aims of the two groups in a modern industrial society.

References

New Brunswick, *Report of the Royal Commission on Finance and Municipal Taxation in New Brunswick,* 1963.

73 ROYAL COMMISSION ON METROPOLITAN SAINT JOHN
(Related Commission)

Appointed   May 29, 1962

Reported   July 10, 1963

Commission   One member; H. Carl Goldenberg (Barrister of
               Montreal)

Purpose   To inquire into the form, method and manner of
               municipal government now existing in any of
               the units located in the County of Saint John,
               the feasibility of amalgamation, and the
               feasibility of alteration of boundaries.

Conclusions/Recommendations

That legislation be enacted to consolidate all school administration within the County of Saint John under a County Board of School Trustees, which shall be responsible for all public education in Grades 1 to 13;

That the Board of School Trustees be appointed, and that it be composed of twelve members, of whom four, including the chairman, shall be appointed by the Provincial Government, and eight by the Common Council, and that their term of office be three years, subject to re-appointment.

References

New Brunswick, *Report of the Royal Commission in Metropolitan Saint John,* [1963].

74 COMMITTEE ON THE FINANCING OF HIGHER EDUCATION IN NEW BRUNSWICK
(Departmental Committee)

Appointed   February 9, 1966

Reported   February, 1967

Committee   Three members; John J. Deutsch (Vice-Principal, Queen's University) chairman

Purpose   To study, in consultation with the universities of the Province and with due regard to the Province's resources, and to make recommendations to the government regarding the types and amounts of assistance to be required by both institutions and students, and to consider and report upon other related matters. [The Report was submitted to the Lieutenant-Governor in Council as a follow-up to the 1964 report of the Royal Commission on Higher Education.]

Conclusions/Recommendations

That further change must be made in the administrative structure of the University of Moncton in order to be equipped to meet successfully its growing responsibilities for providing advanced, specialized and professional education for the Province's French-speaking population;

That provision of adequate facilities for the Saint John branch of the University of New Brunswick needs to be accelerated;

That a permanent Commission on Post-Secondary Education should be established immediately which would have a continuing responsibility for advising the government on the needs and the appropriate pattern for future development.

References

New Brunswick, *Report of the Committee on the Financing of Higher Education in New Brunswick,* 1967.

75 STUDY OF TEACHER EDUCATION AND TRAINING
   (Special Committee)

Appointed   January 4, 1968

Reported   1969

Committee   One member; Donald C. Duffie (President, St. Thomas University)

Purpose   To consider the present and future roles of universities, teachers' colleges and other institutions in meeting the Province's needs in the field of teacher education and training; to assess the adequacy of the relationship and the forms of cooperative effort which now exist among the universities, teachers' colleges and other institutions concerned; and to recommend whatever changes may be required.

Conclusions/Recommendations

That Teacher Training be integrated into Higher Education, given over to the universities, and placed under the Higher Education Commission;

That admission requirements for candidates for teacher training be those of the university;

That there be a continuing selection of candidates for

teacher training;

That curriculum be developed by the university, without prejudice to certification;

That appointment of staff in education be made by the university;

That 'elementary' and 'secondary' teacher training be given in one and the same faculty of education;

That the faculty of education should be subject to the same academic procedures as other faculties of the university;

That practice teaching should be examined and expanded;

That the minimum program for those intending to teach academic subjects in high school should be five years beyond Junior Matriculation;

That the present minimum two year teacher training program for 'elementary' teachers should be increased to a minimum of three and later four years in university.

References

New Brunswick Higher Education Commission, *Teacher Education and Training: A Report*, 1969.

76 A STUDY OF HIGHER EDUCATION IN THE ATLANTIC PROVINCES FOR THE 1970's
(Special Committee)

Appointed   1969

Reported   December, 1969

Committee   Three members; John F. Crean, Michael M. Ferguson, Hugh J. Somers [no chairman designated]

Purpose   To study the present state of higher education

in the three Maritime Provinces and its
future prospects; and to assess existing forms
of cooperative endeavour and new forms that
may be required.

Conclusions/Recommendations

That universities and governments of the Atlantic Provinces
plan to provide the numbers of university places that will
be sought by students as indicated by increasing enrolments
and that adequate financial support be provided;

That governments act with due respect for the autonomy and
freedom necessary to the institutions of higher learning;

That the universities give the highest priority to the
implementation of their agreement in regard to graduate
studies and to a continued search for more effective means
of cooperation and coordination in all areas of higher
education;

That the public relations officers of the universities
review critically their present use of the communications
media, and formulate policies that would give full information on higher education to the taxpayer on whom the
universities depend;

That, whether Maritime political union comes about or not,
there be one university grants committee adequately staffed
to serve the three provinces;

That each institution of higher education set definite
targets of enrolments, not only in general but by
faculties, for three to five-year periods.

References

Association of Atlantic Universities, *Higher Education in
the Atlantic Provinces for the 1970's,* 1969.

[Prepared by the Association of Atlantic Universities for
the Maritime Union Study]

77 TASK FORCE ON SOCIAL DEVELOPMENT AND SOCIAL WELFARE
(Departmental Committee)

Appointed   July, 1970

Reported   September, 1971

Committee   Eleven members; Emery Le Blanc (Former Editor
             of *L'Evangeline*) and H.L. Nutter (Dean of
             Christ Church Cathedral, Fredericton) co-
             chairmen

Purpose   To initiate and promote public dialogue on
             problems in social development and social
             welfare, and on the objectives and proposed
             objectives of government; and to recommend
             broad guidelines to the Government to assist
             in the future development of program prior-
             ities and legislation in the field of social
             development and social welfare.

Conclusions/Recommendations

That the role of education be recognized as a major
component of social development;

That provincial authorities accept in practice the stated
principle that the purpose of public school education in
New Brunswick is to 'provide educational opportunities for
all educable children so that each may develop to the
limit of his capacity and special abilities';

That orientation of the education system be broadened to
'preparation for living' rather than the narrower orientation of 'preparation for work' which appears predominant
at present;

That in the course of teacher training programs, candidates
for certification as teachers be continually assessed
regarding their motivation, ability to relate to students,
and potential effectiveness as teachers;

That since education must prepare a person for living, the
curriculum be restructured at both the elementary and
secondary levels to recognize the primary importance of

instruction in social relationships and physical education; in addition, areas such as music, art, homemaking, and so on must be recognized as essential components of the educational process;

That a French-language section be created within the Department of Education, with full responsibility for the determination of the French-language curriculum, the adoption of French-language textbooks and materials, and the setting of personnel standards and equivalences in qualifications for French-speaking teachers.

References

New Brunswick, *Participation and Development: Report of the New Brunswick Task Force on Social Development,* 1971.

78 STUDY COMMITTEE ON AUXILIARY CLASSES
(Departmental Committee)

Appointed   1971

Reported   1972

Committee   Nine members; G.E.M. MacLeod (Assistant Deputy Minister of Education) and Elizabeth J. Owens (Consultant in Special Education) co-chairmen

Purpose   To study the present operation of Auxiliary Classes in New Brunswick; to study operational models in other provinces of Canada; to make recommendations with respect to the future operation of Auxiliary Classes and to establish and supervise pilot projects for evaluative purposes.

Conclusions/Recommendations

That the term 'trainable mentally retarded' be redefined; and that the term 'cerebral palsied persons' be replaced in the Auxiliary Classes Act with the term 'physically handicapped';

That the Auxiliary Classes Act provide for tutoring for handicapped persons upon application by the District Superintendent to the Minister;

That the Department of Social Services become the supporting agency for adult programs for the handicapped over age 18 years;

That school districts provide transportation for persons under the Auxiliary Classes Act;

That the Department of Education assume the financial responsibility for the maintenance of facilities which house Auxiliary Classes;

That the Interdepartmental Committee on Mental Retardation be charged with the immediate responsibility of investigating the cost-sharing arrangements for the handicapped with the Federal Government.

References

New Brunswick, *The Right to Choose and the Right to be Served: The Report of the Study Committee on Auxiliary Classes,* 1972.

79 COMMITTEE ON THE COMMUNITY USE OF SCHOOL FACILITIES (Departmental Committee)

Appointed   December, 1971

Reported   June, 1973

Committee   Seven members; W.S. Ritchie (New Brunswick Department of Education) chairman

Purpose   To determine, in consultation with school and municipal authorities, community groups, private agencies and the public at large, means by which school facilities may be best utilized; and to explore means whereby a closer liaison may be established between school authorities and community recreation councils, commissions, and departments, in the matter of the planning of new multi-use school-community facilities.

Conclusions/Recommendations

That all schools (public and trade) be made available for use by groups other than regularly scheduled classes;

That future schools be designed with community use in mind;

That school grounds be considered and developed as parks and/or playgrounds for use in after-school and vacation time;

That additional costs be borne 50% by the province and 50% by the local community;

That the control of facilities remain a responsibility of School Boards.

References

New Brunswick, *Report of the Committee on the Community Use of School Facilities*, 1973.

80 COMMITTEE ON SPECIAL EDUCATION
(Special Committee)

Appointed   April, 1972

Reported   January, 1973 [to Ministers of Education of New Brunswick, Newfoundland, Nova Scotia, and Prince Edward Island]

Committee   Ten members; David Kendall (Professor of Special Education, University of B.C.) chairman

Purpose   To inquire into present facilities and pro-grams available in the Atlantic provinces for children requiring special educational consideration, with particular emphasis on those with impairment of sight and/or hearing; to recommend programs of study and training and procedures for assessment of these children; and to recommend to the governments of the Atlantic provinces further direction in this field, bearing in mind the educational systems of the four provinces.

Conclusions/Recommendations

That the governments of the Atlantic Provinces recognize and endorse the right of all handicapped persons to be educated to the maximum of their potential, and develop a comprehensive range of services and programs sufficient to meet the educational needs of all handicapped persons;

That wherever possible and practicable, handicapped persons be educated in regular public school programs, provided that the special needs of the child can be fully met through the service available in the public schools;

That the Governments, through their education systems, give priority to the establishment and development of diagnostic, remedial and special education services within the public schools at both elementary and secondary levels;

That for the purposes of educational administration the governments distinguish between two main categories of handicapped persons: (Category I: the severely handicapped, and Category II: the educationally handicapped).

References

Atlantic Provinces Report of the Special Education Committee to the Ministers of Education, January 1973.

81 COMMITTEE TO EXAMINE HUMAN RIGHTS EDUCATION IN NEW BRUNSWICK
(Departmental Committee)

Appointed   March, 1973

Reported   August, 1973 [to Department of Labour]

Committee	Four members; Russell A. McNeilly (Faculty of Education, University of New Brunswick) chairman
Purpose	To examine Human Rights Education in New Brunswick in particular, and other jurisdictions in general; to document the need for human rights education; to study the possibility of implementing human rights education in all segments of the school and in teacher education institutions; and to consider methods of approach in establishing human rights education.

Conclusions/Recommendations

That the Human Rights Commission of the Department of Labour along with the Department of Education form an inter-ministerial committee to examine textbooks used in the schools of the Province;

That, as soon as possible, the Human Rights Commission in co-operation with the Department of Education plan, design models and prepare guides for pilot programs on human rights education;

That summer projects utilizing a core of graduate students engage in research on the development of programs and curriculum strategies in human rights education for use in the schools;

That the Human Rights Commission consider the appointment of a part-time consultant in human rights education for the coordination of research activities and field developments;

That the Commission along with the Department of Education should organize workshops for teachers during the school year on human rights education and program planning.

References

New Brunswick, *Strategies for Human Rights Education in New Brunswick*, 1974.

82 COMMITTEE ON EDUCATIONAL PLANNING
(Departmental Committee)

Appointed   March, 1973

Reported   November 2, 1973

Committee   Fifteen members; G.E. Malcolm MacLeod
                 (Assistant Deputy Minister of Education) and
                 Arthur A. Pinet (Regional Superintendent of
                 Schools) co-chairmen

Purpose   To review objectively the complete educational
                 system in New Brunswick today and the role of
                 the Department of Education.

Conclusions/Recommendations

That a selective pre-school education program be developed
which would assure the readiness of all pupils to cope with
and benefit from the basic program of the elementary
school;

That a minimum of six years be recommended for the completion of the elementary school program while making provision for the gifted child;

That the philosophy of continuous progress be implemented
in the junior high school;

That research be conducted regarding the effectiveness of
the three-year junior high school as compared to other
types of organization such as the middle school;

That a study be carried out immediately to evaluate the
current junior and senior high summer school programs;

That second languages be taught by specialists;

That the Department at this time not adopt the policy of
implementing immersion programs throughout the Province,
but it be prepared to encourage such programs and offer
assistance wherever possible;

That art, music, and physical education be studied with a

view to providing them with the same status as other parts
of the basic program;

That the Department of Education assume the financial
responsibility for the education of all special education
children;

That the Department move towards a gradual decentralization
of curriculum development;

That the Department of Education establish area resource
centres.

References

New Brunswick, *Education Tomorrow: Report of the Minister's
Committee on Educational Planning,* 1973.

83 TASK FORCE FOR KINDERGARTEN DESIGN
   (Departmental Committee)

Appointed   June, 1974

Reported   December 20, 1974

Committee   Ten members; Cheryl C. Smith (Consultant,
              Department of Education) Anglophone chairman,
              and Rose Marie Roy (Consultant, Department of
              Education) Francophone chairman

Purpose   To propose a program which is not only viable
              for the province of New Brunswick but which
              also reflects a thorough study of the best in
              current research and practice within the field
              of early childhood education.

Conclusions/Recommendations

That the program have the three following basic
characteristics;

That it provide rich and varied learning experiences for
children;

That it be staffed by caring, informed and trained adults;

That it provide a physical environment which is safe as well as attractive and which promotes learning and healthy development.

References

New Brunswick, *Learning in the Play Environment: Report of the Minister's Task Force for Kindergarten Design (Anglophone)* and 'Vivre pour apprendre à Vivre': Rapport du Groupe de Travail Ministériel sur l'Étude des Maternelles (Section Francophone), December 1974.

84 COMMITTEE ON HIGHER EDUCATION IN THE FRENCH SECTOR OF NEW BRUNSWICK
(Special Committee)

Appointed   September 23, 1974

Reported   April 22, 1975

Committee   Three members; Louis Lebel (Judge, St. Quentin), chairman

Purpose   To study the present structure of Francophone higher education which originated with the Deutsch Report in 1962.

Conclusions/Recommendations

That there be a single French Language University for all francophones of New Brunswick;

That Université Acadienne not be responsible for any teaching in English Language, apart from language courses; and that it must however, be the only Institution with a mandate to provide French language education to students in New Brunswick;

That there be created a new university: that this new university replace, as from July 1st, 1976, the University of Moncton, St. Louis Maillet College, and Jesus Mary of

Shippagan;

That Université Acadienne be the legal entity which owns the land, buildings and equipment of the present University of Moncton, of St. Louis Maillet College, and of Jesus Mary College of Shippagan: and that Université Acadienne provide full-time university education on each of these three campuses.

References

Maritime Provinces High Education Commission, *Report of the Committee on Higher Education in the French Sector of New Brunswick*, 1975.

85 TASK FORCE ON SCHOOL FOOD SERVICE IN NEW BRUNSWICK
   (Departmental Committee)

   Appointed   1975

   Reported   October, 1976

   Committee   Three members; Katherine Johnston (Home
                 Economics Consultant) chairman

   Purpose   To survey present situations of school
                 cafeterias with regard to funding, space,
                 facilities, staff and service; to examine
                 policies; to project an adequate school
                 cafeteria policy; to project cost of implemen-
                 tation; and to look at various means of
                 funding.

Conclusions/Recommendations

That the Department of Education in co-operation with other interested government departments develop a policy for school food service which would ensure adequate nourishment for students during the hours they are required to remain at school.

References

New Brunswick, *School Food Service in New Brunswick;
Report of Department of Education and Department of
Health,* 1976.

86 TASK FORCE ON PROVINCIAL TESTING AND EVALUATION
(Departmental Committee)

Appointed   November, 1975

Reported   August, 1976

Committee   Two members; Lionel Bruneau (Principal,
              Nepisiguit High School) and Barry E. Fontaine
              (Principal, Millidgeville North Senior High
              School) co-chairmen

Purpose   To study the question of accountability as it
              relates to provincial responsibility for
              education and to make recommendations on the
              means to achieve it through provincial
              evaluation programs; to determine and make
              recommendations to the Minister on informa-
              tional needs that should and could be met
              through a provincial testing program; and to
              study the need for and make recommendations
              on a Provincial Advisory Committee on
              Evaluation.

Conclusions/Recommendations

That the Department of Education continue to make every
effort to ensure that the general public is made fully
aware of the General Educational Development Tests
Program;

That the Second Language Testing Program should be
encouraged and supported by the Department of Education;

That the Francophone 3, 6 and 9 Testing Program be
continued in some form;

That the criteria of the Co-operative School Evaluation

Program should be revised to focus more on good pedagogical practices rather than specific innovations;

That the current New Brunswick School Achievement Testing Program be discontinued;

That the Department of Education initiate the development of an annual criterion-referenced provincial testing program for grades 5, 8 and 11 with priority on First Language and Mathematics;

That the Department administer to students norm-referenced achievement tests at the end of the 6th, 9th and 12th years every three years.

References

New Brunswick, *Task Force on Provincial Testing and Evaluation Report,* 1976.

87 TASK FORCE ON SCHOOL LIBRARIES
  (Departmental Committee)

  Appointed   November 20, 1975

  Reported   March 4, 1977

  Committee   Nine members; Dale Aiken (New Brunswick
                 Library Council) chairman

  Purpose   To examine present methods of staffing and
                 supporting school libraries, the relationships
                 between extension libraries at the regional
                 level and school libraries, present expendi-
                 tures on school libraries; to make recommen-
                 dations and to consider costs.

Conclusions/Recommendations

That a comprehensive, systematic plan for the development of school libraries in New Brunswick be formulated;

That, on a one-year pilot basis, library co-ordinators or

supervisors be appointed immediately in two Superintenden-
cies, one Anglophone and one Francophone, responsible to
the District Superintendents;

That Provincial library consultants within the Program
Development and Implementation Branches of the Department
of Education and directly responsible to the Directors
of those branches be appointed immediately.

References

New Brunswick, *Report: Task Force on School Libraries*,
1977.

88 SPECIAL COMMITTEE ON STUDENT AID
   (Departmental Committee)

   Appointed   February 9, 1976

   Reported   March 26, 1976

   Committee   Three members; (No chairman designated;
                  Fernand Arsenault, University of Moncton,
                  first listed)

   Purpose   To review the Student Aid Program as it
                  applied to the province and to make recommen-
                  dations.

   Conclusions/Recommendations

   That a Loan Rebate Schedule as outlined be adopted;

   That the Loan Rebate formula apply only to students
   graduating from New Brunswick institutions or outside the
   province where the discipline is not offered;

   That the special bursary program called post-graduate
   grants administered by the Department of Youth be altered
   to assist needy students at the post-graduate level;

   That there be a student advisory body on Student Aid.

References

New Brunswick, *Report to the Cabinet by the Special Committee on Student Aid,* March, 1976.

89 TASK FORCE ON SCHOOL YEAR
   (Departmental Committee)

   Appointed   June 14, 1976

   Reported   February 28, 1977

   Committee   Ten members; Madeleine Girouard (New Brunswick
                  School Trustees' Association) and A.H.
                  Kingett (New Brunswick Teachers' Association)
                  co-chairmen

   Purpose   To make a complete study of school year
                  organization with a view to making recommen-
                  dations, both short-term and long-term,
                  relative to the school year in school
                  districts throughout the Province.

Conclusions/Recommendations

That the year round operation of schools in the province
of New Brunswick is not desirable at this point of time,
and although there is some evidence to support the conclu-
sion that economic savings might be realized, the evidence
is by no means conclusive;

That there is considerable evidence that the year round
operation of schools is neither socially nor educationally
acceptable;

That the school year consist of 195 days;

That the school year begin on the last Monday in August;

That of the 195 days, thirteen days be available for
professional development activities and administrative
purposes.

References

New Brunswick, *Report of Task Force on School Year*, 1977.

QUEBEC

90 COMMITTEE OF THE COUNCIL ON THE SUBJECT OF PROMOTING THE
MEANS OF EDUCATION
(Legislative Committee)

Appointed   May 31, 1787

Reported   1790

Committee   Nine members; William Smith (Chief Justice)
              chairman

Purpose   To investigate the education of youth through-
              out the province and to report, with all
              convenient speed, the best mode of remedying
              the defects, an estimate of the expense, and
              by what means it may be defrayed.

Conclusions/Recommendations

That parish or village free-schools be erected in every
district of the province at the determination of the
Magistrates of the district;

That each district have a free-school in the central or
county town of the district;

That the tuition of the village schools be limited to
reading, writing, and cyphering;

That the instruction in the district or county schools
extend to all the rules of Arithmetic, the Languages,
Grammar, Book-keeping, Gauging, Navigation, Surveying and

the practical branches of the Mathematics;

That a collegiate institution be erected for cultivating the liberal arts and sciences usually taught in the European Universities; the Theology of Christians excepted, on account of the mixture of two Communions, whose joint aid is desirable, as far as they agree, and who ought to be left to find a separate provision for the candidates in the ministry of their respective churches;

That a society be incorporated for the purpose, and that the charter wisely provide against the perversion of the institution to any sectarian peculiarities, leaving free scope for cultivating the general circle of the sciences.

References

Quebec, *Report of the Committee of the Council on the Subject of Promoting the Means of Education,* 1790.

91 ROYAL COMMISSION FOR THE INVESTIGATION OF ALL GRIEVANCES AFFECTING HIS MAJESTY'S SUBJECTS OF LOWER CANADA (Related Commission)

Appointed   1835

Reported   1836

Commission   Three members; Earl of Gosford, chairman

Purpose   To inquire, to deliberate, and to report on the state of education in Lower Canada with a view to the best means of promoting the more general diffusion of sound learning, religious knowledge, and Christian principle.

Conclusions/Recommendations

That a control authority be created;

That trustees and inspectors be elected by the ratepayers in each parish or school district;

That funds for elementary education come from three
sources: first, from a general assessment on all property
within the parish or school district (on the principle
that as education is a matter in which the public good is
concerned, every inhabitant ought to contribute to it in
proportion to his means); secondly, by a provincial grant
(which should never exceed the amount of what is levied by
local assessment); and thirdly, by payment from the
parents of the children in school (for the reason that
what people get for nothing they are apt not to value
highly).

References

Great Britain, Despatches from Lord Glenelg, Colonial
Secretary, July 17, 1835, *Imperial Blue Books,* vol. 51,
1814-37.

Great Britain, 'General Report', *Imperial Blue Books,* vol.
63, 1837-40.

92 ROYAL COMMISSION ON THE AFFAIRS OF BRITISH NORTH AMERICA
(Related Commission)

Appointed   March 31, 1838

Reported   January 31, 1839

Commission   One member; Earl of Durham

Purpose   To inquire into, and, as far as may be
               possible, to adjust all questions depending
               in the said Provinces of *Lower* and *Upper*
               Canada, or either of them, respecting the
               Form and Administration of the Civil Govern-
               ment thereof respectively.

Conclusions/Recommendations

That a scheme be provided by which the children of these
two antagonist races should be brought together (were it
only for purposes of play would be preferable to one by
which they receive a good education apart) by which both

union and instruction were assured to them; such a scheme
to be divested altogether of political and sectarian
tendencies;

That there be some religious instruction in areas on which
all Christians agree, and that different denominations be
afforded the opportunities of still further and more
exclusive religious instruction which they might enjoy
without offending or interfering with each other;

That financial support be based on the American system of
local assessment at least equal to state grants;

That both normal and model schools be provided to supply
competent teachers;

That explicit provisions be made for inspection and supervision, in which the vitality of every system of education
must eventually reside.

References

Great Britain, Despatch from Lord Glenelg, April 21, 1838,
Imperial Blue Books, vol. 10.

Great Britain, 'Durham's Report on the Affairs of British
North America', *Imperial Blue Books*, vol. 10.

Great Britain, Report by Arthur Buller, assistant
commissioner, 'Durham's Report', App. D.

93 SELECT COMMITTEE OF THE LEGISLATIVE ASSEMBLY, APPOINTED TO
ENQUIRE INTO THE STATE OF EDUCATION AND THE WORKING OF THE
SCHOOL LAWS IN LOWER CANADA
(Legislative Committee)

Appointed   February 22, 1853

Reported   June 7, 1853

Committee   Nine members; L.V. Sicotte (Député de Saint-
              Hyacinthe) chairman

Purpose   To enquire into the state of Education in
           Lower Canada, the working of the School Law,
           the efficiency of the Education Department in
           Lower Canada, and the means of rendering more
           effective the Legislative enactments adopted
           for the advancement of Education in *Lower
           Canada*.

Conclusions/Recommendations

That there be an active, energetic, intelligent management
having the right to both advise and enforce;

That there be much closer surveillance by inspectors
conjointly with local authorities, each to help control the
other;

That a Council of Instruction be formed to decide finally
all contestations and difficulties;

That the local authorities be composed of men qualified by
at least an elementary education;

That normal schools be provided;

That teachers receive sufficient payment, and assistance in
old age to such as have been engaged in teaching for at
least thirty years;

That education be divided into two categories; elementary
education as a foundation for all men in society, and
secondary instruction for specialization in classics or
the professions;

That there be more generous expenditure on education.

References

United Canada, *Journals of the Legislative Assembly of the
Province of Canada,* 1853.

United Canada, *Report of the Select Committee of the
Legislative Assembly, Appointed to Enquire into the State
of Education and the Working of the School Laws in Lower
Canada,* 1853.

94 COMMISSION OF INQUIRY INTO THE SCHOOL TRUST IN THE CITY OF
MONTREAL
(General Commission)

Appointed   September 1, 1882

Reported   June 30, 1883

Commission   Five members; Charles Joseph Coursol (Queen's
                 Counsel, Montreal) chairman

Purpose   To hold an investigation: (1) into the admin-
                 istration of the offices of the School
                 Commissioners of the city of Montreal since
                 their organization, (2) into the alleged
                 necessity of increasing the school tax in the
                 said city, and (3) generally into all matters
                 of public interest respecting such schools and
                 the school system in the said city.

Conclusions/Recommendations

That there be a complete change in the personnel of the
Catholic Board even though the Commissioners did not find
anything proved which could in any way, even in the
slightest degree, impeach the honor and integrity of the
individual members of the Board or of Mr. Principal
Archambault;

That there be an increase in the school tax in Montreal
from two-tenths of a cent on the dollar to three-tenths;

That the number of commissioners on each school board
(Catholic and Protestant) be increased to at least nine,
and that of these, three should be appointed by the
government, three by the city council (chosen from each of
the three electoral divisions of Montreal), and three
should be elected directly by the people (Roman Catholics
and Protestants voting separately);

That a concise financial statement be published half-yearly
in the principal newspapers.

References

Quebec, *Journals*, 1884, Sessional Papers, No. 39.

95 COMMISSION OF INQUIRY INTO ALL DEPARTMENTS OF THE
GOVERNMENT
(Related Commission)

Appointed   1883

Reported   1883 (?)   [Sessional Papers destroyed by fire]

Commission

Purpose   To make a general and searching investigation
              into the organization of all the public
              departments.

Conclusions/Recommendations

References

Quebec, *Journals*, 1883.

96 COMMITTEE ON AGRICULTURAL EDUCATION
(Departmental Committee)

Appointed   1891

Reported   May 26, 1891

Committee   Five members; Gédéon Ouimet (Superintendent of
              Public Instruction) chairman

Purpose   To investigate agricultural education at two
              colleges; Ste. Anne de la Pocatière and
              l'Assomption.

Conclusions/Recommendations

That there be government compensation to enable a part of
the farms to be consigned exclusively to student use so

that on the spot farming operations can be used.

References

Québec, *Le Journal d'Agriculture Illustre,* Juin, 1891.

97 COMMISSION OF INQUIRY INTO THE POSSIBILITY OF CREATING A
BOARD OF ROMAN CATHOLIC SCHOOL COMMISSIONERS FOR THE CITY
OF MONTREAL AND ITS *BANLIEUE*
(General Commission)

Appointed	July 29, 1909
Reported	January 9, 1911
Commission	Three members; Raoul Dandurand (Senator) chairman
Purpose	To enquire into the best means to be taken to organize a board of Roman Catholic School Commissioners having jurisdiction over the city of Montreal.

Conclusions/Recommendations

That the idea of dividing the present school board of the
city of Montreal into parochial boards be rejected, and
that the amalgamation into a single board of all the
school municipalities comprised within the present limits
of the city of Montreal be considered.

References

Quebec, *Statutes of the Province of Quebec,* 1909, 9 Ed VII,
c.8.

Quebec, *Sessional Papers,* 1911, No. 68.

98 COMMISSION OF INQUIRY INTO THE EXTENSION OF THE POWERS OF
THE BOARD OF ROMAN CATHOLIC SCHOOL COMMISSIONERS OF
MONTREAL, THE EDUCATION OF JEWISH CHILDREN IN PROTESTANT

SCHOOLS OR IN OTHERS, AND THE FINANCIAL SITUATION OF THE
PROTESTANT SCHOOLS OF VERDUN
(General Commission)

Appointed   July 30, 1924

Reported   December 22 and December 27, 1924

Commission   Nine members; (three Roman Catholic, three
                 Protestant, three Jewish); Lomer Gouin
                 (former Minister of Justice) chairman

Purpose   To investigate the extension of the powers of
                 the Board of Roman Catholic School Commis-
                 sioners of Montreal; the education of Jewish
                 children in Protestant schools or in others;
                 and the financial situation of the Protestant
                 schools of Verdun.

Conclusions/Recommendations

That the Act of 1903 be repealed since it might be
unconstitutional;

That further legislation be enacted to clearly define and
determine the rights of non-Protestants and non-Catholics,
to provide for and assure the undivided control and
administration of the Protestant schools by Protestants as
contemplated by the British North America Act, and to
make provision for the equitable distribution of the cost
of the education of non-Protestants and non-Catholics on
the whole population;

That both the Catholic and Protestant school systems be
maintained in the city of Montreal, and no third system
be created provided that a satisfactory solution can be
found;

That the legal questions be put to higher courts;

That pending further developments in the municipality of
Verdun, the system used for the Catholic schools be
followed;

That within this framework there be a Central Board (the

present Board of Protestant School Commissioners of the City of Montreal) and four local boards representing the four districts.

References

Quebec, *Sessional Papers,* 1925, vol. 58, No. 60.

99 QUEBEC PROTESTANT EDUCATION SURVEY
(Special Committee)

Appointed   November 26, 1937

Reported   December, 1938

Committee   Eleven members; W.A.F. Hepburn (Director of Education, Ayrshire, Scotland) chairman

Purpose   To inquire into and report to the Protestant Committee of the Council of Education on all matters affecting Protestant education in the Province of Quebec.

Conclusions/Recommendations

That the Protestant Committee as now constituted be dissolved and a new Protestant Committee reconstituted with carefully designated representation and powers;

That Protestant district boards of education be organized for the administration and control of all schools outside the area of Montreal;

That school attendance be made compulsory to age fourteen, and, as soon as circumstances permit, be raised to fifteen;

That throughout the Province the length of the school year be ten months;

That teacher training be upgraded and that those responsible never relax their efforts to assemble and retain in their service a staff of gifted, cultured and highly-trained men and women;

That the practice of admitting into teacher training those
who have completed Grade X be discontinued;

That the aim be to reach a stage when completion of Grade
XII could be insisted upon as minimum qualifications;

That approximately a third of teacher training consist of
observing teachers at work and of practising the art of
teaching in different types of schools;

That time, money and teaching skill be freely spent in an
endeavour to give as many as possible of the English-
speaking children of the Province a speaking, reading and
writing command of the French language.

References

Quebec, *Report of the Quebec Protestant Education Survey*,
1938.

100 SOUS-COMITE DE COORDINATION DE L'ENSEIGNMENT A SES DIVERS
DEGRES AU COMITE CATHOLIQUE DU CONSEIL DE L'INSTRUCTION
PUBLIQUE
(Departmental Committee)

Appointed   1951

Reported   November, 1953

Committee   Thirteen members; Omer-Jules Désaulniers
             (Surintendant du Département de l'instruction
             publique) chairman

Purpose   To investigate the multiplicity of institu-
             tions and educational streams existent in the
             province.

Conclusions/Recommendations

That there be uniform terminology;

That all programmes give more consideration to what was
being done at each educational level and by other

institutions;

That more attention be paid to educational psychology and to individual differences;

That there be special classes for the gifted child in order to permit continuous acceleration;

That the differences between complementary and secondary schools be reduced;

That technical specialization not begin too early;

That without betraying their essential character, secondary schools be aware of newer subjects and other courses;

That colleges keep their classical emphasis, but experimental sciences be introduced to all sections;

That universities distinguish very carefully between full university courses and those under university auspices at a lower level;

That certification for degree be consistent.

References

Québec, *Rapport du Sous-Comité de Coordination de L'Enseignment à ses Divers Degrés au Comité Catholique du Conseil de L'Instruction Publique*, 1953.

101 ROYAL COMMISSION OF INQUIRY ON CONSTITUTIONAL MATTERS (Related Commission)

Appointed   February 12, 1953

Reported   1956

Commission   Six members; Thomas Tremblay (Judge in Chief, Quebec) chairman

Purpose   To inquire into constitutional problems, and submit recommendations as to steps to be taken

to safeguard the rights of the Province and
those of municipalities and school corporations; and as part of its mandate, to study
the problem of the distribution of taxes
between the central power, the provinces,
municipalities and school corporations.

Conclusions/Recommendations

That the remedy for provinces that are unable to meet their
financial obligations in the field of education not be
sought in any multiplying or increasing of federal subsi-
dies, but rather in a distribution of fiscal powers which
would assure to each class of government the financial
means necessary to the fulfilment of its obligations.

References

Quebec, *Report of the Royal Commission of Inquiry on
Constitutional Problems,* 1956.

102 COMITE D'ETUDE SUR L'ENSEIGNEMENT AGRICOLE ET AGRONOMIQUE
(Departmental Committee)

Appointed   October 5, 1960

Reported   1961

Committee   Neuf membres; Louis-Marie Regis (ex-doyen de
                 la Faculté de philosophie de l'Université de
                 Montréal) président

Purpose   Pour enquêter sur les problèmes de l'enseigne-
                 ment agricole et agronomique dans la province,
                 y compris la recherche et la vulgarisation,
                 lui faire un rapport de ses constatations et
                 opinions et lui soumettre ses recommandations
                 quant aux mesures à prendre pour réorganiser
                 l'enseignement agricole et agronomique et
                 l'adapter aux exigences nouvelles de
                 l'agriculture.

Conclusions/Recommendations

References

Québec, *Rapport du Comité d'Etude sur l'Enseignement Agricole et Agronomique,* 1961.

103 COMITE D'ETUDE SUR L'ENSEIGNEMENT TECHNIQUE ET
    PROFESSIONNEL
    (Departmental Committee)

    Appointed   January 10, 1961

    Reported   1962

    Committee   Neuf membres; Arthur Tremblay (Directeur
                   adjoint de l'Ecole de Pédagogie et d'orien-
                   tation de l'Université Laval) président

    Purpose   Pour étudier les problèmes relatifs:

             (a) à la structure de l'enseignement technique et
                 professionnel, ses méthodes d'enseignement et
                 ses programmes d'études;

             (b) au recrutement, à la formation et aux condi-
                 tions de travail du personnel dirigeant et
                 enseignant;

             (c) à la sélection et a l'orientation des élèves,
                 au placement des diplômés et a leur intégra-
                 tion au monde du travail;

             (d) à la coordination des institutions
                 d'enseignement technique et professionnel
                 avec les écoles de formation générale et les
                 autres types d'institutions de formation
                 professionnelle.

Conclusions/Recommendations

References

Québec, *Rapport du Comité d'Etude sur L'Enseignement*

Technique et Professionnel, 1962.

104 ROYAL COMMISSION OF INQUIRY ON EDUCATION IN THE PROVINCE OF
    QUEBEC
    (General Commission)

Appointed   April 21, 1961

Reported   April, 1963; October, 1964; March, 1966

Commission   Eight members; Alphonse-Marie Parent (Vice-
              Rector, Laval University) chairman

Purpose   To have a thorough and impartial study of the
              state of education in the Province.

Conclusions/Recommendations

(Included in the 576 recommendations were the following:)

That a Minister of Education be appointed whose function
shall be to promote and coordinate educational services at
all levels, including the private and public sectors;

That a Superior Council of Education be created whose
function is to advise the Minister;

That a Ministry of Education be established by merging the
Department of Education and the Ministry of Youth;

That in the Ministry of Education there be an Associate
Deputy Minister of the Protestant faith;

That the services of the Ministry of Education be grouped
in three Divisions, each headed by a Director General:
the Division of Instruction, the Division of Administration,
the Division of Planning;

That the higher officials of the Ministry of Education be
bilingual;

That all laws concerning education be completely revised;

That a Roman Catholic Committee and a Protestant Committee be established to make regulations concerning the teaching of religion and morals, to assure the religious character of the schools, and to offer suggestions to the Council on problems which may arise when teaching certain subjects;

That a Commission for Elementary and Secondary Education, a Commission for Higher Education, and a Commission for Technical and Specialized Education be established;

That the Department of Education use every means to encourage the training of teachers specialized in education;

That a system of public kindergartens and nursery schools, free, coeducational and of good quality, be developed;

That the organization of elementary education be conceived in accordance with the spirit, the principles and the techniques of the activist (that is, active experience) school;

That the elementary school be of six years duration divided into two equal cycles;

That coeducation in the elementary school be reestablished;

That elementary school discipline be so conceived as to develop a spirit of initiative and sense of responsibility in the pupils;

That the secondary course be of five years' duration; two years devoted to general education, and three years which would allow students to begin to specialize;

That Secondary education be organized in composite schools offering a variety of courses and services corresponding to the varied talents, tastes and needs of young people between twelve and sixteen or seventeen years of age;

That the advisability of establishing coeducation in all public institutions of secondary education be seriously examined in the light of the moral, pedagogical and economic factors involved;

That higher education be revised;

That teacher training be under the jurisdiction of higher education and be revised;

That the school curriculum be revised;

That the public educational system of Quebec respect differences in the religious options of parents and pupils and offer a choice of Roman Catholic, Protestant and non-confessional education, insofar as the requirements for quality in education can be satisfied in each instance;

That the unified school system for Quebec be made up, by law, of both French and English schools;

That a special service for the education of Indian children and adults be instituted;

That Canadian history textbooks be radically amended and corrected in such a way as to make the Amerindian civilization better known and to present a truer picture of American Indians;

That local and regional administration be revised;

That regulations for private educational institutions be revised;

That educational financing be revised;

That elementary and secondary teachers unite in a single professional association in order to promote the coordination of these two stages in education;

That as soon as possible the salaries of men and women teachers be made equal;

That teachers and students, as members of the community of scholars, devote themselves to the continuous growth of dedication to the spirit of research, of regard for competence and of concern for intellectual honesty.

References

Quebec, *Report of the Royal Commission of Inquiry on Education in the Province of Quebec,* Part One, 1963.

105 COMITE D'ETUDE SUR L'EDUCATION DES ADULTES
(Departmental Committee)

Appointed   February 20, 1962

Reported   1964

Committee   Sept membres; Claude Ryan (Editeur, *Le Devoir*) président

Purpose   1. faire le relevé du travail accompli par les divers organismes publics et privés;

2. inventorier et reclassifier les besoins;

3. proposer les grandes lignes de la politique du gouvernement;

4. définir les structures d'organismes provinciaux devant régir l'éducation des adultes.

Conclusions/Recommendations

References

Québec, *Rapport du Comité d'Etude sur l'Education des Adultes,* 1964.

106 COMITE D'ETUDE SUR LES LOISIRS, L'EDUCATION PHYSIQUE ET LES SPORTS
(Departmental Committee)

Appointed   February 20, 1962

Reported   1964

<u>Committee</u>	Huit membres; René Bélisle (Surintendant de la division de la récréation du service des parcs de la Ville de Montréal) président
<u>Purpose</u>	To study the broad field of leisure, physical education, and sports.

<u>Conclusions/Recommendations</u>

That because of the growing importance of leisure, adequate recreation services be provided;

That proper legislation establish minimum standards for recreation organizations;

That care be taken to ensure adequate control of professional sports.

<u>References</u>

Québec, *Rapport du Comité d'Etude sur les Loisirs l'Education Physique et les Sports,* 1964.

107 COMMISSION D'ENQUETE SUR L'ENSEIGNEMENT DES ARTS AU QUEBEC
(Related Commission)

<u>Appointed</u>	31 mars 1966
<u>Reported</u>	août 1968
<u>Commission</u>	Six membres; Marcel Rioux (Professeur de sociologie à l'Université de Montréal) président
<u>Purpose</u>	Pour étudier toutes les questions relatives à l'enseignement des arts, y compris les structures administratives, l'organisation matérielle des institutions affectées à cet enseignement et la coordination de ces institutions avec les écoles de formation générale.

Conclusions/Recommendations

Que l'enseignement public des arts, à quelque niveau que
ce soit, relève exclusivement du Ministère de l'Education;

Que le Ministère de l'Education assume toute la
responsabilité de la réforme générale de l'enseignement des
arts;

Que soit reconnu, en principe et dans les faits, le droit
de l'enfant à l'éducation artistique;

Que l'éducation artistique au niveau préscolaire soit
considéreé comme la base même de la formation de l'enfant;

Que l'éducation artistique à l'élémentaire soit l'une des
bases essentielles de la formation de l'enfant; que les
matières suivantes soient inscrites aux programmes: la
rythmique et la danse, le jeu dramatique, les activités
plastiques et la musique; et qu'une durée hebdomadaire
d'environ sept heures et demie leur soit consacrée;

Qu'au niveau secondaire l'éducation artistique soit
considérée comme l'un des champs fondamentaux de
l'enseignement polyvalent;

Que l'éducation artistique devinne l'une des formes de
l'éducation permanente et qu'elle soit considérée selon
les perspectives suivantes:
(a) comme une éducation essentielle aux études de formation
    générale;
(b) comme une reconversion professionnelle des adultes
    désirant faire carrière dans les arts, ainsi qu'un
    perfectionnement des artistes desireaux de parfaire
    leur formation;
(c) comme une reconversion et un perfectionnement d'ordre
    culturel pour tout individu.

References

Québec, *Rapport de la commission d'enquête sur
l'enseignement des arts au Québec,* août 1968.

108 COMITE INTERMINISTERIEL SUR L'ENSEIGNEMENT DES LANGUES AUX
NEO-CANADIENS
(Departmental Committee)

Appointed   [   ]

Reported   27 janvier 1967 [au Ministère de l'Éducation
                et Ministère des Affaires Culturelles]

Committee   Dix membres; Réné Gauthier (Directeur général
                de l'Immigration) président

Purpose   D'examiner l'orientation et l'option
                linguistique des Néo-Québécois, à la lumière
                notamment de l'étude du français par les
                adultes et du type d'école fréquentée par
                les enfants.

Conclusions/Recommendations

D'assumer désormais la responsabilité totale de
l'organisation des cours de langues aux immigrants et de
prendre sans délai toutes les mesures utiles pour que de
tels cours soient efficacement mis à la disposition des
immigrants dans tout le Québec;

De faire en sorte que ce service spécialisé soit assuré de
la collaboration la plus large des commissions scolaires
locales et régionales;

De créer un comité pédagogique interministeriel dans lequel
les Ministères de l'Education et des Affaires Culturelles
(et tous autres ministères intéressés éventuellement)
collaboreraint à l'établissement des programmes, à la
définition des méthodes, à la sélection des enseignants, au
choix des manuels et du matériel didactique et à l'octroi
des attestations;

Qu'il soit clairement reconnu que la responsabilité et la
mise en oeuvre d'une politique scolaire pour les enfants
néo-canadiens incombent directement et exclusivement au
gouvernement du Québec, notamment à son Ministère de
l'Education agissant, en l'occurrence, en étroite liaison
avec la Direction générale de l'Immigration;

Que tous les moyens d'information, d'accueil et d'incitation soient employés, avec le concours actif du gouvernement et de tous les organismes publics, afin d'amener les immigrants à opter pour l'école de langue française;

D'établir concrètement et d'appliquer rigoureusement, dans les plus courts délais, une politique dynamique de priorité du francais, particulièrement comme langue du travail, de l'affichage et de la communication.

References

Québec, *Rapport: Comité interministériel sur l'enseignement des langues aux Néo-Canadiens,* janvier 1967.

109 CONSEIL DE RESTRUCTURATION SCOLAIRE DE L'ILE DE MONTREAL
(Departmental Committee)

Appointed   30 septembre 1967

Reported   28 octobre 1968

Committee   Dix-huit membres; Joseph L. Pagé (Vice-
                   président de la Commission des écoles
                   catholiques de Montréal) président

Purpose   De promouvoir la régionalisation et la
                   démocratisation de l'administration scolaire
                   dans l'île de Montréal.

Conclusions/Recommendations

Qu'il soit reconnu que tout corps public qui a une responsabilité dans l'administration scolaire sur l'île de Montréal, a pour objectif premier d'assurer, à tous les élèves sans distinction, un enseignement de bonne qualité et favorable au plein épanouissement de la personnalité de chacun dans un juste respect de pluralisme religieux et de la dualité linguistique et culturelle qui caractérisent la région métropolitaine de Montréal;

Que le gouvernement adopte une législation fixant le statut des droits linguistiques au Québec, qu'il établisse

une politique de la langue et de l'immigration, et que ces
dispositions s'accompagnent de mesures propres à favoriser
la priorité concrète du français;

Que, sur l'île de Montréal, les programmes d'études
puissent conduire tout élève terminant ses études
secondaires à parler couramment la langue officielle que
n'aura pas été sa langue principale d'instruction et que,
normalement, pour obtenir un diplôme de fin d'études il
doive réussir au préalable un examen oral et écrit en
langue seconde.

References

Québec, *Rapport au Ministre de L'Education: Conseil de
Restructuration Scolaire de l'île de Montreal*, octobre
1968.

110 COMMISSION D'ENQUETE SUR LE DIFFEREND ENTRE LES PARTIES A
    LA NEGOCIATION ... DANS LE SECTEUR SCOLAIRE
    (Judicial Commission)

Appointed   2 avril 1968

Reported   1968

Commission   Un membre; Jean-Charles Simard (Juge de la
              Cour provinciale)

Purpose   Pour faire enquête sur le différend; cette
              commission ne peut rendre une décision ni
              formuler de recommandations mais seulement
              constater les faits pertinents.

Conclusions/Recommendations

Les parties se sont buteés a un sérieux obstacle: celui
de la définition de 'membre du personnel enseignant'.
L'obstacle est d'autant plus sérieux qu'il infère tout le
problème de la juridiction ou du champ d'application de la
convention collective.

References

Québec, *Rapport de la Commission d'enquête constituée en vertu de l'article 16 de la Loi assurant le droit de l'enfant à l'éducation et instituant un nouveau régime de convention collective dans le secteur scolaire (15-16, Elizabett II, chapitre 63)*, 1968.

111 COMMISSION OF INQUIRY ON THE POSITION OF THE FRENCH
LANGUAGE AND ON LANGUAGE RIGHTS IN QUEBEC
(Related Commission)

Appointed   December 9, 1968

Reported   December, 1972

Commission   Five members; Jean-Denis Gendron (Vice-doyen
                 de la Faculté des lettres à l'Université
                 Laval) président

Purpose   To make an inquiry into and submit a report on
                 the position of French as the language of
                 usage in Québec, and to recommend measures
                 designed to guarantee the linguistic rights
                 of the majority as well as the protection of
                 the rights of the minority; and the full
                 expansion and diffusion of the French
                 language in Québec in all fields of activity
                 and also at the educational, cultural, social
                 and economic levels.

Conclusions/Recommendations

That the Government of Québec proceed to legislate forthwith to proclaim French as the Official Language of the
Province of Québec, and to proclaim French and English as
the two National Languages of the Province of Québec; thus
making French the Provincial *Official Language* in Québec,
and French and English the Provincial *National Languages*
in Québec;

That the Government of Québec proceed, -- by legislation,
administrative decrees and practice, and also voluntary,
persuasive or facultative, community measures -- to make
French a language that is useful and necessary in

communications within all fields of activity in commerce
and industry and the work *milieu* in general, in the
Province of Québec;

That the Government of Québec require all children enrolled
in English-speaking schools in the Province of Québec to
acquire a mastery of French from the earliest possible age,
and all children enrolled in French-speaking schools to
acquire a mastery of English from the earliest possible age.

References

Québec, *Report of the Commission of Inquiry on the Position
of the French Language and on Language Rights in Québec*,
vol. 2 'Language Rights', December 1972.

112 COMMISSION D'ETUDE DE LA PROPAGANDE POLITIQUE DANS
L'ENSEIGNEMENT
(Departmental Committee)

Appointed   19 novembre 1970

Reported   15 mars 1971

Committee   Un membre; Gérard Dion (Professeur au
               département des relations industrielles à la
               Faculté des Sciences sociales de l'Université
               Laval)

Purpose   Pour étudier les plaintes qui lui parvenaient
               touchant la propagande politique et
               l'endoctrinement auxquels se seraient
               indûment livrés certains professeurs dans
               l'exercice de leurs fonctions auprès des
               élèves.

Conclusions/Recommendations

Qu'on établit un code d'éthique professionnelle pour les
enseignants et la création d'un poste permanent
d'ombudsman dans le domaine de l'éducation.

References

Québec, *Rapport au Ministre de l'Éducation: Le Commissaire - Enquêteur Gérard Dion,* mars 1971.

113 COMITE INTERMINISTERIEL POUR ENTREPRENDRE L'ETUDE DU
PROBLEME DE LA DISTRIBUTION DES IMPRIMES, PERIODIQUES ET
LIVRES DE POCHE
(Departmental Committee)

Appointed   octobre 1972

Reported   15 janvier 1973

Committee   Cinq membres; Pierre de Grandpré (Conseiller
               culturel à la Délégation générale du Québec à
               Paris) président

Purpose   D'examiner à fond les conditions dans
               lesquelles s'opère au Québec la diffusion des
               périodiques et des livres de poche et de
               présenter au Ministre des Affaires culturelles
               des recommandations propres à améliorer la
               situation.

Conclusions/Recommendations

Que le développement d'une véritable industrie québécoise
de biens culturels constitue la meilleure garantie de
l'indépendance et du développement culturel des citoyens
du Québec.

References

Québec, *Rapport sur la distribution des périodiques et du
livre de poche au Québec,* janvier 1973.

114 COMMISSION D'ETUDE DE LA TACHE DES ENSEIGNANTS DE
L'ELEMENTAIRE ET DU SECONDAIRE
(Departmental Committee)

Appointed   15 décembre 1972

Reported   mars 1975

Committee   Huit membres; Jean-Noël Faucher (Ministère de
               l'Education) coordonnateur

Purpose   De proposer des méthodes et/ou systèmes
               pouvant permettre une utilisation optionale
               des ressources humaines actuellement
               affectées au système d'éducation, compte tenu
               des orientations pédagogiques du Ministère,
               des dispositions financières et des priorités
               collectives du Québec; et d'examiner les
               existants tant au Québec qu' à l'étranger.

Conclusions/Recommendations

Que le ministère de l'Education et les commissions
scolaires fassent connaître et vulgarisent les orientations et les objectifs pédagogiques, qu'ils identifient
clairement ceux qu'ils imposent et ceux qu'ils proposent et
qu'ils en évaluent au préalable les implications sur les
tâches des enseignants;

Que le ministère de l'Education, au niveau élémentaire
(incluant l'enfance inadaptée), mette en application
graduellement les recommandations du Conseil supérieur de
l'éducation et du groupe COMMEL concernant l'implantation
de spécialistes en langue seconde, en éducation physique
et en musique, libérant ainsi les enseignants
l'équivalent d'une période journalière d'enseignement
(environ 45 minutes) leur permettant de se consacrer à
d'autres activités professionnelles et d'améliorer la
qualité de leur enseignement.

References

Québec, *Rapport de la C.E.T.E.E.S.: Commission d'étude de
la tâche des enseignants de l'élémentaire et du secondaire,*
mars 1975.

115 COMITE PROVINCIAL DE L'ENFANCE INADAPTEE
(Departmental Committee)

Appointed   15 décembre 1972

Reported   2 septembre 1976

Committee   Sept membres; Thérèse Baron (Sous-ministre
adjoint à l'éducation) présidente

Purpose   De préparer des recommandations relatives à
une meilleure coordination régionale et
provinciale des ressources publiques et
privées en éducation de l'enfance inadaptée;
et de préparer, pour le bénéfice du ministère
de l'Education, des recommandations relatives
aux politiques générales qui régissent
l'éducation des enfants en difficulté
d'apprentissage et d'adaptation.

Conclusions/Recommendations

Que le ministère de l'Education adapte, en concertation
avec les organismes concernes, et rende publique une
politique officielle d'éducation de l'enfance en difficulté
d'adaptation et d'apprentissage;

Que cette politique favorise le développement intégral et
optimal de l'enfant en difficulté d'adaptation et
d'apprentissage par l'utilisation d'une approche pédagogique axée sur le potentiel de l'enfant et par
l'établissement d'une communication harmonieuse et d'un
fonctionnement intègre entre tous les services et toutes
les personnes responsables de l'enfant.

References

Québec, *L'Education de l'enfance en difficulté d'adaptation
et d'apprentissage au Québec,* 1976.

116 COMMISSION D'ETUDE SUR LA CLASSIFICATION DES ENSEIGNANTS
(Departmental Committee)

Appointed   8 février 1973

Reported   février 1975

Committee   Quatre membres; Roger Laberge (Ministère de
                 l'Education) président

Purpose   A étudier les systèmes de classification des
                 enseignants des autres provinces canadiennes
                 ainsi que de certains états américains.

Conclusions/Recommendations

Que le gouvernement crée une commission provinciale qui, à
la lumière des travaux de la commission d'étude, aurait
comme mandat d'établir et de reviser au besoin les
principes et le plan de classification des enseignants,
d'élaborer les règles nécessaires à l'évaluation des
études faites hors du Québec et des compétences particulières;

Que les membres de cette commission soient issus des
organismes d'éducation et des associations qui sont
concernés par cette question, soit les commissions
scolaires, les collèges, le gouvernement, les universités
et les associations d'enseignants.

References

Québec, *Rapport de la commission d'étude la classification
des enseignants*, février 1975.

117 CONSEIL SUPERIEUR DE L'EDUCATION SUR L'ETAT ET LES BESOINS
    DE L'ENSEIGNEMENT COLLEGIAL
    (Departmental Committee)

Appointed   15 février 1973

Reported   juillet 1975

Committee   Vingt-quatre membres; Jean-Marie Beauchemin
                 (Sous-ministre associé au ministère de
                 L'Education) président

Purpose   De demander au Conseil supérieur de l'Educa-
                 tion un avis, dans le cadre de la loi qui le
                 régit, sur l'état et les besoins de

l'enseignement collégial, c'est-à-dire sur les résultats atteints à ce jour, sur les problèmes qu'il suscite et sur les orientations à retenir pour son développement ultérieur, tant sur le plan administratif que pédagogique.

Conclusions/Recommendations

Que le ministère de l'Education considère l'identification des besoins éducatifs comme une priorité et comme une condition préalable à la definition des objectifs de formation post-secondaire et de ses divers programmes;

Que l'organisation de l'enseignement post-secondaire dispensé par les collèges permette aux étudiants de réaliser les objectifs de leur programme dans des temps variables ajustés à leurs possibilités et à leur rythme;

Que l'on reconnaisse que pour atteindre les objectifs qu'il poursuit, l'étudiant puisse choisir ses activités ou dans l'institution qui offre le programme ou en dehors de celle-ci;

Que le collège soit structuré sur le module, unité de base qui administre le programme.

References

Québec, *Le Collège: Rapport sur l'état et les besoins de l'enseignement collégial*, 1975.

118 COMITE D'ETUDE SUR LA RECHERCHE ET L'ENSEIGNEMENT EN TECHNOLOGIE DU BOIS
(Departmental Committee)

Appointed   janvier 1974

Reported   octobre 1974

Committee   Six membres; Jean Poliquin (faculté de Foresterie et de Géodésie, université Laval) président

Purpose   De définir les objectifs de la province
             concernant la recherche et l'enseignement en
             technologie du bois; de déterminer le plus
             clairement possible les carences actuelles
             dans ce domaine; et de définir les principaux
             moyens nécessaires pour répondre aux besoins
             fixés et pour régler les principaux problèmes
             existants.

Conclusions/Recommendations

Que le ministère de l'Education et les universités
s'emploient à assurer la priorité qu'il importe d'accorder
à ce secteur de façon à ce que le programme puisse être
accessible aux étudiants aux trois cycles universitaires.

References

Québec, *L'Enseignement et la recherche en sciences et
technologie de bois,* octobre 1974.

119 COMITE D'ETUDE SUR LA CREATION DE L'INSTITUT DES SPORTS DU
    QUEBEC
    (Departmental Committee)

    Appointed   7 février 1974

    Reported   24 mai 1974 [au Ministre d'Etat responsable
                   du Haut-Commissariat à la Jeunesse, aux
                   Loisirs et aux Sports]

    Committee   Quinze membres; Claude Bouchard (Directeur,
                   Laboratoire des sciences, de l'activité
                   physique, de l'Université Laval) président

    Purpose   D'étudier l'ensemble de la question de la
                   création de l'Institut des Sports du Québec
                   et d'émettre des recommandations au sujet de
                   tous les aspects importants de son développe-
                   ment.

Conclusions/Recommendations

Que les organismes et les institutions du Québec reconnais-
sent, pour les fins de leurs programmes de sport, les
quatre catégories suivantes de participants: le débutant,
l'espoir, l'élite québécoise, l'élite canadienne et
internationale;

Que le loi spéciale créant l'Institut des Sports du Québec
assure la participation des institutions universitaires,
des collèges et des municipalités au niveau décisionnel de
l'Institut des Sports du Québec.

References

Québec, *Comité d'étude sur la création de l'institut des
sports du Québec,* mai 1974.

120 GROUPE DE TRAVAIL SUR L'EDUCATION PHYSIQUE ET LE SPORT A
L'ECOLE
(Departmental Committee)

Appointed   mars 1974

Reported   avril 1975

Committee   Onze membres; Claude Beauregard (Bureau des
              sous-ministres) président

Purpose   D'élucider et d'articuler au moins sommaire-
              ment les concepts de sport scolaire,
              d'éducation physique, d'activité physique,
              d'activité de mouvement et d'activité de
              plein air pour les fins des niveaux élémen-
              taire et secondaire; et de proposer un plan
              de développement du sport scolaire et de
              l'éducation physique aux niveaux élémentaire
              et secondaire dans la perspective d'un
              developpement prioritaire au niveau élémen-
              taire.

Conclusions/Recommendations

Que le groupe de travail ministériel mandate le Comité
d'étude sur les objectifs de l'éducation physique et du

sport en milieu scolaire afin que ce dernier développe et
élabore des taxonomies particulières aux objectifs de
l'éducation physique d'ordre cognitif, social et affectif,
culturel et esthétique et qu'il donne au Comité d'étude
les moyens financiers de mener ses travaux à bonne fin.

References

Québec, *Rapport du groupe de travail sur l'éducation
physique et le sport à l'école,* avril 1975.

121 COMITE D'ETUDE SUR LA READAPTATION DES ENFANTS ET
ADOLESCENTS PLACES EN CENTRE D'ACCUEIL
(Departmental Committee)

Appointed   1 février 1975

Reported   22 décembre 1975

Committee   Huit membres; Manuel G. Batshaw (Directeur
               Général, Services Communautaires Juifs,
               Montréal) président

Purpose   D'étudier les méthodes couramment utilisées ou
               qui pourraient l'être pour la réadaptation des
               pensionnaires reçus dans les centres d'accueil
               de transition et de réadaptation pour jeunes
               mésadaptés sociaux, tout en tenant compte de
               la coordination optionale avec les activités
               professionnelles pouvant être assumées par les
               Centres de Services Sociaux.

Conclusions/Recommendations

Que le Ministère de l'Education du Québec voit à ce que le
développement des Services à l'Enfance Inadaptée tant au
niveau primaire que secondaire ne soit pas uniquement des
projets-pilotes ou émargeant au budget inadmissible des
commissions scolaires, mais fasse bien partie des priorités
budgétaires du Ministère;

Que conjointement avec le Ministère des Affaires Sociales,
des Centres de Jour soient organisés pour les mésadaptés

socio-affectifs graves tant au niveau primaire que secondaire;

Que les écoles aient le personnel nécessaire pour assurer
la récupération scolaire, la compréhension des comporte-
ments difficiles des jeunes et l'attitude adéquate pour les
aider à se contrôler et se développer normalement, et que
les programmes appropriés à ces fins soient disponibles
sans déplacer l'enfant.

References

Québec, *Rapport du comité d'étude sur la réadaptation des
enfants et adolescents placés en centre d'accueil*, décembre
1975.

122 GROUPE DE TRAVAIL SUR L'INSTITUT D'HISTOIRE ET DE
CIVILISATION DU QUEBEC
(Departmental Committee)

Appointed   23 juin 1976

Reported   21 février 1977

Committee   Huit membres; Guy Frégault (Sous-ministre aux
                Affaires culturelles) président

Purpose   De présenter des recommandations sur
                l'opportunité d'établir un Institut d'histoire
                et de civilisation du Québec; et d'indiquer,
                s'il y a lieu, ce que pourrait être un tel
                institut et, notamment: son statut; son
                mandat; sa composition; son mode de fonc-
                tionnement; les pouvoirs qui lui seraient
                utiles ou nécessaires; la participation
                éventuelle des organismes, tant publics que
                privés, oeuvrant dans les secteurs de
                l'histoire, des sciences humaines et des
                sciences physiques.

Conclusions/Recommendations

Que l'implantation de cet Institut québécois de recherche

sur la culture s'impose;

Que cette originalité s'inscrit en premier lieu dans les
trois principales fonctions qu'il assumera: (1) poursuivre
des recherches à long terme sur la nature et l'évolution de
la culture québécoise; (2) conduire des investigations sur
le développement culturel du Québec; (3) aménager la
concertation des études québécoises et contribuer à une
meilleure diffusion des travaux qui en résulteront.

References

Québec, *Rapport du groupe de travail sur l'institut
d'histoire et de civilisation du Québec*, février 1977.

123 COMITE D'ETUDE SUR LA SITUATION DES ENSEIGNANTS RELIGIEUX
(Departmental Committee)

Appointed   6 octobre 1976

Reported   15 juillet 1977

Committee   Dix membres; Guy Monfette (Directeur général,
                Commission administrative du régime de
                retraite) président

Purpose   D'étudier la situation dans laquelle se
                trouvent les religieux enseignants et les
                religieux enseignants laïcisés depuis le 1er
                juillet 1965 par rapport aux autres enseig-
                nants à qui le Régime de retraite des
                fonctionnaires de l'enseignement était appli-
                cable.

Conclusions/Recommendations

Que le Gouvernement du Québec accorde, pour chaque année
d'enseignement en excédent des années rachetées en vertu
de l'article 81 du Régime de retraite des employés du
gouvernement et des organismes publics, un crédit de rente
égal à 1% du traitement admissible annuel au 30 juin 1977,
aux enseignants religieux et aux enseignants religieux
laïcisés après le 30 juin 1965 qui cotisent audit Régime

et qui rachètent ou ont racheté la totalité des années
d'enseignement que leur permet l'article 81 audit Régime.

References

Québec, *Rapport du comité 'ad hoc' constitué pour étudier
la situation des enseignants religieux et des enseignants
religieux laïcisés après le 30 juin 1965 en regard de leur
protection à la retraite,* juillet 1977.

124 COMMISSION D'ETUDE SUR LES UNIVERSITES
(Departmental Committee)

Appointed   20 juillet 1977

Reported   31 janvier 1978

Committee   Huit membres; Pierre Angers (Professeur à
                l'Université du Québec à Trois-Rivières)
                président

Purpose   De déterminer et analyser les indicateurs de
                l'avenir qui permettront de mieux cerner les
                choix qui s'offrent, de formuler les
                hypothèses, de dégager des problèmes
                prioritaires, d'indiquer des voies de solu-
                tions.

Conclusions/Recommendations

Si l'une des principales fonctions de l'université est de
jouer un rôle dans l'évolution de la culture, elle devra
envisager de former un type d'homme qui, au-delà des
langages disjoints de la réussite matérielle, puisse se
faire entendre de la collectivité et participer au
gouvernement des hommes. Comment toutefois, établir cette
nouvelle perspective pédagogique sans que ne s'engage
également une discussion sur le discours politique et
social sans lequel tout projet éducatif demeure vain? Nous
souhaiterions donc que l'université soit en mesure de
restaurer l'idéal qui lui permettrait de donner un sens à
l'accumulation et à la diffusion des connaissances, et de
les maîtriser avant justement que l'homme n'en devienne la

victime;

Si l'université refusait d'éclairer la société dans la
mesure de ses moyens et acceptait de se faire dicter son
avenir sans participer à l'effort pour la définir, bref si
elle faisait passer ses fonctions de formation avant ses
fonctions critiques, elle ne pourrait guère demeurer long-
temps encore 'le lieu où se poursuit sans contrainte
l'expérience de l'esprit'.

References

Québec, *Commission d'étude sur les universités: Document
de consultation,* janvier 1978.

ONTARIO

125 COMMITTEE ON EDUCATION
   (Legislative Committee)

   Appointed   April 10, 1835

   Reported   February 25, 1836

   Committee   Three members; Charles Duncombe (Member for
                    Oxford) chairman

   Purpose   To obtain the best plans and estimates of a
                    Lunatic Asylum and such information as may be
                    considered relative to the management and
                    good government of such institutions, and also
                    respecting the system and management of
                    Schools and Colleges.

Conclusions/Recommendations

That education of youth be provided in direct reference to
the wants of the world;

That teachers in colleges be prepared to work as long hours
as those in high schools and academies and primary schools;

That women be encouraged to make a career in teaching;

That religious training be provided in separate schools if
this is the only way to guarantee a moral man;

That teachers be better qualified and better trained;

That normal schools be provided;

That competent common school teacher inspectors be appointed to prevent the disqualified from entering into the responsible profession of teaching;

That new areas of scientific study and of the inductive system whereby students collect facts and accumulate ideas from observation which is superseding the former arbitrary copying system learned from books alone be encouraged.

References

Upper Canada, *Journal of the House of Assembly of Upper Canada*, 1835.

Upper Canada, *Journals*, 1836, App. Vol. 1.

126 COMMISSION OF INQUIRY INTO THE PUBLIC DEPARTMENTS OF THE PROVINCE
(Related Commission)

Appointed   October 21, 1839

Reported   January 22, 1840 (Report of Education
                Committee)

Commission   Nineteen members; Robert Baldwin Sullivan
                (Member of Legislative Council) chairman
                (Three education commissioners; John McCaul)

Purpose   To investigate the business, conduct and
                organization of the several Public Departments
                in the Province, and to report on the state of
                the said several Departments, and what changes
                in the system of conducting the public busi-
                ness in the said several Departments would be
                beneficial;

                And to ascertain the state of all School Funds;
                to examine into the past and present state of
                Education throughout the Province; to frame
                such a plan as will appear to be the best

calculated to afford the best possible kind
of Education to the community at the least
possible expense; to institute an inquiry with
reference to the constitution of King's
College University, and also to the lands
forming its endowment; and to investigate
generally all matters of public interest.

Conclusions/Recommendations

That provision for professional education, that is,
theology, law, and medicine, which is very deficient be
improved;

That no grammar school master be appointed without an
examination of his qualifications as a scholar and a
teacher, for it often happens that excellent scholars are
wholly unfit for the office of teachers;

That adequate salaries be paid to teachers;

That normal schools and model schools be provided;

That curriculum and textbooks be revised;

That a Board of Commissioners be provided;

That there be increased financial aid to education.

References

Upper Canada, *Journals*, 1839-40, App. Vol. 2.

127 RYERSON'S REPORT ON A SYSTEM OF PUBLIC ELEMENTARY
INSTRUCTION FOR UPPER CANADA
(Departmental Committee)

Appointed   1844

Reported   March 27, 1846

Committee   One member; Egerton Ryerson (Assistant
              Superintedent of Education)

Purpose   To devise such measures as may be necessary
                to establish the most efficient system of
                Instruction.

Conclusions/Recommendations

That in adopting measures for the advancement of the
education of the people, the Administration of Canada is
but following the example of the most enlightened Governments, and, like them, laying the foundation for the
strongest claims to the esteem of the country and the
gratitude of posterity.

References

United Canada, *Report on a System of Public Elementary
Instruction for Upper Canada,* [1846]

128 COMMISSION OF INQUIRY INTO THE AFFAIRS OF KING'S COLLEGE
    UNIVERSITY AND UPPER CANADA COLLEGE
    (Special Committee)

Appointed   July 20, 1848

Reported   July 31, 1851

Committee   Three members; Joseph Workman (Physician)
                chairman

Purpose   To inquire into the affairs of King's College
                University and Upper Canada College.

Conclusions/Recommendations

That the business transactions of a wealthy corporation,
extending over a period of twenty-two years, have been
unravelled and brought from a state of unintelligible
complexity and confusion into a proper business shape.

References

United Canada, *Journals,* 1849, App. Vol. No. 2, III.

United Canada, *Journals*, 1851, App. No. 4, EEE.

129 ROYAL COMMISSION ON AFFAIRS AND FINANCIAL CONDITIONS OF
TORONTO UNIVERSITY AND UNIVERSITY COLLEGE
(General Commission)

Appointed   October 28, 1861

Reported   May 29, 1862

Commission   Three members; James Patton (Vice-Chancellor,
               University of Toronto) chairman

Purpose   To enquire into the affairs and financial
               conditions of Toronto University and
               University College.

Conclusions/Recommendations

That expenditure has been upon a scale disproportionate to
its uses and requirements, as well as inexpedient when the
necessity for public aid to sustain the higher educational
interests of the country is considered;

That so long as the University and University College have
no inducements to practice economy, there will, from the
nature of things, be large expenditure without corresponding results; and so long as the other Colleges having
University powers can see no advantage from affiliation, as
is undoubtedly the case under the present system, they
will not only decline to unite, but will inevitably
continue to occupy a position of rivalry and of remon-
strance;

That within a really National University all classes and
denominations will be impartially provided with those
opportunities for higher education which may be in accordance with their convictions, and none suffer wrong or
disability because of their preference;

That the standard of University education will be uniform,
and Degrees of equal value, because all will be tested by

one curriculum and by one Board of Examiners, and
endorsed by the same authority; although each Institution
will be at liberty, without interference, to teach by such
mode as the authorities thereof may deem best.

References

United Canada, 'Commission on Affairs and Financial Conditions of Toronto University and University College',
Province of Canada *Sessional Papers*, 1863, No. 19.

130 SPECIAL REPORT ON POPULAR EDUCATION IN EUROPE AND THE
    UNITED STATES
    (Departmental Committee)

Appointed   1866

Reported   March 4, 1868

Committee   One member; Egerton Ryerson (Superintendent of
               Education)

Purpose   To make an educational tour of observation
               and enquiry into the working and progress of
               the systems of Public Instruction in the chief
               educating countries of America and Europe,
               that we might avail ourselves, as far as
               possible, of the experience of both Hemis-
               pheres in simplifying and improving our own
               system and methods of diffusing education and
               useful knowledge among all classes of the
               population.

Conclusions/Recommendations

References

United Canada, 'Special Report on Popular Education in
Europe and the United States', *Journals*, 1867-68.

131 SELECT COMMITTEE TO ENQUIRE INTO THE MANAGEMENT AND
WORKING OF THE EDUCATION DEPARTMENT
(Legislative Committee)

Appointed   November 10, 1868

Reported   January 19, 1869

Committee   Twenty-three members; M.C. Cameron (Member for
              Toronto East) chairman

Purpose   To examine into the working of the Common and
              Grammar School System of Ontario, together
              with the Department of Public Instruction.

Conclusions/Recommendations

That this report is an ample vindication of the Chief
Superintendent, and all who assisted him, from the imputa-
tions long and recklessly thrown upon them by a portion of
the public press and other parties; an unquestionable
testimony to the fidelity, efficiency and economy with
which the Department of Public Instruction has been conducted in its various branches and details.

References

Ontario, *Report on the Education Department by a Large
Select Committee of the Legislative Assembly of Ontario*,
1869.

132 PROVINCIAL FARM COMMISSION
(Departmental Committee)

Appointed   1873

Reported   January 31, 1874

Committee   Eight members; David Christie (former
              President, Provincial Agricultural Associa-
              tion) chairman

Purpose   To consider the whole subject of the future

organization and management of the newly
acquired Provincial Farm.

Conclusions/Recommendations

(Forty-eight separate conclusions included everything from
choosing a suitable name, to the best means of laying out
the fields.)

References

Ontario, *Report of the Commissioner of Agriculture and Arts
for 1873*, App. G.

133 LEGISLATIVE COMMITTEE TO ENQUIRE INTO THE MANAGEMENT OF THE
AGRICULTURAL COLLEGE AND MODEL FARM
(Legislative Committee)

Appointed   December 2, 1874

Reported   December 19, 1874

Committee   Five members; James Bethune (Member for
              Stormont) chairman

Purpose   To enquire into the management of the
              Agricultural College and Model Farm.

Conclusions/Recommendations

That in the opinion of the Committee, the Government was
fully justified, on the facts disclosed, in dispensing
with the services of the Principal; present conditions and
management seemed satisfactory; and it was not in the
public interest to pursue the inquiry further.

References

Ontario, *The Daily Globe*, December 18, 1874.

134 COMMISSION OF INQUIRY INTO CHARGES AGAINST THE CENTRAL

COMMITTEE OF EXAMINERS OF THE EDUCATION DEPARTMENT
(Judicial Commission)

Appointed   September 24, 1877

Reported   December 31, 1877

Commission   One member; Christopher Salmon Patterson
               (Justice of the Court of Appeal)

Purpose   To enquire into and report upon charges that
               there is within the Central Committee a 'ring',
               the members of which have dishonorable rela-
               tions with the publishing house of Adam
               Miller & Co., of Toronto; and that in the
               preparation of examination papers in connec-
               tion with the Public and High Schools, there
               has been collusion between members of the
               Central Committee and other parties interested
               in the work or results of the examinations.

Conclusions/Recommendations

That the clear result of the whole evidence is that
neither charge has any support from affirmative proof;
that the charges have not been allowed to be disposed of as
simply unproved, but that both have been conclusively
rebutted.

References

Ontario, *Sessional Papers,* A1878, No. 11.

135 COMMISSION TO INVESTIGATE CERTAIN CHARGES AGAINST DR.
    SAMUEL MAY OF THE EDUCATION DEPARTMENT
    (Departmental Committee)

    Appointed   December 30, 1881

    Reported   February 16, 1882

    Committee   One member; E.J. Senkler (Judge, Lincoln
                   County)

Purpose   To enquire into certain charges preferred by
               a member of the Legislative Assembly of
               Ontario, against Samuel P. May, Doctor of
               Medicine, Superintendent of the Educational
               Museum and Library, and lately of the
               Depository of the Education Department.

Conclusions/Recommendations

That no evidence was given to support this charge, and it
is not sustained.

References

Ontario, *Sessional Papers*, A1882, No. 55.

136 COMMISSION OF INQUIRY INTO AN INCIDENT AT THE AGRICULTURAL
    COLLEGE
    (Judicial Commission)

Appointed   January, 1884

Reported   [   ]

Commission   One member; John Winchester (Inspector of
               Legal Offices)

Purpose   To inquire into and report in respect to an
               incident at the Agricultural College involv-
               ing Mr. Hunt, the Assistant Master.

Conclusions/Recommendations

References

Handwritten entry dated 25 January 1884 in the Order in
Council Book in the Executive Council Office, Toronto.

137 SPECIAL INQUIRY INTO CONDITIONS OF THE FRENCH SCHOOLS IN
    THE UNITED COUNTIES OF PRESCOTT AND RUSSELL

(Departmental Committee)

Appointed   1887 (?)

Reported   March 25, 1887

Committee   One member; O. Dufort (Assistant Inspector of
              Public Schools)

Purpose   To investigate conditions of the French
              schools in the united counties of Prescott
              and Russell.

Conclusions/Recommendations

References

Ontario, 'Report of the Assistant Inspector of Public
Schools upon the conditions of the French Schools in the
United Counties of Prescott and Russell', 1887.

138 COMMISSION OF INQUIRY INTO THE FIRE AT THE GOVERNMENT FARM
    (Judicial Commission)

Appointed   November, 1888

Reported   [   ]

Commission   Two members; Archibald Blue (Deputy Minister
              of Agriculture) and John Winchester (Inspector
              of Legal Offices)

Purpose   To investigate the cause of the fire at the
              Government Farm.

Conclusions/Recommendations

References

Ontario, *Annual Report of the Agricultural College*, 1888.

139 SURVEY OF LEADING SCHOOLS OF TECHNOLOGY IN THE UNITED
STATES
(Departmental Committee)

Appointed	1888
Reported	February 4, 1889
Committee	Two members; George Ross (Minister of Education) chairman
Purpose	To survey the leading schools of technology in the United States.

Conclusions/Recommendations

That as a rule all the institutions visited in the United
States were built with very little regard to architectural
effect, and not one of them would compare with the
University of Toronto in external appearances although
they were all much superior in internal arrangements.

References

Ontario, *Report of the Minister of Education on the Subject
of Technical Education,* 1889.

140 SPECIAL INQUIRY INTO THE SCHOOLS IN THE COUNTIES OF
PRESCOTT, RUSSELL, ESSEX, KENT, AND SIMCOE
(Departmental Committee)

Appointed	May 13, 1889
Reported	August 22, 1889
Committee	Three members; John J. Tilley (Inspector of County Model Schools) chairman
Purpose	To visit the Public Schools of the Counties of Prescott, Russell, Essex, Kent and Simcoe, for the purpose of making full and careful enquiry by personal inspection and any other way that may be deemed expedient, into the teaching of

> English in the Public Schools of the said
> counties in which the French language is
> taught, and the observance of the Regulations
> of the Education Department generally by
> teachers, trustees and other school officers
> therein; and to consider and report in what
> way the study of English may be most success-
> fully promoted among those accustomed to the
> use of the French language as their mother
> tongue.

Conclusions/Recommendations

That there are some schools in which the time given to
English and the use of that language in the school are
too limited, but even in these, more attention is paid to
English than formerly, and the use made of it in the work
of instruction is greater than it was a few years ago;

That in dealing with these schools, in order to raise them
to a higher standard, and to secure a satisfactory teaching of the English language in them, time must be allowed
and patience must be exercised;

That there is reason to believe that whatever changes may
be necessary to render these schools more efficient, and
to advance the children more rapidly and intelligently in
the knowledge of English, will be welcomed by the French
people themselves; that on the whole the people take a
deep interest in the education of their children;

That a special school be established for the training of
French teachers in the English language;

That special institutes be held for the immediate benefit
of the teachers now employed in the French Schools;

That the attention of the teachers be called at once to
the necessity of making greater use of the oral or conver-
sational method in teaching English;

That a bilingual series of readers -- French and English --
be provided for the French Schools in Ontario;

That the use of unauthorized text-books in the schools be

discontinued.

References

Ontario, *Sessional Papers*, 1890, No. 7.

Ontario, *Sessional Papers*, 1894, No. 4.

141 SPECIAL INQUIRY INTO THE SCHOOLS IN THE COUNTIES OF
PRESCOTT, RUSSELL, ESSEX, KENT, AND SIMCOE
(Departmental Committee)

Appointed	May 29, 1893
Reported	August 9, 1893
Committee	Three members; John J. Tilley (Inspector of County Model Schools) chairman
Purpose	To consider and report what progress, if any, has been made in the study of English since the date of the last report, and also as to what benefits, if any, have resulted from and by the establishment of the Model School.

Conclusions/Recommendations

That the backward condition of these schools which are
described as inferior in their knowledge of English, must
be attributed mainly to the inability of the teachers to
speak the English language freely; and that the teacher
who finds it difficult to express his thoughts in English
to pupils who know even less English than himself,
naturally uses the language which both he and they understand;

That a much larger number of teachers are now competent to
make effective use of English in the work of instruction
than was indicated in the former report; and that it is
gratifying to notice the decided advance made by the
schools as a whole during the past four years.

References

Ontario, *Sessional Papers,* 1894, No. 4.

142 COMMISSION OF INQUIRY AS TO THE ONTARIO AGRICULTURAL
COLLEGE AND EXPERIMENTAL FARM
(Judicial Commission)

Appointed   June 8, 1893

Reported   July 29, 1893

Commission   Three members; John Winchester (Inspector of
               Legal Offices) chairman

Purpose   To inquire into the want of harmony said to
               prevail in the Agricultural College and
               Experimental Farm at the City of Guelph
               amongst the staff, officers and others con-
               nected with the said institution, or some of
               them, and into the conduct of said persons
               so far as the Commissioners may deem the
               interests of the institution to require.

Conclusions/Recommendations

That it is in the interest of the institution that the
rules, regulations and by-laws in connection with the
institution be rigidly enforced;

That it is absolutely necessary that there be only one
head of the institution, and he alone responsible to the
Minister for the proper discharge of the duties of all the
staff and officers connected therewith.

References

Ontario, *Report of the Commission of Inquiry as to the
Ontario Agricultural College and Experimental Farm,* 1893.

143 SPECIAL INQUIRY INTO THE SEPARATE SCHOOLS OF OTTAWA
(Departmental Committee)

Appointed   1895

Reported   February 12, 1896

Committee   Three members; William Scott (Toronto Normal
             School) chairman

Purpose   To inquire into the charges made against Mr.
             Inspector White by the Rev. Mr. Flamien
             representing the Christian Brothers and to
             visit the Separate Schools of the City of
             Ottawa for the purpose of making full and
             careful inquiry by personal inspection, and
             any other way that may be deemed expedient,
             into the methods of teaching in the said
             schools, the training of pupils in the
             various subjects prescribed in the course of
             study, the text books used by the pupils, and
             the extent to which the English language is
             taught in the schools where the French
             language prevails.

Conclusions/Recommendations

References

Ontario, *Sessional Papers*, 1896, No. 1.

144 COMMISSION OF INQUIRY INTO THE DISCIPLINE AND OTHER
    MATTERS IN THE UNIVERSITY OF TORONTO
    (General Commission)

Appointed   April 6, 1895

Reported   April 27, 1895

Commission   Five members; Thomas Wardlaw Taylor (Chief
             Justice of Manitoba) chairman

Purpose   To inquire into all complaints that may be
             submitted by any student, or by any person on
             behalf of any student, in respect to the

discipline or exercise of authority by the
Councils of the University of Toronto and
University College, and into all causes that
led to the friction alleged to exist between
such students and the said Councils, and into
all matters bearing thereon; also into the
qualifications, conduct, teaching and
efficiency of any member of the Faculties of
the University of Toronto and University
College against whom any charge or complaint
may be laid before the Commissioners; and to
inquire into the respective powers of the
various governing bodies of the University of
Toronto and University College, and, so far as
may be deemed necessary, into all matters
bearing on the administration of such bodies
since the date of the proclamation of the
Revised Statutes of the Province of Ontario,
chaptered two hundred and thirty, and
entitled 'An Act respecting the Federation of
University of Toronto and University College
with other Universities and Colleges', including their dealing with the discipline of
students and the various societies and associations of students.

Conclusions/Recommendations

That the University Council and University College Council
were within their jurisdiction in dealing with the case as
they did;

That the statements were not properly facts, they were
mere assertions;

That the students completely failed to show any justification for their alleged belief.

References

Ontario, *Report of the Commissioners on the Discipline and
Other Matters in the University of Toronto,* 1895.

145 COMMISSION OF INQUIRY INTO COST OF TEXT BOOKS
(General Commission)

> Appointed   November 12, 1897
>
> Reported   January 10, 1898
>
> Commission   Three members; Edward Morgan (York County Judge) chairman
>
> Purpose   To enquire as to the cost of text books in the Province of Ontario and elsewhere, and to the royalty paid on all text books used in the Public and High Schools.

Conclusions/Recommendations

That, since experts were all united in speaking in terms of high praise as to the literary quality and educational value of all school books now in use in the Public and High Schools of Ontario, and since the Readers were of excellent and durable quality, attractive in appearance, selling for a retail price not excessive, and infinitely better adapted for use in Ontario schools than either the Irish or American series, there seemed little reason for recommending changes;

That the policy of publishers paying royalties to authors was considered the best way of obtaining a book of acceptable calibre and of ensuring any necessary revisions and should be continued;

That the continued development of a Canadian text book literature was a wise and judicious policy and should be encouraged.

References

Ontario, *Text Book Committee*, 1897.

146 COMMISSION OF INQUIRY INTO THE MATTERS REFERRED TO IN A
RESOLUTION OF THE SENATE OF THE UNIVERSITY OF TORONTO
(Judicial Commission)

Appointed   February 2, 1905

Reported   May 16, 1905

Commission   Five members; W.R. Meredith (Chief Justice of
              Ontario) chairman

Purpose   To investigate certain anonymous communica-
              tions reflecting on the conduct of President
              Loudon and Professor McLennon in connection
              with the awarding of the 1851 Exhibition
              Scholarships in the years 1900 and 1904, and
              in other matters.

Conclusions/Recommendations

That although the Commissioners felt there had been no
intentional deviousness in awarding the 1900 scholarship,
they were of the opinion that under the circumstances the
recommendation that the scholarship should be awarded to
Mr. Patterson was irregular, and should not have been
made;

That the general charges affecting the capacity, character
and conduct of the President were not supported by the
evidence and were unfounded, but that the evidence showed
that the Presidency was heavily weighted with a multiplicity of duties not necessarily attaching to the office and
of such a nature as in the judgment of the Commissioners
to interfere seriously with the general oversight and careful co-ordination which were necessary to efficient and
harmonious working in any large institution;

That the President be relieved of some of the duties which
in their nature are less closely connected with his office;

That in respect of duties essential to his office, the
President's hands be strengthened by a clear definition of
his responsibilities and powers and by the increase thereof
where necessary.

References

Ontario, *Report of the Commissioners Appointed to Inquire
into and the Matters Referred to in a Resolution of the*

Senate of the University of Toronto Passed on the 20th Day of January, 1905.

147 ROYAL COMMISSION ON THE UNIVERSITY OF TORONTO
(General Commission)

Appointed   October 3, 1905

Reported   April 4, 1906

Commission   Seven members; Joseph W. Flavelle (Financier) chairman

Purpose   To inquire into and report upon:

(a) A scheme for the management and government of the University of Toronto in the room and stead of the one under which the said University is now managed and governed.

(b) A scheme for the management and government of University College, including its relations to and connection with the said University of Toronto.

(c) The advisability of the incorporation of the School of Practical-Science with the University of Toronto.

(d) Such changes as in the opinion of the Commissioners should be brought about in the relations between the said University of Toronto and the several Colleges affiliated or federated therewith, having regard to the provisions of the Federation Act.

(e) Such suggestions and recommendations in connection with or arising out of any of the subjects thus indicated as in the opinion of the said Commissioners may be desirable.

Conclusions/Recommendations

That the administration of the University be divided
between a Board of Governors (chosen by the Lieutenant-
Governor-in-Council) which would possess the general oversight and financial control, and a Senate (representative
of the federated and affiliated institutions and the
faculties and graduates) and Faculty Councils which would
direct the academic work and policy;

That the connecting bond between the Governors and the
Senate be the President.

References

Ontario, *Report of the Royal Commission on the University
of Toronto*, 1906.

148 COMMISSION OF INQUIRY INTO COST AND PRICES OF TEXT BOOKS
(General Commission)

Appointed   July 12, 1906

Reported   January 31, 1907

Commission   Two members; T.W. Crothers (St. Thomas
Barrister) chairman

Purpose   To enquire into and report upon the reason-
ableness of the present prices of School Text
Books now on the authorized list, and to
enquire into the prices of such publications
elsewhere.

Conclusions/Recommendations

That it is clear that text book publishing in Ontario has
fallen behind the times and that most of the books produced today are no better than those produced twenty years
ago, whereas in the United States and Great Britain great
progress has been made;

That if a satisfactory and modern set of readers cannot be
secured one should be prepared by the Department, the
copyright of all selections secured, the plates made, and

the printing be given out by tender, under proper specifications to one firm;

That since the price of nearly all the high school books
was too high, prices could be materially reduced without
depriving the publishers of a fair profit;

That the Government investigate the free text book systems
in vogue in Manitoba, the City of Toronto, and may cities
of the United States.

References

Ontario, *Report of Text Book Committee*, 1907.

149 COMMISSION OF INQUIRY TO INVESTIGATE THE WORKINGS OF THE
BLIND INSTITUTE AT BRANTFORD, AND THE DEAF AND DUMB
INSTITUTE AT BELLEVILLE
(Judicial Commission)

Appointed   October 5, 1906

Reported   1907 (?)

Commission   One member; Alexander John Russell Snow
              (Toronto Barrister)

Purpose   To investigate the workings of the Blind
              Institute at Brantford, and the Deaf and Dumb
              Institute at Belleville.

Conclusions/Recommendations

References

Ontario, Order-in-Council dated October 5, 1906, Executive
Council files.

150 SURVEY OF TECHNICAL EDUCATION IN THE UNITED STATES AND
EUROPE

(Departmental Committee)

Appointed   1909

Reported   [   ]

Committee   One member; John Seath (Superintendent of
              Education)

Purpose   To visit Great Britain, France, Germany and
              Switzerland and examine the instruction given
              in the trade schools at certain centres in
              those countries.

Conclusions/Recommendations

References

Ontario, *Sessional Papers*, 1910, No. 16.

151 SPECIAL INQUIRY INTO THE ENGLISH-FRENCH SCHOOLS, PUBLIC
    AND SEPARATE, IN THE COUNTIES OF ESSEX AND KENT AND ELSE-
    WHERE IN THE PROVINCE
    (Departmental Committee)

Appointed   November 4, 1910

Reported   March 6, 1912

Committee   One member; F.W. Merchant (Chief Inspector
              of Schools)

Purpose   To investigate and report upon the English-
              French Schools, Public and Separate, of the
              Province.

Conclusions/Recommendations

References

Ontario, *Journals*, 1912.

152 SURVEY OF THE SYSTEMS OF INDUSTRIAL AND TECHNICAL INSTRUC-
TION IN EUROPE
(Departmental Committee)

Appointed   1913 (?)

Reported   1913

Committee   One member; F.W. Merchant (Director of
             Industrial and Technical Education)

Purpose   To investigate the systems of industrial and
             technical instruction in Europe.

Conclusions/Recommendations

References

Ontario, *Journals*, 1914.

153 COMMISSION OF INQUIRY INTO MEDICAL EDUCATION IN ONTARIO
(Related Commission)

Appointed   September 29, 1915

Reported   October 13, 1917

Commission   One member; Frank E. Hodgins (Supreme Court
             Justice)

Purpose   To investigate medical education in Ontario.

Conclusions/Recommendations

That the whole subject seemed to require a thorough
inquiry into the standing, capacity, and numbers of those
who desired to bring about any radical change, as well as
into the educational record and constitution of the bodies
advocating or resisting it, and a candid consideration of
the results of all of those parties and to the interests
of the public of the Province as well.

References

Ontario, *Report and Supporting Statements on Medical Education in Ontario,* 1917.

154 COMMISSION OF INQUIRY INTO CERTAIN COMPLAINTS AGAINST THE INTERNAL DISCIPLINE AND MANAGEMENT OF THE ONTARIO SCHOOL FOR THE BLIND, BRANTFORD
(Judicial Commission)

Appointed   April 26, 1916

Reported   February 12, 1917

Commission   One member; N.B. Gash (King's Counsel)

Purpose   To enquire into certain complaints made to the Department of Education of the Province against the internal discipline and management of the Ontario School for the Blind, Brantford, and the report upon the same, as well as the general administration, conduct and welfare thereof, and any other matters or questions arising thereout, or in the course of the inquiry.

Conclusions/Recommendations

(There were five pages of recommendations under the headings: Constitution, Management and Discipline; Literary Department; Gymnasium, Physical Exercises and Fire Drill; Physical, Social and Moral; Printing; School Premises; Extension of Manual or Vocational Training; Administration and Inspection; Prevention of Blindness and Conservation of Vision; The Adult Blind.)

That there be closer supervision by the principal and his assistants;

That the discipline of the institution be more strictly under the supervision of the superintendent, and where physical punishment is needed, only the strap be used;

That an open-air skating rink, as well as a slide for tobogganing or sleighing, be laid out on the grounds for use by the students during the winter months. The natural features of the grounds can be used for the latter.

References

Ontario, *Royal Commission to Inquire into the Administration, Management and Welfare of the Ontario School for the Blind,* 1917.

155 COMMISSION OF INQUIRY INTO THE CARE AND CONTROL OF THE MENTALLY DEFECTIVE AND FEEBLE-MINDED IN ONTARIO (Related Commission)

Appointed   November 18, 1917

Reported   October 18, 1919

Commission   One member; Frank E. Hodgins (Supreme Court Justice)

Purpose   To inquire into the care and control of the mentally defective and feeble-minded in Ontario.

Conclusions/Recommendations

That it is in the schools that the most useful work can be done in ascertaining the mental condition of the vast majority of children between the ages of 8 and 14 years, now increased to 18 years under the Adolescent School Attendance Act, 1919;

That special classes need trained teachers whose powers of observation have been quickened and informed by previous technical study;

That it is of great importance that these classes should be designated as for special training, as there is a distinct value to be got by avoiding the error of treating the children in them ostensibly as feeble-minded;

That it is comparatively easy to form these classes in
urban centres where one school in a district can be
equipped with a specially trained teacher and supplied with
the necessary and appropriate aids to the teaching
required;

That there should be thorough provision for physical,
manual and vocational training and for physical development, as this saves very many from institutional life;

That the end to be aimed at is that when their schooling is
done they may remain with their families and, under their
care and supervision, progress in the direction of self-
support in the community or pass into training schools
specially fitted for their highest development in manual
and industrial efficiency.

References

Ontario, *Report on the Care and Control of the Mentally
Defective and Feeble-Minded in Ontario,* 1919.

156 COMMISSION OF INQUIRY INTO THE BUILDING DEPARTMENT OF THE
BOARD OF EDUCATION OF THE CITY OF TORONTO
(Judicial Commission)

Appointed   January 9, 1918

Reported   [   ]

Commission   One member; Haughton I.S. Lennox (Supreme
                 Court Justice)

Purpose   To inquire into and report upon the Building
                 Department of the Board of Education of the
                 City of Toronto as requested by said body.

Conclusions/Recommendations

References

Ontario, Order-in-Council, dated January 9, 1918,

Executive Council files.

157 COMMISSION OF INQUIRY INTO THE ADMINISTRATION, MANAGEMENT,
CONDUCT, DISCIPLINE, EQUIPMENT, AND WELFARE OF THE
VICTORIA INDUSTRIAL SCHOOL
(Judicial Commission)

Appointed   January 29, 1920

Reported   April 15, 1921

Commission   Three members; John Waugh (Chief Inspector of
Public and Separate Schools) chairman

Purpose   To inquire into and report upon the administration, management, conduct, discipline,
equipment and welfare of The Victoria
Industrial School, and any other matters or
questions arising thereout or in the course
of the inquiry.

Conclusions/Recommendations

That the Victoria Industrial School at Mimico be replaced
by: a Reception and Observation Home visited regularly
by a psychiatrist, or physician, and an educational
official; a Training School to provide for older boys
with strongly marked anti-social tendencies; a Provincial
Auxiliary School to take charge of normal unfortunates,
retarded and physically defective boys;

That the organization be flexible enough to permit
regrouping, or transfer from one school to another when
found necessary or advisable;

That especial attention be given to making the lives of
the boys as happy and homelike as possible if permanent
improvement is to be accomplished.

References

Ontario, Order-in-Council dated January 29, 1920,
Executive Council files.

158 ROYAL COMMISSION ON UNIVERSITY FINANCE
(General Commission)

Appointed   October 27, 1920

Reported   February 10, 1921

Commission   Six members; Henry J. Cody (former Minister of Education) chairman

Purpose   (a) to inquire into and report upon a basis for determining the financial obligations of the Province toward the University of Toronto, and the financial aid which the Province may give to Queen's University of Kingston and the Western University of London; (b) to recommend such permanent plan of public aid to the said Universities as shall bear a just and reasonable relation to the amount of the legislative grants to primary and secondary education, and (c) to make such suggestions on any of the above subjects as may seem, in the opinion of the Commission, to be desirable.

Conclusions/Recommendations

That there be substantially increased financial aid to higher education;

That for the maintenance of the Provincial University and of University College the basis of support in the 1906 Act be restored, that is, a yearly sum equal to 50 percent of the average of the succession duties for the preceding three years;

That annual maintenance grants, to be adjusted every five years, be paid to Queen's and Western Universities;

That for urgently needed buildings, capital grants of $1,500,000 to the University of Toronto, $800,000 to Western, and $340,000 to Queen's be awarded;

That if future enrollment made it necessary, the transfer of present first-year university work to collegiate institutes and high schools be considered;

That a Department of Graduate Studies and Research be organized in the Provincial University as soon as practicable.

References

Ontario, *Report of Royal Commission on University Finance,* 1921.

159 COMMISSION ON INQUIRY INTO EXAMINATION IRREGULARITIES (Judicial Commission)

Appointed   1921

Reported   [   ]

Commission   One member; J.H. Putman (Inspector of Public Schools)

Purpose   To investigate the theft of examination papers during the 1921 examinations.

Conclusions/Recommendations

References

Minutes of University Matriculation Board, November 27, 1922.

Ontario, *Journals,* 1923.

160 SPECIAL COMMITTEE TO INVESTIGATE THE ORGANIZATION AND ADMINISTRATION OF THE UNIVERSITY OF TORONTO (Legislative Committee)

Appointed   June 8, 1922

Reported   May 2, 1923

Committee   Nine members; E.C. Drury (Member for Halton)

chairman

Purpose   To investigate the organization and admini-
                 stration of the University of Toronto, includ-
                 ing its relation with Federated Colleges and
                 with the Toronto General Hospital and to
                 make any recommendations which the committee
                 desire in the public's interest.

Conclusions/Recommendations

References

Ontario, *Journals*, 1922.

Ontario, *Report of Special Committee Appointed by the
Legislature to Inquire into the Organization and Administration of the University of Toronto*, 1923.

161 COMMISSION OF INQUIRY INTO THE BUILDING DEPARTMENT OF THE
    OTTAWA SCHOOL BOARD
    (Judicial Commission)

Appointed   March 21, 1924

Reported   [   ]

Commission   One member; John A. McDonald (Ottawa Public
                 School Board Trustee)

Purpose   To inquire into and report on the Building
                 Department of the Ottawa Public School Board.

Conclusions/Recommendations

References

Ontario, Order-in-Council dated March 21, 1924, Executive
Council files.

162 COMMISSION OF INQUIRY INTO AFFAIRS OF THE OSHAWA BOARD OF
EDUCATION
(Judicial Commission)

Appointed   September 1, 1925

Reported   [   ]

Commission   One commissioner; Judge Ruddy (Ontario County
               Judge) [Judge Ruddy declined, and information
               is not available as to whether a replacement
               was named.]

Purpose   The Oshawa Board of Education desired an
               investigation into the affairs of the Board
               for the past three years.

Conclusions/Recommendations

References

Ontario, Order-in-Council dated September 1, 1925,
Executive Council files.

163 SPECIAL INQUIRY INTO THOSE SCHOOLS IN THE PROVINCE
ATTENDED BY PUPILS WHO SPEAK THE FRENCH LANGUAGE
(Departmental Committee)

Appointed   October 21, 1925

Reported   August 26, 1927

Committee   Three members; F.W. Merchant (Chief Director
               of Education) chairman

Purpose   To investigate those schools in the Province
               attended by pupils who speak the French
               language with a view of determining the
               efficiency of the schools, means for improving
               the instruction, and plans for securing a
               more constant supply of qualified teachers for
               the schools.

Conclusions/Recommendations

That the necessity for securing better instruction in
English and in French and of improving the general status
of the schools is so urgent it be made the responsibility
of two special officers to be appointed by the Department
of Education, a Director of English Instruction and a
Director of French Instruction; and that the duty of these
officers be to keep themselves constantly in touch with the
schools in all parts of the Province, to study all phases
of the problems presented, and to cooperate with inspectors and teachers in setting up standards and in devising
ways and means to make instruction effective.

References

Ontario, *Report of the Committee Appointed to Enquire into
the Conditions of the Schools Attended by French-Speaking
Pupils*, 1927, App.A.

164 COMMISSION OF INQUIRY INTO OTTAWA COLLEGIATE CONDITIONS
(Judicial Commission)

Appointed   October 26, 1926

Reported   January 6, 1927

Commission   One member; John Fosbery Orde (Supreme Court
               Justice)

Purpose   To enquire into and report upon the condi-
               tions alleged by Rev. E.B. Wyllie to exist in
               the Ottawa Collegiate Institute.

Conclusions/Recommendations

That there was not a tittle of evidence to indicate that at
any of these school dances had there ever been any immoral
or improper or objectional conduct or drinking;

That Dr. Wyllie has failed completely to justify his
statements, and that, so far as the evidence discloses,
there is no reason to believe that any of the conditions

which he alleged as rendering it unsafe for parents to send their children to the Ottawa Collegiate Institute exist at all, or that the management and supervision of the schools and of the social activities of the pupils are not as efficient and perfect as is reasonably possible.

References

Ontario, Order-in-Council dated October 26, 1926, Executive Council files.

Ontario, *Royal Commission on Ottawa Collegiate Conditions*, 1927.

165 COMMITTEE TO INVESTIGATE THE COSTS OF EDUCATION IN ONTARIO
(Departmental Committee)

Appointed   May, 1935

Reported   March 25, 1938

Committee   Eight members; D. McArthur (Deputy Minister of Education) chairman

Purpose   To investigate the costs of education in Ontario.

Conclusions/Recommendations

That the total cost of education as well as the cost per pupil in elementary and secondary schools increased steadily from 1910 to 1930, but since that year has declined gradually;

That the increase in the cost of education was due (a) to the demand on the part of parents and employers for a longer period of training for youth in secondary schools and for a type of training which involved relatively large capital expenditures for buildings and equipment and (b) to the necessity for employing a larger number of teachers and to an increase in the salaries of teachers, due largely to the post-war increase in the cost of living;

That the decline in the cost of education since 1930 has
been due chiefly to a reduction in teachers' salaries;
that during the next ten years there should be a reduction
in the amounts required annually for the retirement of
debentures; and that during this period teachers' salaries
are likely to be increased rather than reduced, because of
a decline in the supply of teachers;

That the attendance at secondary schools is not likely to
decline until there is an extension of opportunities for
the employment of adolescents, and, consequently, that the
number of teachers required is not likely to be reduced;

That criticism of the cost of education has been directed
chiefly to the incidence of the taxes required for its
payment, and, particularly, to the unequal distribution of
the burden of taxation between real estate and other forms
of property, between different municipalities, and between
different groups in the same municipality;

That it is desirable that the burden of taxation on real
estate should be reduced, and that, as a means to that end,
consideration should be given to the taxation by the
Province of other forms of wealth and to the distribution
of the proceeds of such taxation to the municipalities in
the form of increased grants in aid of education;

That there is great inequality in the assessed value of the
taxable property of secondary school districts and of
public school and separate school sections throughout the
Province, and, consequently, in the mill rates of the
taxation which must be imposed for the support of education.

References

Ontario, *Report of the Committee of Enquiry into the Cost
of Education in the Province of Ontario,* 1938.

166 ROYAL COMMISSION ON EDUCATION
   (General Commission)

Appointed   March 21, 1945

Reported   December 15, 1950

Commission   Twenty-one members; John Andrew Hope (Supreme
             Court Justice) chairman

Purpose   To inquire into and report upon the provin-
             cial education system, and without derogating
             from the generality thereof, including
             courses of study, text books, examinations,
             financing, and the general system and scheme
             of elementary and secondary schools involving
             public schools, separate schools, continuation
             schools, high schools, collegiate institutes,
             vocational schools, schools for the training
             of teachers and all other schools under the
             jurisdiction of the Department of Education,
             as well as the selection and training of
             teachers, inspectors, and other officials of
             such schools, and the system of provincial and
             local school administration.

Conclusions/Recommendations

(Major recommendations included:)

That the province's school system be reorganized into a
three phase 6-4-3 programme;

That publicly supported Roman Catholic separate schools
terminate at grade 6;

That the official language of instruction and communication
in all publicly supported schools of Ontario be English;

That school districts throughout the province be totally
reorganized in order to create larger units of administration;

That a new system of grants and educational financing be
created;

('Non-disagreement' recommendations included:)

That there be expanded research and experimentation in
education;

That there be province-wide improvement in library facilities;

That there be multiple authorization of textbooks;

That education keep abreast of audio-visual and other teaching techniques;

That there be closer medical and dental supervision of students;

That there be a gradated counselling service;

That there be less stress on external examinations;

That there be more diversified technical training;

That there be closer concern for exceptional children.

References

Ontario, *Report of the Royal Commission on Education in Ontario,* 1950.

167 MINISTER'S COMMITTEE ON THE TRAINING OF SECONDARY SCHOOL TEACHERS
(Departmental Committee)

Appointed   February 23, 1961

Reported   1962

Committee   Twelve members; F.G. Patten (Superintendent of Secondary Schools) chairman

Purpose   To investigate:

1. Admission requirements of colleges of education and the courses at universities leading thereto.

2. The curriculum in special subjects and summer courses therein.

3. Practice teaching in all its aspects.

4. Diplomas, certificates, and degrees.

5. The relationship of the colleges to the universities and to the Department of Education in matters both academic and non-academic.

6. The relationship of the academic and the professional education of teachers, in both time and arrangement.

Conclusions/Recommendations

(There were 148 recommendations under the headings of Staff, Admission Requirements, Courses, Theoretical Instruction, Practice Teaching, Evaluation, Extra Responsibilities, The Student, Summer Courses, Finances, Location and Structure.)

That at least two new colleges of education be established in different parts of the province, and that such new colleges follow the pattern of graduate school attached to a university;

That modern facilities be provided for the Ontario College of Education which would continue as a graduate school;

That secondary teacher training be a post-graduate year at a college of education rather than any scheme of concurrent training in academic and professional subjects.

References

Ontario, *Report of the Minister's Committee on the Training of Secondary School Teachers,* 1962.

168 SELECT COMMITTEE ON MANPOWER TRAINING
(Legislative Committee)

Appointed   April 18, 1962

Reported   March 27, 1963

Committee   Eleven members; J.R. Simonett (Member for
              Frontenac-Addington) chairman

Purpose   To investigate the entire range of manpower
              training and development programs in Ontario:
              full-time courses in secondary schools, trade
              schools, and technical institutes as well as
              part-time extension programs therein; train-
              ing for employable unemployed as well as
              measures designed to upgrade those already
              employed; and formal apprenticeship programs
              as well as less formalized methods for
              occupational betterment and advancement.

Conclusions/Recommendations

That although many of the attributes of the whole man can
be imparted to the student or worker at the same time he
receives his vocational preparation, the time which can be
devoted to such matters will leave much to be desired;

That for this reason the tremendous variety of academic and
cultural enrichment courses which are being offered in
night classes in many centres across the Province is very
welcome;

That it does seem reasonable to assert that unless we turn
out employable men we cannot hope to develop whole men;

That historically, Ontario has tended to emphasize academic
preparation, often at the expense of vocational education
and training; and that it is vital that this imbalance be
corrected as quickly as possible.

References

Ontario, *Report of the Select Committee on Manpower
Training,* 1963.

169 ONTARIO COMMITTEE ON TAXATION
    (Related Commission)

Appointed   February 26, 1963

Reported   August 30, 1967

Commission   Five members; Lancelot J. Smith (Chartered
Accountant, Toronto) chairman

Purpose   To inquire into and report upon the taxation
and revenue system of Ontario and its
municipalities and school boards in relation
to their expenditures, the tax and revenue
sources available to them, their debts and
other financial obligations, with a view of
determining whether, within the constitutional
limitations existing and having regard to
present and potential financial requirements,
such tax and revenue system is as simple,
clear, equitable, efficient, adequate and as
conducive to the sound growth of the Province
as can be devised.

Conclusions/Recommendations

That public education is peculiarly well suited to local
government, and whether the criterion is a reasonably open
market for teacher's services, diversity and experimentation in education, or the need for school programs that
are accommodated to regional peculiarities, local authority
over education hold out greater promise than central
administration;

That if it is to be more than an illusion, such local
authority must be marked by a genuine degree of autonomy,
and to be genuine, governmental autonomy must have a basis
in the revenue system;

That the requisitioning powers of public school boards,
separate school boards and boards of education be terminated, and that these boards levy their own taxes to be
collected through bills issued for the purpose by municipalities and payable at times distinct from those at which
municipal tax bills are payable.

References

Ontario, *The Ontario Committee on Taxation: Report,* 1967.

170 ROYAL COMMISSION ON METROPOLITAN TORONTO
(Related Commission)

Appointed   June 20, 1963

Reported   June 10, 1965

Commission   One member; H. Carl Goldenberg (Barrister of Montreal)

Purpose   To inquire into and report upon

(a) the structure and organization of the Municipality of Metropolitan Toronto and, more particularly of the Metropolitan Council and the Metropolitan School Board, their functions and responsibilities and the relations with the area municipalities and the local school boards respectively and with municipalities and planning boards within the Metropolitan Toronto planning area,

(b) the purposes and objectives of the establishment of the Metropolitan Corporation and the Metropolitan School Board, the extent of the accomplishment of such objectives and whether such objectives can be better achieved under a new or revised system of local government, having regard to the past and future development and needs,

(c) the boundaries of the metropolitan area and of the area municipalities and their suitability in the light of the experience gained through the operations of the metropolitan government, with due regard to probable future urban growth within or beyond the present metropolitan limits and future service requirements,

(d) any related matters affecting the government

of the Toronto metropolitan region.

Conclusions/Recommendations

That the Metropolitan Toronto Board of Education be responsible for developing an acceptable and uniformly high standard consistent with area-wide formulae for most major
items of expense, while the local districts be allowed
some discretionary fiscal powers for special purposes,
such as experimentation;

That the varying school rates in the area be replaced by a
uniform tax rate for public schools.

References

Ontario, *Report of the Royal Commission on Metropolitan
Toronto*, 1965.

171 GRADE 13 STUDY COMMITTEE
(Departmental Committee)

Appointed   February, 1964

Reported   June 26, 1964

Committee   Seventeen members; Fred A. Hamilton (Director
               of Education, Guelph) chairman

Purpose   To inquire into the nature and function of
               Grade 13.

Conclusions/Recommendations

That the secondary school proper conclude at Grade 12;

That beyond this, two-year community colleges be provided
in addition to the existing pattern of universities,
teachers' colleges, and polytechnical institutes;

That the university-preparatory courses be offered not in
Grade 13 but in Grade 12, and (as the Matriculation Year)
be but one of a number of programmes offered in that grade;

That the preparatory programme include studies in breadth
and in depth;

That until this ideal situation was accomplished, course
content in Grade 13 be somewhat lightened, some credit be
given for a student's term work, and Departmental examinations be shorter with more options.

References

Ontario, *Report of the Grade 13 Study Committee,* 1964.

172 SELECT COMMITTEE ON YOUTH
    (Legislative Committee)

Appointed   May 8, 1964

Reported   April 6, 1967

Committee   Fourteen members; Sylvanus Apps (Member for
              Kingston) chairman

Purpose   To conduct a comprehensive inquiry into and
              report upon the special needs of youth, with
              particular reference to educational, cultural,
              recreational, and employment opportunities, as
              well as the health, welfare and sports
              facilities now available to youth, and the
              steps to be taken which in the opinion of the
              Committee would ensure a wider participation
              by youth in the life of the community.

Conclusions/Recommendations

That a separate Provincial Department of Youth, with its
own Cabinet Minister be formed at the earliest convenience
of the Legislature;

That sex education be undertaken by the schools as part of
a core of social subject matter that would include family
living, alcohol, drugs, and smoking;

That a course in civics compiled and supervised by the

Department of Education be given in elementary and secondary schools;

That physical education and physical fitness be encouraged;

That guidance facilities be improved;

That teachers be given more training in the behavioural sciences of applied psychology, child development and sociology at the Teachers' Colleges;

That school facilities be made available to responsible groups within the community at token rates;

That equality of opportunity in education, recreation and job opportunities be provided for Indian citizens;

That the Ontario Government request the Federal Government to establish an Office of Education.

References

Ontario, *Votes and Proceedings of the Legislative Assembly of the Province of Ontario,* No. 69.

Ontario, *Report of the Ontario Legislative's Select Committee on Youth,* 1967.

173 MINISTER'S COMMITTEE ON THE TRAINING OF ELEMENTARY SCHOOL TEACHERS
(Departmental Committee)

Appointed   September 28, 1964

Reported   March 29, 1966

Committee   Eighteen members; C.R. MacLeod (Superintendent of Public Schools) chairman

Purpose   1. to examine the teacher training programme now being followed at the Ontario Teachers' Colleges;

2. to examine other selected teacher training programmes;

3. to recommend changes that might be made immediately to improve the present One-year Course;

4. to develop, in some detail, what the committee considers to be an ideal programme for the training of teachers for the elementary schools of Ontario;

5. to suggest the successive steps that might be taken, over a period of time, to achieve the implementation of this ideal programme.

Conclusions/Recommendations

(Included in the 47 recommendations were the following:)

That responsibility for certification of teachers continue to rest with the Minister of Education;

That the program for teacher education be provided by the university; and that it be of four years' duration leading to a baccalaureate degree and professional certification, and elementary and secondary teacher education be offered within the same university faculty or college where feasible;

That all candidates for teacher education comply with regular university admission requirements and share the privileges and responsibilities of the students in other faculties;

That liberal arts professors and professors of education cooperate closely in preparing and carrying out the program of teacher education;

That approximately 75% of the four-year program be devoted to academic studies and approximately 25% to professional preparation;

That the four main components in teacher education be a liberal or academic education, foundations of education, curriculum and instruction, practice teaching;

That alternate routes of preparation include a concurrent plan, a consecutive plan, and an internship plan;

That programs be challenging, and there be opportunity for specialization;

That carefully chosen committees of selection appraise candidates' suitability for the teaching profession and recommend acceptance or rejection;

That the recruitment of capable students be undertaken cooperatively by the Department of Education, the Ontario Teachers' Federation, Colleges of Education, and local boards of trustees;

That every effort be made to attract to the staffs of the colleges competent scholars and distinguished and successful teachers;

That post-graduate study for teachers be encouraged.

References

Ontario, Department of Education memorandum dated September 28, 1964.

Ontario, *Report of Minister's Committee on the Training of Elementary School Teachers,* 1966.

174 COMMITTEE ON AIMS AND OBJECTIVES OF EDUCATION
(Departmental Committee)

Appointed   June 10, 1965

Reported   June 12, 1968

Committee   Twenty-two members; E.M. Hall (Supreme Court
               Justice) and L.A. Dennis (Secretary, Provin-
               cial Committee on Aims and Objectives) co-
               chairmen

Purpose   1. to identify the needs of the child as a
               member of society;

            2. to set forth the aims of education for the
               educational system of the Province;

            3. to outline objectives of the curriculum for
               children in the age groups presently desig-
               nated as Kindergarten, Primary, and Junior
               Divisions;

            4. to propose means by which these aims and
               objectives may be achieved;

            5. to submit a report for the consideration of
               the Minister of Education.

Conclusions/Recommendations

(Among the 258 recommendations grouped under the headings
of The Learning Program, Special Learning Situations, The
World of Teaching, and Organizing for Learning, were the
following.)

That a continuum for public education consisting of a
minimum of kindergarten and 12 additional years be established;

That the Grade 13 year be phased out as soon as possible
and its curriculum areas absorbed within the 12-year
continuum;

That the lock-step system of organizing pupils, such as
grades, streams, programs, etc., be eliminated, and
learners be permitted to move through the school in a
manner which will ensure continuous progress;

That horizontal and vertical divisions of pupils, such as
elementary, secondary, academic, vocational and commercial
be removed;

That learning experiences be organized around general areas
such as Communications, Environmental Studies, and the
Humanities;

That French or English be designated as the second
language to be offered for study;

That student learning profiles that reveal the individual
progress and experience of each student throughout the
learning continuum be developed;

That the use of class standing, percentage marks, and
letter grades be abandoned in favor of parent and pupil
counselling as a method of reporting individual progress;

That the use of formal examinations be abandoned except
where the experience would be of value to students planning to attend universities where formal examinations may
still be in use;

That schools and school districts as demonstration schools
and areas for particular projects and investigations be
selected;

That decision-making related to curriculum design and
implementation be located at the school board level and
in particular at the individual school level;

That, where the membership in the Indian community agrees,
the transfer of all federal schools on Indian reserves to
school boards be negotiated with the Federal Government,
the continuing costs of this program to remain a federal
responsibility;

That a Teaching Profession Act be enacted which will make
teaching a self-governing profession with powers to
license and to discipline its members, these powers to be
exercised through an organization to be known as the
College of Teachers of Ontario;

That all teachers' organizations be consolidated into one
association to be known as the Ontario Teachers Association;

That each faculty of education be allowed to develop its
curriculum and its operations freely;

That the focus be upon the processes of learning rather
than upon the acquisition of a methodology of teaching;

That professional and academic studies be included which will stress child development and psychology;

That, within the faculties, methods be employed, such as co-operative teaching, programmed instruction, field trips, group research, etc., in order to stimulate the student to accept them as a regular part of teaching practice.

References

Ontario, *Curriculum Bulletin,* Vol. 1 No. 2, May, 1965.

Ontario, *Living and Learning: The Report of the Provincial Committee on Aims and Objectives of Education in the Schools of Ontario,* 1968.

175 COMMISSION TO STUDY THE DEVELOPMENT OF GRADUATE PROGRAMS IN ONTARIO UNIVERSITIES
(Special Committee)

Appointed   August, 1965

Reported   November, 1966

Committee   Three members; John W.T. Spinks (President, University of Saskatchewan) chairman

Purpose   To study matters concerning the quality, need, introduction and expansion of graduate education and research in Ontario and the financial support for these programmes.

Conclusions/Recommendations

That the Provincial Government adopt a method of determining university operating and capital grants such as will permit rational forward planning with respect to graduate studies and research;

That the Province take appropriate steps to ensure co-operation and co-ordination between the universities in the field of graduate studies and research, with a view both to develop excellence and to economize resources;

That steps be taken to develop a number of centres of
excellence in the universities of Ontario, which might
achieve an international respect and renown;

That an Ontario Universities Research Council be established;

That the Ontario Universities Research Council be asked to
assume responsibility for the Ontario Graduate Fellowship
Program;

That the Provincial Government adopt a plan of adequate
support for those graduate students not supported by
Federal and private plans;

That the Provincial Government make provision for adequate
research facilities;

That an Ontario Provincial Universities Library be established;

That a provincial University of Ontario be established to
co-ordinate Ontario universities.

References

Ontario, *Report of the Commission to Study the Development
of Graduate Programmes in Ontario Universities,* 1966.
(Submitted to the Committee on University Affairs and the
Committee of Presidents of provincially-assisted universities).

176 MINISTER'S COMMITTEE ON RELIGIOUS EDUCATION
    (Departmental Committee)

    Appointed   January 27, 1966

    Reported   February 2, 1969

    Committee   Seven members; J. Keiller MacKay (former
                   Lieutenant-Governor of Ontario) chairman

    Purpose   To examine and evaluate the present program;

to receive representations from all interested
bodies about the effectiveness and desira-
bility of the program; to consider suggestions
for changes and improvement; to study means by
which character building, ethics, social
attitudes and moral values and principles may
best be instilled in the young; to consider
the responsibility of the Public Schools in
these matters; and to make recommendations
thereon for the information and consideration
of the Minister.

Conclusions/Recommendations

That the present course of study in religious education in
the elementary schools of Ontario be discontinued, and that
its aims as set out in related legislation, programs of
studies, regulations, and guide books, be abandoned;

That in the elementary schools of Ontario opening
exercises consisting of the National Anthem and a prayer,
either of universal character appealing to God for help in
the day's activities, or the Lord's Prayer, be held in the
home rooms each morning;

That in the secondary schools of the province opening
exercises consisting of the National Anthem and either a
prayer of universal character or the Lord's Prayer, be
held at the beginning of any student assembly but not
daily in the classroom;

That the high duty of public education to foster character
building be discharged through a clearly understood,
continuously pursued, universal program pervading every
curricular and extracurricular activity in the public
school system from the beginning of elementary to the close
of secondary education;

That the acquisition of information about and respect for
all religions be recognized as an essential objective of
the educational system from kindergarten to grade 13. This
should be achieved by a program of incidental teaching and
study, not through a formal syllabus;

That a formal course of study dealing with the principal

religions of the world be offered as one of the optional
courses in grades 11 and 12 in the secondary schools;
instruction in these courses to be given by members of the
history department;

That in addition to the assumption by the teachers'
colleges, future faculties of education, and colleges of
education, of the teacher-training responsibilities in
relation to the new program as outlined in the body of
this report, the Department of Education should provide for
the professional development of the present teaching body
through the planning and encouragement of workshops,
summer courses, and other appropriate in-service activities.

References

Ontario, *Report of Committee on Religious Education in the
Public Schools of the Province of Ontario,* 1969.

177 TASK FORCE ON SCHOOL HEALTH SERVICES
(Departmental Committee)

Appointed   April, 1967

Reported   December, 1972 [to Minister of Health]

Committee   Ten members; Jean F. Webb (Chief, Maternal and
             Child Health Service) chairman

Purpose   To examine school health programs and services
             in order to develop guidelines for the
             organization and delivery of health services
             in schools in Ontario.

Conclusions/Recommendations

That School Health Services be administered as an integral
part of the community health program;

That the Chairman of the School Health Coordinating Committee be a member of the School Board staff;

That a health assessment of each student be carried out on

or before entry into the school system;

That vision screening be carried out three times and hearing screening twice during schooling;

That tuberculin testing be done on all school entrants and at age 15;

That health information gathered in a uniform manner through School Health Services be tabulated at regular intervals and used to evaluate current health needs and the effectiveness of programs in meeting these needs.

References

Ontario, *Report of the Task Force on School Health Services*, December 1972.

178 COMMITTEE ON FRENCH LANGUAGE SCHOOLS IN ONTARIO
(Departmental Committee)

Appointed   November 24, 1967

Reported   November 28, 1968

Committee   Eleven members; R.R. Bériault (Department of
              Education Policy and Development Council)
              chairman

Purpose   To look at the broad spectrum of French
              language education in Ontario and to advise
              the Government as to the procedures required
              to provide adequate opportunities in the
              public education system for those who are
              French-speaking.

Conclusions/Recommendations

That a special committee (the French Language Committee) be created to represent the views of the Franco-Ontarians to the school boards;

That steps be taken at the departmental level to establish

special elementary schools for English-speaking pupils whose parents wish to have them achieve proficiency in the two official languages of this country;

That teachers in French-language schools follow the same pedagogical principles and basic instructional guidelines as teachers in other Ontario schools;

That the French-language secondary schools be given the opportunity of coming into contact with educational and cultural developments of the French-speaking society at large, either in Canada or in other French-speaking countries;

That wherever possible, French be the language of instruction in all subjects of the curriculum, with the exception of English;

That an effort be made to recruit teachers for French-language schools from other provinces of Canada and from French-speaking countries;

That staffs of French-language schools and universities encourage young French-speaking students to enter the teacher profession.

References

Ontario, *Report of the Committee on French Language Schools in Ontario,* 1968.

179 COMMISSION ON THE GOVERNMENT OF THE UNIVERSITY OF TORONTO
(Special Committee)

Appointed   December 1968

Reported   October 16, 1969

Committee   Nine members; L.E. Lynch (Chairman of
               Philosophy, St. Michael's College) and A.J.
               Webster (Graduate Student in Political
               Economy) co-chairmen

Purpose   To examine the whole structure of the
               University of Toronto.

Conclusions/Recommendations

That meetings of all university councils and committees be
open to members of the university community, university
media, the mass media, and members of the general community;

That appropriate standard rating questionnaires be
developed and administered routinely every year for all
courses and teachers, so that broadly-based objective
information is generated;

That promotions not involving tenure and below the rank of
full professor be made by the chairman of the department on
the advice of the departmental personnel committee;

That promotions to full professor and the award of tenure
be made by the dean on the advice of an ad hoc personnel
committee of the faculty council;

That faculty, college and departmental councils take
responsibility for defining their long-term objectives,
and relating those needs to developments in the university
as a whole;

That the students in every department form a department
students' union or club, and that this body be recognized
as the legitimate representative voice of the students in
any given department;

That any part of the university which administers its own
degree or diploma programme be known as a faculty, and
that the term 'division' be reserved for a section of a
faculty.

References

Toward Community in University Government, University of
Toronto Press, 1970. [Described as 'an independent commission of the university community as a whole']

180 COMMISSION ON POST-SECONDARY EDUCATION IN ONTARIO
(Departmental Committee)

Appointed   April 15, 1969

Reported   December 20, 1972 [to Minister of University
               Affairs]

Committee   Thirteen members; Douglas T. Wright (Chairman,
               Committee on University Affairs) first chair-
               man; D.O. Davis (Council of Regents, Colleges
               of Applied Arts and Technology) final chair-
               man

Purpose   To consider, in the light of present provi-
               sions for university and other post-secondary
               education in Ontario, the pattern necessary to
               ensure the further effective development of
               post-secondary education in the Province
               during the period to 1980, and in general
               terms to 1990, and make recommendations
               thereon.

Conclusions/Recommendations

That socially useful alternatives to post-secondary
education be provided;

That community involvement in manpower programs be established;

That legislation, structures and programs be devised to
facilitate the return to learning opportunities for
professionals, salaried employees, wage earners, and all
other persons residing in Ontario;

That, where possible, institutions of post-secondary education provide part-time students with a range and quality of
learning opportunities equal to those available to full-
time students;

That provision be made for employees to have the right to
time off for study;

That the present grade 13 standard of education be

attainable in 12 years, allowing individuals entry to all forms of post-secondary education after 12 years of schooling;

That there be established within the open educational sector an Open Academy of Ontario;

That the Government of Ontario adopt policies that would permit the establishment of a number of small, limited charter colleges;

That discrimination on the basis of sex in all sectors and on all levels of post-secondary education in Ontario, with regard to pay, rank and advancement, be abolished;

That efforts be made in the field of continuing education to provide appropriate educational and cultural services to adults among the native peoples.

References

Ontario, *The Learning Society: Report of the Commission on Post-Secondary Education in Ontario,* 1972.

181 STUDY COMMITTEE ON RECREATION SERVICES IN ONTARIO
    (Departmental Committee)

Appointed   June, 1969

Reported   1970

Committee   Thirty members; R. Secord (Director of Youth
               and Recreation Branch) chairman

Purpose   To make recommendations regarding the provi-
               sion of recreation services designed to
               obtain maximum benefits for the people of
               Ontario.

Conclusions/Recommendations

That services related to community recreation presently divided among several provincial departments be consolidated within the jurisdiction of a single and, if necessary, new provincial administration;

That the Ontario educational system examine completely its philosophy in relation to community development and community leisure services;

That boards of education be encouraged to extend the use of their facilities and services for leisure and community use;

That consultative services for the formulation of educational curriculum in leisure be provided without delay by the Department of Education to the Ontario educational system;

That schools provide some recreation programs based on their special resources during non-school time;

That boards of education, the local community college and the university strive to achieve and maintain a high level of operative coordination.

References

Ontario, *Report of the Study Committee on Recreation Services in Ontario,* 1970.

182 TASK FORCE ON INDUSTRIAL TRAINING
(Departmental Committee)

Appointed   October 1970

Reported   1973 [To Minister of Colleges and Universities]

Committee   Six members; W.R. Dymond (Chairman, Department of Public Administration, University of Ottawa) chairman

Purpose   To study existing industrial training programs and to make recommendations.

Conclusions/Recommendations

That a single branch to be known as the Employer-centered Training Branch in the Ministry of Colleges and Universities be constituted, to be responsible for the development and co-ordination of all employer-centred training programs, including apprenticeship, in the province;

That an Employer-centred Training Division be established in each College of Applied Arts and Technology;

That a Vocational Counselling Service be established as part of the Ministry of Colleges and Universities.

References

Ontario, *Training for Ontario's Future: Report of the Task Force on Industrial Training,* 1973.

183 COMMITTEE OF INQUIRY INTO NEGOTIATION PROCEDURES CONCERNING ELEMENTARY AND SECONDARY SCHOOLS OF ONTARIO (Departmental Committee)

Appointed   November 5, 1970

Reported   June, 1972

Committee   Three members; R.W. Reville (Judge of County of Brant) chairman

Purpose   To inquire into the process of negotiation between teachers and school boards and the roles of the various professional and trustee organizations in the bargaining process.

Conclusions/Recommendations

That the concept of professionalism must, by necessity, imply a sense of obligation to one's work. The teacher concentrates on the efficiency of his technique and on constant improvement of his performance. Matters such as remuneration, or the race or religion of pupils are relegated to a position of secondary importance.

Notwithstanding, the desire to improve one's financial status is not necessarily incompatible with one's obligations to his profession, but may indeed be fundamental in maintaining the high degree of excellence expected of that profession. Nevertheless, society demands that any such attempt be carried out in a professionally irreproachable manner;

That the negotiating entities consist on the one side of the teachers employed by a local school board, and on the other side, of the local board of trustees;

That a persistent disagreement between the parties as to any of the items that are subject to negotiations be referred to an adjudicator who is a member of a permanent Adjudicative Tribunal consisting of a chairman, one or more vice-chairmen and a number of part-time members, appointed by the Lieutenant Governor-in-Council on the advice of the Minister of Education, and financed by the Government of the Province of Ontario through the budget of the Ministry of Education; and further that the decision of the adjudicator be final and binding on both parties.

References

Ontario, *Professional Consultation and the Determination of Compensation for Ontario Teachers*, 1972.

184 ROYAL COMMISSION ON BOOK PUBLISHING
(Related Commission)

Appointed   December 23, 1970

Reported   December 1, 1972

Commission   Three members; Richard Rohmer (Queen's
               Counsel, Author) chairman

Purpose   To examine the publishing industry in Ontario
               and throughout Canada with respect to its
               position within the business community, the
               functions of the publishing industry in terms
               of its contributions to the cultural life and

education of the people of the Province of
Ontario and Canada; and the economic, cultural,
social or other consequences for the people of
Ontario and of Canada, of the substantial
ownership or control of publishing firms by
foreign or foreign-owned or foreign-
controlled corporations or by non-Canadians.

Conclusions/Recommendations

That a specialized agency, the Ontario Book Publishing
Board, be appointed to act as an interface between the
Canadian book industry and the public;

That the Board develop and administer a program of title
grants to Ontario-based, Canadian-owned publishers to
assist the publication of completed book manuscripts by
Canadian authors;

That the Board develop a program of assistance to bring
about the re-issue of out-of-print Canadian works;

That the Board devise and introduce a program of annual
Ontario Literary awards;

That the Ontario Institute for Studies in Education set as
one of its important program objectives the development
and evaluation of Canadian learning materials;

That teacher-training institutions provide special training in the evaluation of learning materials;

That the principle underlying the former book stimulation
grants be re-introduced into the special book listings
(Circulars 14 and 15) of the Ministry of Education.

References

Ontario, *Canadian Publishers and Canadian Publishing*, 1972.

185 COMMITTEE ON YEAR-ROUND USE OF SCHOOLS
(Departmental Committee)

Appointed   April 5, 1971

Reported   November 8, 1972

Committee   Eight members; first G.H. Waldrum (Director,
                Supervision Branch, Ministry of Education) and
                then Gladys R. Mannings (Assistant Superinten-
                dent, Supervision Branch) chairman

Purpose   To consider the overall feasibility and wisdom
                of a year-round use of schools, or of an
                extended school year, and patterns of
                'semestering'.

Conclusions/Recommendations

That boards may submit to the Minister of Education for
approval, plans for an experimental, innovative re-
scheduling of the school year for its elementary or secondary schools, or for both;

That experimental schedules may provide for the establishment of summer school programs and vacations during June,
July and August;

That school boards should carefully explore alternatives
before any re-scheduling of the school year is undertaken
and should inform the public they serve through an
organized program of communication with teachers, parents,
students, and the business community.

References

Ontario, *Report of Committee on Year-Round Use of Schools,*
November, 1972.

186 COMMITTEE ON THE COSTS OF EDUCATION
    (Departmental Committee)

Appointed   April 21, 1971

Reported   1972 to 1977

<u>Committee</u>   Seven members; T.A. McEwan (President,
            Beckton, Dickinson and Co.) chairman

<u>Purpose</u>   To examine the costs of education for the
            elementary and secondary schools of Ontario
            in relation to the aims and objectives, pro-
            grams, priorities, and the like, of the educa-
            tional system and to evaluate the programs in
            the light of the experience with them, the
            requirements of the present day, and in terms
            of the expenditures of money for them.

Conclusions/Recommendations

That Stratford Teachers' College, Peterborough Teachers'
College, Ottawa Teachers' College, and Hamilton Teachers'
College be closed; that other designated Teachers' Colleges
be integrated with university Faculties of Education; and
that they train, as specified, elementary or elementary and
secondary teachers;

That the Ministry of Education and local school boards make
careful analyses of expected enrolments and accommodation
needs;

That the Ministry of Education take a leadership role in
the development of transportation policy and assist school
boards in their efforts to achieve efficient and economical
transportation services;

That the Ministry of Education establish a Planning unit
responsible for the development on a continuing basis of an
integrated, comprehensive plan for quality education in
Ontario in accordance with accepted goals and expectations
determined by concensus of those concerned; and that each
school board give first priority to the development of a
'plan for planning';

That the Ministry of Education reaffirm its earlier commitment to the principle of decentralization of decision-
making in education to the maximum extent possible;

That changes be made in the financing of education.

References

Ontario, *Committee on the Costs of Education,* Interim
Reports, 1972 through 1977.

187 MINISTERIAL COMMISSION ON FRENCH LANGUAGE SECONDARY
EDUCATION
(Departmental Committee)

Appointed   October 1, 1971

Reported   February 17, 1972

Committee   One member; T.H.B. Symons (Vice-Chancellor of
                Trent University)

Purpose   To inquire into the effectiveness of the
                legislation to implement a program of French
                language education in the schools in Ontario;
                and to direct particular attention to the
                establishment, operation, and progress of
                French language secondary schools and French
                language classes in secondary schools.

Conclusions/Recommendations

That the legislative provisions for the French Language
Committee be retained, but that the functions of this
committee be clarified and strengthened;

That the board consult with the French Language Committee
on all matters affecting the establishment, program, and
administration of French language schools, wings, or
classes before any final decisions regarding such matters
are taken by the board;

That a Linguistic Rights Commission in Education for
Ontario be created;

That the Department of Education deal in French with the
French language schools of the province;

That the Standing Committee on French Language Schools
review procedures and set new criteria for the approval of
texts for French-speaking students;

That admission requirements to French language Teachers'
Colleges and Colleges of Education be progressively brought
into line with those for English-speaking candidates.

References

Ontario, *Ministerial Commission on French Language
Secondary Education,* 1972.

188 EDUCATIONAL RESOURCES ALLOCATION SYSTEM TASK FORCE
(Departmental Committee)

Appointed   November, 1971

Reported   1973 to 1975

Committee   Sixteen members; J.S. Stephen (Assistant
              Deputy Minister) chairman

Purpose   To develop, in co-operation with local school
              systems in Ontario, a resource allocation
              system that will emphasize planning for
              effective decision-making by educational
              authorities.

Conclusions/Recommendations

That Boards be requested to prepare annually, for the
communities they serve, a three-year plan describing and
forecasting all proposed changes in programs and services;

That the Ministry of Education utilize the Educational
Resources Allocation System as a comprehensive decision-
making approach in all its internal programs.

References

Ontario, *Report of the Educational Resources Allocation
System Task Force to the Minister of Education,* 1975.

189 SELECT COMMITTEE ON ECONOMIC AND CULTURAL NATIONALISM

(Legislative Committee)

Appointed   December 17, 1971

Reported   1973

Committee   Eleven members; Russell D. Rowe (M.P.P. for
             Northumberland) chairman

Purpose   To review the Report of the Interdepartmental
             Task Force on Foreign Investment and the
             current status of opinion and information on
             economic and cultural nationalism in Canada.

Conclusions/Recommendations

That legislation be introduced to provide that within five
years all chancellors, boards of governors or equivalent,
presidents, vice-presidents, deans and chairmen of departments at universities in Ontario be Canadians;

That universities be directed to advertise all academic
vacancies well in advance of the date on which it is
intended offers will be made, in at least the two periodi-
cals which are likely to reach the widest audience among
prospective Canadian candidates in the discipline for
which applicants are sought;

That plans be established to develop graduate programs
likely to attract the highest international reputation and
the ablest degree candidates from both Canada and abroad;

That each university in Ontario establish machinery to
assure that very substantially higher percentages of its
new faculty appointments are Canadian citizens on appointment, and that a similar high proportion have obtained
most or all of their graduate training at Canadian
universities;

That all universities be required to submit, on an annual
basis, and by department, the citizenship and countries of
undergraduate and graduate training of all new appointees,
tenured faculty, department heads and other academic ranks,
departures from strength, and persons on limited term
appointments;

That the Ontario Human Rights Code be amended to enable
universities to ask for citizenship of applicants for
teaching positions, and to permit discrimination in favour
of Canadian citizens in faculty appointments to universities in Ontario.

References

Ontario, *Interim Report of the Select Committee on
Economic and Cultural Nationalism,* 1973.

190 SELECT COMMITTEE ON THE UTILIZATION OF EDUCATIONAL
FACILITIES
(Legislative Committee)

Appointed   December 17, 1971

Reported   June, 1973; December, 1973; July, 1974;
              February, 1975

Committee   Eleven members; Charles E. McIlvene (M.P.P.
              for Oshawa) chairman

Purpose   To inquire into the potentialities and possi-
              bilities for the increased use of educational
              facilities throughout Ontario at all levels,
              including post-secondary facilities.

Conclusions/Recommendations

That the Government of Ontario, through the Provincial
Secretary for Social Development, adopt, as the basis for
the development of general policy guidelines, a system of
community education which will emphasize the need for
integration and coordination of educational and other
community resources, services and facilities; equality of
opportunity and access; and frameworks for local community
involvement in decision-making;

That the Ministers of Education, Health, Community and
Social Services, and Colleges and Universities work
together with the Provincial Secretary for Social Development;

That general policy guidelines be adopted to encourage the development of programs that recognize the growth of leisure as an important and positive element in the life of the individual and of the community;

That community education be stressed in the teacher training curricula of the province's teacher colleges and faculties of education;

That arts, sports and other recreational activities be totally integrated into the school process;

That a Council on Open Education be established.

References

Ontario, *'What happens next is up to you': Final Report: Select Committee on the Utilization of Educational Facilities*, February, 1975.

191 TASK FORCE ON THE SCHOOL YEAR
(Departmental Committee)

Appointed   June, 1972

Reported   September 1, 1972

Committee   Eleven members; H.K. Fisher (Director, Supervisory Services Branch, Ministry of Education) chairman

Purpose   To study the question of school closing dates and the length of the school year.

Conclusions/Recommendations

That for all schools operated by a board, the school year shall be defined within the calendar year as being 200 school days of which a minimum of 185 school days shall be designated as instructional days;

That each school board shall establish a pattern of attendance for students and staff within the defined school year

which will reflect the particular needs of the schools and
which may re-define the school year for the board as being
more than 200 days;

That such patterns be subject to the annual approval of the
Ministry of Education.

References

Ontario, *Report: Task Force: The School Year*, September,
1972.

192 STUDY TEAM ON THE SHARING OR TRANSFERRING OF SCHOOL
FACILITIES
(Departmental Committee)

Appointed   November, 1972

Reported   February 1, 1973

Committee   Six members; R.J. Christie (Former Chairman,
                Borough of York, Board of Education) and J.A.
                Marrese (Chairman, Metropolitan Separate
                School Board) co-chairmen

Purpose   To study the sharing or transferring of school
                facilities.

Conclusions/Recommendations

That the Minister of Education provide for the mandatory
establishment of a joint planning council of public and
separate school boards, wherever such boards share common
or overlapping attendance areas;

That the Minister of Education strongly recommend to school
boards who may be experiencing problems with large-scale
transferrals that the pairs of boards concerned agree upon
dates for the determination of the final number of transfers for the following year;

That legislation be established to ensure that school
boards, both public and separate, have representatives on

local planning boards and access to complete information on the development of new areas.

References

Ontario, *Report of the Study Team on the Sharing or Transferring of School Facilities,* February, 1973.

193 MINISTERIAL COMMITTEE ON THE TEACHING OF FRENCH (Departmental Committee)

Appointed   June 12, 1973

Reported   September, 1974

Committee   Twelve members; Robert Gillin (Curriculum Services Officer, Ministry of Education) chairman

Purpose   To develop improved curriculum and techniques for teaching French to the English-speaking students of Ontario, and at the same time to review the aims and objectives of French language courses in our schools.

Conclusions/Recommendations

That French be introduced at the Kindergarten, Primary, or at the latest, the Junior level, and that from whatever level it is introduced, a carefully articulated program be provided to the end of the secondary level;

That, at whatever grade French is introduced, a daily class be offered to the end of the Junior Division;

That, beginning at Grade 7, each individual Board declare French to be either a compulsory or an optional subject;

That French teachers take the initiative in developing Canadian Studies courses;

That the Ministry of Education encourage the production of materials with Canadian content for all levels of the

French program;

That immediate steps be taken to ensure that there is an
adequate supply of teachers capable of teaching French
immersion classes and of teaching in French in other areas
of the curriculum both in elementary and secondary schools
to meet current needs.

References

Ontario, *Report of the Ministerial Committee on the Teaching of French*, 1974.

194 MINISTERIAL COMMISSION ON THE ORGANIZATION AND FINANCING OF
THE PUBLIC AND SECONDARY SCHOOL SYSTEMS IN METROPOLITAN
TORONTO
(Departmental Committee)

Appointed   June 13, 1973

Reported   June, 1974

Committee   Four members; Barry Lowes (former Chairman of
Metropolitan Toronto School Board) chairman

Purpose   To inquire into the structure, operation and
financing of the public and secondary school
systems in Metropolitan Toronto.

Conclusions/Recommendations

That Area Boards of Education move to establish families of
schools as their primary unit of educational administration;

That the two-tier structure of educational governance be
retained;

That the powers of the Metropolitan Toronto School Board be
modified, that these powers be designated, and that all
residual powers and responsibilities remain with the Area
Boards;

That Metropolitan Toronto be considered a region of the Province by the Ministry of Education.

References

Ontario, *Report of the Ministerial Commission on the Organization and Financing of the Public and Secondary School Systems in Metropolitan Toronto,* [1973]

195 ROYAL COMMISSION ON METROPOLITAN TORONTO
(Related Commission)

Appointed   September 10, 1974

Reported   June 15, 1977

Commission   One member; John P. Robarts (former Premier of Ontario)

Purpose   To examine, evaluate and make appropriate recommendations on the structure, organization and operations of local government within the Metropolitan Toronto area, including all municipal governments, boards and commissions.

Conclusions/Recommendations

That the boundaries of area municipalities and area boards of education in Metropolitan Toronto continue to coincide;

That the direct educational responsibilities of the Metro-politan Toronto School Board be transferred to the area boards of education, with provision to ensure that no child is thereby denied access to appropriate educational services;

That health-related costs and services of the school system, including those for special education, be paid from municipal public health budgets;

That the collection of education taxes in Metropolitan Toronto continue to be the responsibility of the area municipalities.

References

Ontario, *Report of the Royal Commission on Metropolitan Toronto,* 1977.

196 TASK FORCE ON THE EDUCATIONAL NEEDS OF NATIVE PEOPLES OF ONTARIO
(Departmental Committee)

Appointed   October 23, 1974

Reported   June 30, 1976 [to Minister of Colleges and
              Universities, Minister of Culture and Recrea-
              tion, and the Minister of Education]

Committee   Nine members; [no chairman designated]

Purpose   To study the educational needs of the native
              peoples.

Conclusions/Recommendations

That a teacher-training programme be developed with the aid
of Indian education specialists, so as to make it more
appropriate to the educational background, heritage, and
needs of the people of native ancestry;

That all teaching staff employed in schools serving native
students be required to participate in cross-cultural
sensitivity and awareness sessions, as well as workshops
in up-to-date teaching techniques;

That native counsellor training programmes provide immersion courses in native culture and history, together with
sound counselling techniques;

That native peoples be involved in the development of
curriculum and programmes of study, text design, the
writing of resource materials, the evaluation of present
curriculum as it relates to native peoples, and that they
be consulted before any new native studies material is
introduced into the schools;

That governments (both federal and provincial) adjust their
policies and practices so that native peoples are involved
in all phases of the education of their children and are
in a position to assume more responsibility for the provision of that education.

References

Ontario, *Summary Report of the Task Force on the Educational Needs of Native Peoples of Ontario,* June, 1976.

197 INTERIM COMMITTEE ON FINANCIAL ASSISTANCE FOR STUDENTS
(Departmental Committee)

Appointed   January, 1975

Reported   January 31, 1977

Committee   Nine members; J. Stefan Dupré (Chairman of
               Ontario Council on University Affairs) and
               Norman A. Sisco (Chairman of Council of
               Regents for the Colleges of Applied Arts and
               Technology) co-chairmen

Purpose   To advise the Minister of Colleges and Univer-
               sities of the financial arrangements required,
               in the long run, to assist students pursuing
               their post-secondary studies or training and
               to recommend the administrative steps and
               procedures considered most desirable for
               implementing these arrangements.

Conclusions/Recommendations

That a new program of student assistance to be called the
Optional Loan and Need-Tested Grant Program (OLANG) be
instituted which is designed to increase the accessibility
of post-secondary education to students from low-income
backgrounds; to foster accessibility for all students; to
be simple to administer; to encourage individual responsibility and broaden the effective range of individual
choice; and to operate entirely under the jurisdiction of
the Government of Ontario.

References

Ontario, *Report of the Interim Committee on Financial Assistance for Students*, January, 1977.

198 STUDY OF WOMEN AND ONTARIO UNIVERSITIES
(Departmental Committee)

Appointed   March, 1975

Reported   October, 1975 [to Minister of Colleges and
              Universities]

Committee   Gail McIntyre (independent consultant)

Purpose   To investigate the current status of women in
              Ontario universities; to identify issues of
              concern to women students, faculty and sup-
              port staff; and to recommend an action plan to
              eliminate inequalities between women and men.

Conclusions/Recommendations

That each institution issue a policy statement affirming
its commitment to positive action to achieve equal opportunity for women;

That each institution assign responsibility at a senior
level for the coordination, design, and implementation of
measures for achieving equal opportunity for all women in
the university community;

That each institution which has not already done so, conduct a formal study of the status of women students,
faculty and staff;

That each university design and implement a program to
increase the participation of women in graduate schools;

That, when recruiting faculty and staff, each institution
conduct an active search for women candidates;

That the Ministry of Colleges and Universities review

annually the enrolment patterns of male and female students
at the under-graduate and graduate levels, degrees granted
by sex and field, representation of faculty by sex, rank
and field, new faculty by sex, rank and field, faculty
salaries by sex, rank and field, and senior administrative
appointments in order to determine progress on a province-
wide basis; and that this data be made public.

References

Ontario, *Women and Ontario Universities*, October, 1975.

199 ROYAL COMMISSION ON VIOLENCE IN THE COMMUNICATIONS
INDUSTRY
(Related Commission)

Appointed   May 7, 1975

Reported   June, 1977

Commission   Three members; Julia Verlyn La Marsh (Privy
               Councillor) chairman

Purpose   To study the effect on society of the increas-
               ing exhibition of violence in the communica-
               tions industry and to determine if there is
               any connection or a cause and effect relation-
               ship between this phenomenon and the incidence
               of violent crime in society.

Conclusions/Recommendations

That the great weight of research into the effects of
violent media content indicates potential harm to society;

That we find a constantly increasing flow of television
violence at all hours, including those when children are
watching, in a cynical attempt to maximize audiences;

That television's escalation of violence is drawing other
sections of the media along like the tail of a comet;

That we do not believe in censorship but we do believe in

providing more and better alternatives for public entertainment, information and education, and we believe that it
is only just to demand accountability beyond the balance
sheet from those who take a profit from communications;

That wide-scale changes in present procedures should be
initiated to the end that the communications industry, by
diminishing the exploitation of violence, will reflect
more accurately the quality of life to which most
Canadians aspire.

References

Ontario, *Report of the Royal Commission on Violence in the
Communications Industry,* [1977].

200 ROYAL COMMISSION OF INQUIRY ON ALGOMA UNIVERSITY COLLEGE
(Judicial Commission)

Appointed   March 10, 1976

Reported   June 30, 1976; July 30, 1977; November 15,
               1977

Commission   One member; John W. Whiteside (Faculty of Law,
               University of Windsor)

Purpose   To inquire into, study and report upon all
               aspects of the management of Algoma University
               College bearing upon its effective operation.

Conclusions/Recommendations

That the existing major elements of the corporation and the
college, namely, the Board of Directors, the Academic
Council and the Membership of the corporation be disbanded
for a period which should not exceed one year; and that an
interim trusteeship be appointed in order that it may take
immediate action to assure recovery of the college from
its present problems and to institute appropriate proceedings to plan for the future;

That the undergraduate programme of Algoma University

College be terminated at June 30, 1978; that the Algoma College Association corporation be reorganized to assume the role of a regional education planning council at the earliest date; and that a substructure be created within the corporation to be known as Outreach Algoma to establish, finance and administer such educational and cultural programs, particularly in the areas of outreach, continuing education, research and development, as may be recommended by the planning council, within the means and resources available to the corporation.

References

Ontario, *Reports of the Royal Commission of Inquiry: Algoma University College: June 30, 1976 - November 15, 1977.*

201 COMMISSION ON THE REFORM OF PROPERTY TAXATION IN ONTARIO
    (Related Commission)

Appointed   May 5, 1976

Reported   March, 1977

Commission   Ten members; Willis L. Blair (Ontario
                Municipal Board, Toronto) chairman

Purpose   To review proposals with respect to property
                taxation in Ontario.

Conclusions/Recommendations

That assessment of all government property be pooled and assigned between the public and separate elementary schools in the same proportion as the taxable assessment assigned by the owners and occupants of residences; and that the pooling of taxable assessment be extended to incorporate all taxable assessment in respect of which a senior government will make payment in lieu of taxes;

That public school boards and separate school boards each be permitted to assign the taxable assessment of their own real property to the support of their respective school systems.

References

Ontario, *Report of the Commission on the Reform of Property Taxation in Ontario,* 1977.

202 WORK GROUP ON EVALUATION AND REPORTING
(Departmental Committee)

Appointed   November 26, 1976

Reported   April 15, 1977

Committee   Seven members; Claudette Foisy-Moon (Executive
                Assistant, Ontario Teachers' Federation)
                chairman

Purpose   To study how best to improve testing and
                evaluation in the classroom and how best to
                give teachers and parents a clear understand-
                ing of how their children are progressing.

Conclusions/Recommendations

That, in conjunction with teachers, trustees, and administrative officials, the Ministry develop, publish, and
distribute to teachers, manuals, resource guides, hand-
books, and information kits on evaluation, testing and
reporting, which describe as comprehensively as possible
how each function can be carried out effectively;

That the Ministry and the Ontario Teachers' Federation
jointly fund, organize, and conduct in-service professional
development for teachers in the areas of evaluation,
testing, and reporting;

That the Ministry make every effort to develop programs
and resources in the areas of evaluation, testing, and
reporting that would take into account the needs of the
Francophone students of the province;

That an advisory committee on evaluation and reporting be

established, and which would include evaluation in the broader context of curriculum design.

References

Ontario, *Report of the Work Group on Evaluation and Reporting,* April, 1977.

203 COMMISSION ON DECLINING SCHOOL ENROLMENTS IN ONTARIO
(Departmental Committee)

Appointed   August 24, 1977

Reported   October 31, 1978

Committee   One member; R.W.B. Jackson (former Director,
                Ontario Institute for Studies in Education)
                chairman

Purpose   To study the implications of declining school
                enrolments in Ontario.

Conclusions/Recommendations

That since there is nothing we can do to stop the steady decline in enrolment of children and youth in our schools, we must learn to live with this phenomenon and strive to maintain the quality of education we provide in light of the unfavourable economic, social and financial conditions which prevail at present and which promise to remain our lot for many years to come;

That school boards increase their cooperation with each other in the design of programs and development of curriculum materials;

That the Ministry of Education play an active role in cooperation with the boards in providing empathetic guidance personnel able to increase the awareness of students of the range of options open to them;

That the Ministry of Education and the boards encourage the Native Peoples to exercise their rights of involvement in

board and school affairs, including by seeking board
membership;

That all teachers be prepared for teaching in a multi-
cultural society;

That the teaching profession begin work together on: (a)
early retirement plans; (b) job sharing plans, including
night school and summer school jobs; (c) elimination of
large classes; (d) encouragement of most kinds of part-time
continuing employment; (e) encouragement or transfers,
exchanges, and leaves of absence; (f) encouragement of in-
service training, including retraining for teaching, as
well as for related or even unrelated jobs in business and
industry.

References

Ontario, *Implications of Declining Enrolment for the
Schools of Ontario: A Statement of Effects and Solutions,*
October, 1978.

MANITOBA

204 COMMISSION OF INQUIRY INTO THE WISDOM AND ADVISABILITY OF
ESTABLISHING AND MAINTAINING AN AGRICULTURAL COLLEGE
(General Commission)

Appointed   August 1, 1901

Reported   February 26, 1903

Commission   Seven members; William Patrick (Principal,
              Manitoba College) chairman

Purpose   To investigate agricultural education in the
              province and to inquire into the wisdom and
              advisability of establishing and maintaining
              an agricultural college.

Conclusions/Recommendations

That an agricultural college be established as soon as
possible;

That the foundation for the work of the agricultural
college be laid in the rural public schools of the
Province;

That attendance at these schools be made compulsory;

That rural schools be combined in districts sparsely
settled;

That greater attention be paid to English composition,
arithmetic, and handwriting.

References

Manitoba, *Sessional Papers*, 1903, No. 17.

205 ROYAL COMMISSION ON THE UNIVERSITY OF MANITOBA
(General Commission)

Appointed   September 26, 1907

Reported   November 30, 1909

Commission   Seven members; J.A.M. Aikins (King's Counsel)
               chairman

Purpose   To enquire into the government and management
               of the University of Manitoba; its financial
               status; relations with the several affiliated
               colleges; the nature, scope and method of
               teaching at the University; the suitability
               and sufficiency of the present building and
               premises; and other related matters.

Conclusions/Recommendations

That there be more monetary aid;

That there be a larger site;

That the office of president be created.

(Three separate reports were submitted with two commissioners supporting the *status quo*, two presenting a strong
plea for an unfettered state university, and the other
three proposing a sort of compromise whereby the provincial
government would appoint a controlling board of twelve
members to handle general administration, but the autonomy
of the affiliated colleges would be respected in academic
matters.)

References

Manitoba, *Sessional Papers*, 1910, No. 9.

206 COMMISSION OF INQUIRY INTO AIMS AND METHODS IN INDUSTRIAL
EDUCATION
(General Commission)

Appointed   August 26, 1910

Reported   February 26, 1912

Commission   Twenty-five members; G.R. Coldwell (King's
              Counsel) chairman

Purpose   To enquire into aims and methods in industrial
              education.

Conclusions/Recommendations

That vocational training be supported as a means of discov-
ering special aptitudes and fulfilling broader potentials,
of raising the status of the worker, and of contributing
to the industrial progress of the community;

That the foundation for such training be laid in the
elementary school with regularly-organized industrial work
in the higher grades;

That vocational and general education supplement one
another;

That evening classes for adult education be provided;

That teachers be specially trained;

That at some future date a technical college be established.

References

Manitoba, *Sessional Papers*, 1912, No. 3.

207 SPECIAL REPORT ON BILINGUAL SCHOOLS IN MANITOBA
(Departmental Committee)

Appointed   1915 (?)

Reported   January 15 and March 1, 1916

Committee   One member; Charles K. Newcombe (Superintendent
             of Education)

Purpose   To investigate bilingual schools in Manitoba.

Conclusions/Recommendations

That of all the children enrolled in Manitoba, one out of
every six received his education in a bilingual school
(16,720 out of a total enrolment of 100,963). There were
126 French bilingual schools in operation, employing 234
teachers, with an enrolment of 7,393 pupils and an average
attendance of 3,465.27; there were 111 Ruthenian or Polish
bilingual schools, employing 114 teachers, with an enrolment of 6,513 pupils and an average attendance of 3,884.96;
there were 61 German bilingual schools, employing 73
teachers, with an enrolment of 2,814 and an average attendance of 1,840.61.

References

Manitoba, *Special Report on Bilingual Schools in Manitoba,*
1916.

208 COMMISSION OF INQUIRY INTO ALL MATTERS PERTAINING TO THE
    MANITOBA AGRICULTURAL COLLEGE
    (Judicial Commission)

    Appointed   July 14, 1916

    Reported   January 30, 1917

    Commission   One member; Alexander C. Galt (Court of King's
                 Bench Judge)

    Purpose   To investigate and inquire into all matters
                 pertaining to the said Manitoba Agricultural
                 College, and the contracts entered into there-
                 for, and the expenditure of public money in
                 respect thereof, and the sub-contracts let

therefor, the persons interested in such sub-contracts, and the amounts paid to the sub-contractors.

Conclusions/Recommendations

References

Manitoba, *Sessional Papers*, 1917, No. 17.

209 COMMISSION ON STATUS AND SALARIES OF TEACHERS
(Departmental Committee)

Appointed   September 25, 1919

Reported   [   ]

Committee   Five members; Alfred A. Hill (Education
                Advising Board) chairman

Purpose   To enquire into the serious situation of the
                Province arising from the shortage of tea-
                chers, the inequality of qualifications and
                the uncertainty as to salaries.

Conclusions/Recommendations

That teacher qualifications be upgraded;

That experience be recognized for salary purposes;

That a larger unit for the administration of school affairs
be adopted;

That salary schedules have sufficient elasticity to permit
revision;

That, since the work in public schools was at least equally
important with that in high schools and collegiates, the
pay, therefore, be equally high;

That more young men and women of superior qualifications
and character be sought to give leadership to the future.

References

Manitoba, *Report of Committee on Status and Salaries of Teachers,* 1919.

210 SPECIAL COMMISSION ON THE POSSIBILITY OF READJUSTING THE
RELATIONS OF THE HIGHER INSTITUTIONS OF LEARNING
(Special Committee)

Appointed   1923

Reported   1923

Committee   One member; William S. Learned (Carnegie
              Foundation)

Purpose   To investigate the possibility of readjusting
              the relations of the higher institutions of
              learning.

Conclusions/Recommendations

That the university be transferred to the fine and extensive St. Vital property of the Manitoba Agricultural
College;

That the affiliated colleges build residences at the new
location.

References

Manitoba, *Report of the Commission on the Possibility of
Readjusting the Relations of the Higher Institutions of
Learning,* [1923].

[Sponsored by The Carnegie Foundation]

211 ROYAL COMMISSION ON EDUCATION
(General Commission)

Appointed   June 13, 1923

Reported   January, 1924 and January, 1925

Commission   Five members; Walter C. Murray (President,
             University of Saskatchewan) chairman

Purpose   To enquire into (a) the needs of the more
            recently settled and less developed districts
            of the province for better educational
            facilities (b) the better adaptation of the
            elementary and secondary schools to the needs
            of the communities they serve (c) the possi-
            bility of readjusting the relations of the
            higher institutions of learning so as to
            provide for their extension in the future,
            lessen the burden of their support, and
            increase their service to the province.

Conclusions/Recommendations

That legislative grants and special grants be given to
equalize school support;

That a curriculum committee be formed with representation
from the agricultural, industrial, commercial and professional life of the province;

That all normal school students be required to take a full
course of one year;

That the teachers' pension fund be established on a sound
actuarial basis;

That rural schools be used for practice-teaching purposes;

That adequate inspectorial supervision of rural schools be
provided.

References

Manitoba, *Report of the Educational Commission,* 1924 and
1925.

212 COMMISSION OF INQUIRY INTO IMPAIRMENT OR DEPLETION OF

UNIVERSITY OF MANITOBA FUNDS
(Judicial Commission)

Appointed   September 24, 1932

Reported   March 27, 1933

Commission   Three members; W.F.A. Turgeon, (Court of
              Appeal Judge) chairman

Purpose   To inquire into impairment or depletion of
              University of Manitoba funds.

Conclusions/Recommendations

That the Board of Governors be enlarged;

That no member of the Board have any financial interest in
university administration;

That security regulations be tightened.

References

Manitoba, 'Royal Commission on Impairment of University of
Manitoba Trust Fund', 1933.

213 SELECT COMMITTEE TO ENQUIRE INTO THE ADMINISTRATION AND THE
    FINANCING OF THE PUBLIC EDUCATIONAL SYSTEM OF THE PROVINCE
    (Legislative Committee)

    Appointed   April 6, 1934

    Reported   February 26, 1935

    Committee   Ten members; R.A. Hoey (Member for St.
                  Clements) chairman

    Purpose   To enquire into the administration and the
                  financing of the public educational system of
                  the province.

    Conclusions/Recommendations

That an inquiry be made into the cost of text books;

That a Salary Adjustment Board be formed to alleviate the diversity of salaries being paid to teachers, often in adjacent districts, for similar services;

That obligatory regulations with regard to school board-teachers contracts be inserted into the Public Schools Act;

That taxes be increased to make possible larger contributions on the part of the central authority.

References

Manitoba, *Journals,* 1935.

214 SPECIAL REPORT ON EDUCATION IN MANITOBA
(Special Committee)

Appointed   1937

Reported   February and March, 1938

Committee   One member; D.S. Woods (Dean of Education, University of Manitoba)

Purpose   To assess education in Manitoba as part of a survey of the economic and social life of the province.

Conclusions/Recommendations

That, for all types of community irrespective of racial characteristics, the people of Manitoba are elementary school conscious and are becoming, more and more secondary school conscious;

That the evidence of this investigation would indicate that elementary school facilities, in so far as they may be provided in one-room rural and small and large graded schools, have been made available to almost every home in the province;

That provision for secondary education, measured by numbers and nearness of schools, bears a direct relationship to one or more of the following factors: age of settlement, racial characteristics of the population, and the economic ability of the area;

That industrial changes and depressed economic conditions have produced a new problem for secondary education in that employment is not readily available for young people between the ages of fifteen and twenty who would normally leave school for gainful occupations;

That, as a result of the changes which have occurred in the population of the secondary school, that institution has been called upon to provide for many whose interests are included towards practical subjects, as well as for those looking toward professional pursuits.

References

Manitoba, *Education in Manitoba*, February, 1938, Part I, and March, 1938, Part II.

215 SPECIAL SELECT COMMITTEE ON EDUCATION
(Legislative Committee)

Appointed   March 10, 1944

Reported   March 9, 1945

Committee   Fifteen members; Ivan Schultz (Member for Mountain) chairman

Purpose   To enquire and report upon:

(a) The administration and financing of the public school system of the province;

(b) Equalization of educational opportunity throughout the province, with particular reference to elementary and technical education;

(c) Technical education in the light of the present-day and post-war needs;

(d) The provision for, and control of, admission of students to various faculties of the University of Manitoba;

(e) Any and all matters relating to the above, including curriculum, training of teachers and post-war education.

Conclusions/Recommendations

That larger units of school administration be instituted;

That local boards with certain specific and definite powers be kept, however, in order to retain local interest;

That educational standards for the whole province be set by departmental decree;

That the equalization of educational opportunity be further assured by financial stabilization which would include uniform assessment and provincial assumption of 50% of the basic operational costs of education;

That courses and programmes be provided to fit the varying needs of different pupils with different capabilities and interests;

That the teaching profession be upgraded;

That higher salaries be paid; more men be encouraged to enter this field; but that the period of Normal School training not be extended at this time;

That a survey of the situation with regard to adult education be made forthwith by the Department of Education and the University of Manitoba, with a view to close co-operation in this field.

References

Manitoba, *Journals*, 1944.

Manitoba, *Report of the Special Select Committee of the Manitoba Legislative Assembly on Education,* 1945.

216 ROYAL COMMISSION ON ADULT EDUCATION
(General Commission)

Appointed   August 21, 1945

Reported   April 8, 1947

Commission   Five members; A.W. Trueman (President,
                 University of Manitoba) chairman

Purpose   To investigate the work now being carried on
                 in the whole field of adult education in the
                 Province of Manitoba, to advise and make
                 recommendations to the Government of Manitoba
                 on the co-ordination of such work in order to
                 eliminate all overlapping, duplication and
                 conflict, to advise as to whether the whole
                 field is now being adequately covered and, if
                 not, as to what steps should be taken to
                 cover that portion which is not.

Conclusions/Recommendations

That the role of the provincial government in adult education be three-fold: to secure the greatest and most
effective use of federal government resources; to assure
maximum efficiency in the educational participation of
provincial departments concerned; and to provide financial
support to voluntary agencies without interfering with
their educational policies;

That the adult educational efforts of the three departments
of Agriculture, Education, and Health and Welfare be better
co-ordinated;

That the university, as an educational institution of major
significance for adult education, assume the responsibility for deciding what part it would play;

That a department of extension replace the faculty

committees used heretofore;

That voluntary agencies be encouraged in their vital work but that some sort of broad administrative organization be provided to ease the complexities and ensure the maximum results;

That the Government take the initiative in calling a conference of representatives of all voluntary agencies in order to establish an effective Manitoba Adult Education Council;

That library facilities be improved, and greater use be made of educational films, particularly those provided by the National Film Board;

That educational facilities be widened for handicapped groups such as the blind and deaf so that they might be able to support themselves, educate themselves, and adjust themselves to other groups.

References

Manitoba, *Report of the Manitoba Royal Commission on Adult Education,* 1947.

217 SELECT SPECIAL COMMITTEE APPOINTED TO STUDY AND REPORT ON ALL PHASES OF THE PENSION SCHEME FOR TEACHERS (Legislative Committee)

Appointed   March 11, 1946

Reported   February 11, 1948

Committee   Six members; John Cameron Dryden (Member for Morris) chairman

Purpose   To study and report on all phases of the pension scheme then in operation and to make suggestions.

Conclusions/Recommendations

That a teacher retirement system of the joint-contributing
type be instituted with contributions from the teachers
and from public funds.

References

Manitoba, 'Report of the Select Special Committee appointed
to study and report on all phases of the pension scheme for
teachers established under The Teachers' Retirement Fund
Act', 1948.

218 GREATER WINNIPEG INVESTIGATION COMMISSION
    (Related Commission)

Appointed   September 6, 1955

Reported   1959

Commission   Five members; J.L. Bodie, (Mayor of East
                Kildonan) chairman

Purpose   To study the metropolitan development of
                Greater Winnipeg.

Conclusions/Recommendations

That the establishment of a metropolitan school district
would ensure that all pupils throughout the Greater
Winnipeg area obtained the same educational opportunity
and that the cost of education was borne equally by the
metropolitan community;

That a metropolitan administration -- 'the Municipality of
Metropolitan Winnipeg' -- be formed.

References

Manitoba, *Report and Recommendations: Greater Winnipeg
Investigating Commission,* 1959.

219 SURVEY COVERING COSTS AND OTHER FACTORS IN CONNECTION WITH

THE ESTABLISHMENT OF A DENTAL COLLEGE IN THE PROVINCE OF
MANITOBA
(Departmental Committee)

Appointed   1956

Reported   August, 1956

Committee   One member; K.J. Paynter (Chairman, Post
               Graduate Studies, University of Toronto)

Purpose   To inquire into the costs and other factors in
               connection with the establishment of a Dental
               College in the Province of Manitoba.

Conclusions/Recommendations

References

Manitoba, *Concerning the Establishment of a School of
Dentistry in Manitoba: A Report to the Government of the
Province of Manitoba,* 1956.

220 STUDY COMMITTEE ON PHYSICAL EDUCATION AND RECREATION
    (Departmental Committee)

Appointed   March 19, 1957

Reported   1958

Committee   Five members; F.W. Kennedy (Head of Physical
               Education, University of Manitoba) chairman

Purpose   To investigate provincial needs in physical
               education and recreation.

Conclusions/Recommendations

That the Physical Education Branch be made an integral part
of the Department of Education;

That physical education receive more emphasis in the school

curriculum;

That specialization in physical education be offered at the
diploma or degree level in provincial teacher training
institutions;

That a provincial director of recreation be provided;

That the Government assist in a programme for training
recreational leaders and providing better facilities.

References

Manitoba, *Physical Education and Recreation in Manitoba*,
1958.

221 ROYAL COMMISSION ON EDUCATION
    (General Commission)

<u>Appointed</u>   May 15, 1957

<u>Reported</u>   November 30, 1959

<u>Commission</u>   Five members; Ronald Oliver MacFarlane
                (former Deputy Minister of Education, Manitoba)
                chairman

<u>Purpose</u>   To study and report on all aspects of educa-
                tion in Manitoba, up to University level, and
                without limiting the generality of the fore-
                going, in particular to study and report on
                the following:

                1. administration;
                2. finance;
                3. buildings and equipment;
                4. curriculum and standards;
                5. supply, training, certification and terms of
                   employment of teachers;
                6. inspection and field services;
                7. special groups, such as blind, deaf, physi-
                   cally and mentally handicapped;
                8. special services such as audio, visual,

library, correspondence;
9. scholarships and bursaries;
10. official trustee and special schools;
11. school attendance and its enforcement;
12. advisory and statutory boards and committees.

Conclusions/Recommendations

That, since Manitoba bears a far smaller share of the cost of education than in most other provinces, more financial aid be given;

That equalization of educational opportunity be sought;

That larger administrative units be adopted;

That entrance requirements into teacher training be upgraded;

That Manitoba Teachers' College be made an affiliated college of the University of Manitoba, or, if this were unfeasible, that it be transferred to the Faculty of Pedagogy;

That pedagogical courses be of such weight and content that they could be recognized for credit towards a pedagogical degree;

That standards for inspectors be raised (five years of academic training, plus two years of professional training, plus seven years of successful teaching in the province).

References

Manitoba, *Report of the Manitoba Royal Commission on Education,* 1959.

222 SURVEY OF READING
(Departmental Committee)

Appointed   May 1, 1962

Reported   January, 1967

Committee   Twenty-one members (Advisory Board); W.M.
Sibley (Dean of Arts and Science, University
of Manitoba) chairman

Purpose   To examine the programme for the teaching of
reading in elementary grades with a view to
its improvement.

Conclusions/Recommendations

That the Manitoba Reading Program remain under continuous
evaluation and review in all its aspects to ensure a
pattern of development that is sequential, continuous,
flexible, and up-to-date;

That in-service training in reading be provided for
teachers on a continuous basis and that courses in
developmental reading, diagnostic and remedial techniques,
and children's literature be incorporated into the program
for teachers in training at the Faculties of Education;

That school districts and divisions be encouraged to
establish a public relations program to acquaint parents
with the reading teaching methods used in their schools.

References

Manitoba, *Reading: A Report of the Advisory Board to the
Minister of Education,* January 1967.

223 ROYAL COMMISSION ON LOCAL GOVERNMENT ORGANIZATION AND
FINANCE
(Related Commission)

Appointed   February 13, 1963

Reported   April 28, 1964

Commission   Five members; Roland Michener (former Speaker
of House of Commons) chairman

Purpose   To inquire into local government organization
and finance.

Conclusions/Recommendations

That a solution to the problem of costs of education be
found by broadening the base of taxation for the financial
support of public schools so that the costs will be spread
as generally as the benefits throughout the province, in
contrast to the old system by which these costs were
borne only by the real property taxpayers of the locality.

References

Manitoba, *Report of the Manitoba Royal Commission on Local
Government Organization and Finance,* 1964.

224 STUDY OF THE EDUCATION OF HANDICAPPED CHILDREN IN MANITOBA
    (Special Committee)

Appointed	October, 1963
Reported	July 15, 1965 [to the Premier]
Committee	One member; John A. Christianson (former M.L.A. for Portage la Prairie)
Purpose	To conduct a comprehensive study to determine the kind and numbers as well as the geographical distribution of handicapped children within the province, to conduct a comprehensive survey of facilities and programs, and to make recommendations.

Conclusions/Recommendations

That local and provincial governments co-operate to
develop programs to provide educational opportunities for
children with mental or physical handicaps;

That the handicapped child be educated in regular schools
and helped to remain in his own home wherever possible;

That the public school system be reorganized on a non-
graded basis;

That greater emphasis in basic teacher training be placed on the fundamental principles of child development;

That the education of trainable retarded children be the responsibility of the various School Boards;

That legally blind children with some degree of residual vision be educated as partially sighted children and be given all educational opportunities recommended for partially sighted children;

That programs of auditory training for the very young deaf child be organized;

That placement in the Manitoba School for the Deaf be made only after complete assessment of the child's physical and mental ability;

That the Departments of Education and Health, working with the Manitoba Medical Association develop a positive screening policy to attempt to identify all physically handicapped children at as early an age as is practicable;

That all physically handicapped children be educated in regular classes as long as they are able to function successfully.

References

Manitoba, *A Study of the Education of the Handicapped Children in Manitoba,* 1965.

225 LOCAL GOVERNMENT BOUNDARIES COMMISSION
(Departmental Committee)

Appointed   August 18, 1966

Reported   September, 1970 [to Minister of Municipal
             Affairs]

Committee   Eleven members; R.G. Smellie (former M.L.A.
             for Birtle-Russell) chairman

Purpose   To make such inquiries as are deemed necessary, so as to enable the Commission to recommend the territory to be included in and the boundaries of Local Government within the Province.

Conclusions/Recommendations

That it was very apparent that a major part of rural Manitoba was not yet ready to undertake such a massive reorganization of the education system [the Provisional Plan], particularly when such a reorganization to many of them seemed designed to hasten the end of the rural way of life;

That the goals and criteria were still valid but that a structure must be designed to allow a greater degree of local participation in the effort to reach these goals;

That the most immediate solution to this 'local planning' concept seemed to be to allow the individual existing school divisions to be the local planning authority;

That as the basic premise of the Final Education Plan the theory that a *regional system* built around existing school divisions offered the best combination of a pooling of resources and a retention of local planning control over the education system to be developed within the specific region.

References

Manitoba, *Final Plan for the Educational Structure in Manitoba outside of the Interlake Area and the Metropolitan Winnipeg Study Area,* September 1970.

226 CORE COMMITTEE ON THE REORGANIZATION OF THE SECONDARY SCHOOL
(Departmental Committee)

Appointed   July, 1969

Reported   1973

Committee   Thirty-five members; S.A.V. Bullock (Director
             of Curricula) chairman

Purpose   To make recommendations concerning the revi-
             sion of the entire process of secondary
             education in the province, including the aims,
             objectives, philosophy, structure, and
             curriculum.

Conclusions/Recommendations

That continuous progress and the individualization of
student programs be adopted as the priorities of all
secondary schools;

That a balance be maintained within the total school program between studies of a general nature and those that are
of more immediate local interest and application;

That larger numbers of teachers be involved in curriculum
development at the local level;

That there be greater utilization of group and individual
counselling;

That a program of intensive in-service training focusing
on this report be provided for trustees, divisional
administrators, and secondary-school principals;

That the professional preparation of teachers, both pre-
service and in-service, be modified to ensure that the
knowledge, skills, and attitudes developed will be
complementary to the requirements for successful development of the proposals in this report.

References

Manitoba, *The Secondary School: Report of The Core
Committee on The Reorganization of The Secondary School*,
1973.

227 TASK FORCE ON TEXT BOOK EVALUATION
    (Departmental Committee)

Appointed   1972

Reported   November, 1973

Committee   Six members; Caroline B. Cramer (Manitoba
               Human Rights Commission) chairman

Purpose   To explore ways and means of ensuring a
               reasonable limitation on bias in materials
               used for educative purposes.

Conclusions/Recommendations

That the Minister of Education approach the Council of
Ministers to request the Canadian Publishers to develop
mechanisms to carry out a content analysis of all basic
texts; and request publishers and authors to incorporate
into their works, contributions made by various groups of
people in Canadian society;

That the Faculty of Education through pre-service studies
and the Department of Education through in-service programs,
provide training of all school personnel which will incorporate the study of bias and prejudice, the effects of
discrimination and stereotyping, the legislation affecting
rights and responsibilities, the declarations of human
rights, and which will develop the skills to identify and
cope with bias and prejudice in learning materials;

That the Minister of Education direct his department
through its Curriculum Branch, to continue its present
procedures for the evaluation of textual materials, and
include evaluation for bias and discrimination as one of
the criteria applied by the various curriculum and
materials selection committees.

References

Manitoba, *Report of the Task Force on Text Book Evaluation,*
1973.

228 TASK FORCE ON POST-SECONDARY EDUCATION IN MANITOBA
    (Departmental Committee)

Appointed   February, 1972

Reported   July, 1973 [to Minister of Colleges and
               Universities Affairs]

Committee   Seven members; Michael Oliver (President of
               Carleton University) chairman

Purpose   To survey the educational needs of Manitoba in
               relation to post-secondary education, to
               assess the adequacy of existing facilities and
               resources for fulfilling those needs, and to
               make recommendations for post-secondary
               development and the institutional arrangements
               by which this development may best be
               achieved.

Conclusions/Recommendations

That full-time enrolment at the University of Manitoba not
exceed 15,000 students, graduate and undergraduate, by
1980-81;

That the Universities Division of the Commission on Post-
Secondary Education work out with the three universities an
acceptable plan for enrolment control;

That Brandon University concentrate exclusively on undergraduate education, following its liberal arts tradition;

That the University of Winnipeg continue to operate
primarily as an undergraduate institution;

That each university establish a committee on the status
of women;

That Keewatin Community College develop its program in
mining technology and establish programs in forestry and
conservation; and that it broaden its offerings to include
practical nursing and social aid courses;

That Assiniboine Community College and Brandon University
continue to develop close coordination;

That a regional organization for post-secondary education

be established to make learning opportunities accessible to all Manitoba citizens;

That a committee representing the public schools, the universities and colleges, and the community at large be set up to undertake a study of methods of evaluating student achievement at the shifting boundary between secondary and post-secondary education;

That a Commission on Post-Secondary Education be established.

References

Manitoba, *Report of the Task Force on Post-Secondary Education in Manitoba*, 1973.

229 TASK FORCE ON GOVERNMENT ORGANIZATION AND ECONOMY (Special Committee)

Appointed   November 16, 1977

Reported   March 31, 1978

Committee   Four members; Sidney J. Spivak (Member for River Heights) and Conrad S. Riley (Winnipeg business executive) co-chairmen

Purpose   To review and study the organization of the Executive Government of the province and the various departments thereof, the Crown agencies and the boards and commissions that perform duties and functions under various Acts of the Legislature to ascertain whether any improvement in the administration of government can be achieved.

Conclusions/Recommendations

That all curriculum development work should be centralized in the Program Development Branch (School Program Division) and not be dispersed as at present in Native Education, Small Schools, Frontier School Division and other branches;

That an attempt be made to consolidate some of the
current operating grants;

That a study be conducted to determine what student and
teacher records are needed in the Department;

That School Boards and funded agencies be encouraged to
conform to the same restraints and economies as provincial
government departments and agencies.

References

Manitoba, *Report on Government Organization and Economy*,
Vol. I & II, April, 1978.

SASKATCHEWAN

230 ROYAL COMMISSION ON MUNICIPAL ORGANIZATION
(Related Commission)

Appointed   October 3, 1906

Reported   August 30, 1907

Commission   Five members; J.W. Smith (Mayor of Regina) and
                P. Ferguson (Ex Councillor of Indian Head)
                co-chairmen

Purpose   To inquire into municipal organization in the
                province.

Conclusions/Recommendations

That school district accounts be subject to government
inspection;

That school taxes be collected by the municipalities on
demand by the board of school trustees.

References

Saskatchewan, *Report of the Municipal Commission*, 1907.

231 COMMISSION OF INQUIRY INTO MORANG TEXT BOOK CONTRACT
(Judicial Commission)

Appointed   January 13, 1909

Reported   March 9, 1909

Commission   Two members; E.L. Wetmore (Chief Justice of
                Saskatchewan) chairman

Purpose   To investigate text book contracts.

Conclusions/Recommendations

That the evidence satisfied the Commissioners that there
was no graft -- in any sense of the word -- in the deal,
and that the Morang set was equal, if not superior, to any
readers in use in Canada, and equal to any in the United
States; that the prices paid for the Morang readers were
less than the price paid by the Government of Manitoba for
books of the same character, and which were shown to be
inferior in manufacture.

References

Saskatchewan, 'Royal Commission on Morang Text Book
Contract', 1909.

232 ROYAL COMMISSION ON AGRICULTURAL AND INDUSTRIAL EDUCATION,
    CONSOLIDATION OF SCHOOLS, TRAINING AND SUPPLY OF TEACHERS,
    COURSES OF STUDY, PHYSICAL AND MORAL EDUCATION
    (General Commission)

    Appointed   May 9, 1912

    Reported   November 15, 1913, and September 1, 1914

    Commission   Five members; Duncan P. McColl (Superintendent
                  of Education) chairman

    Purpose   To enquire into agricultural education in
                  public and high schools, technical education,
                  consolidation of schools, training and supply
                  of teachers, courses of study and text-books
                  for public and high schools, physical educa-
                  tion, and other related matters.

Conclusions/Recommendations

That systematic efforts be made to introduce more generally
into the public schools the subjects of nature study and
school gardening, manual training and elementary household
science and to provide in the more advanced schools such
instruction and training as will prepare teachers and
leaders in these departments;

That young men and young women of Saskatchewan be
encouraged to enter the teaching profession;

That teacher training be upgraded;

That consolidation of schools be encouraged and districts
wishing to consolidate receive such guidance and assistance from the Department of Education as conditions seem
to warrant.

References

Saskatchewan, *Report of the Saskatchewan Educational Commission on Agricultural and Industrial Education, Consolidation of Schools, Training and Supply of Teachers, Courses
of Study, Physical and Moral Education, with Recommendations,* 1915.

233 GENERAL SURVEY AND INVESTIGATION OF THE INCIDENCE OF
TAXATION IN THE URBAN MUNICIPALITIES OF SASKATCHEWAN
(Special Committee)

Appointed   1917

Reported   November 5, 1917

Committee   One member; Robert Murray Haig (Department of
             Economics, Columbia University)

Purpose   To investigate the incidence of taxation in
             the urban municipalities of Saskatchewan.

Conclusions/Recommendations

That high schools and collegiate institutes in Saskatchewan
are municipally controlled institutions which receive their

financial support primarily from taxes levied by the cities and towns, whereas the students are often drawn from a wide territory, and consequently the urban taxpayers are called upon to bear the total cost of high schools which serve both city and country.

References

Saskatchewan, *Taxation in the Urban Municipalities of the Province of Saskatchewan*, 1917.

234. SURVEY OF EDUCATION IN THE PROVINCE OF SASKATCHEWAN (Special Committee)

Appointed   June 7, 1917

Reported   January 20, 1918

Committee   One member; Harold W. Foght (Bureau of Educa-
                tion, Washington)

Purpose   To survey the system of education in
                Saskatchewan.

Conclusions/Recommendations

That everywhere on the North American Continent today and particularly in those sections where economic and civic life is most dynamic, there is a deepseated public feeling that educational institutions have not kept pace with the rapidly advancing life of modern civilization;

That Saskatchewan, in common with the other prairie provinces of Canada, is dominated by people of progressive type -- forward looking people, who have shown a striking determination to escape the hindering influence of back-eastern conservatism by taking action before their educational institutions shall become affected with inertness, resulting in failure to respond to the changing life of their democratic civilisation;

That the people of the Province have failed to use the schools as fully as they should have done;

That the prevailing system of school organization and administration in rural districts particularly, is no longer adequate for modern uses;

That abnormal opportunities in other occupations and other causes have conspired to make it difficult to train and keep in the profession an adequate number of well-prepared teachers;

That the courses of study in elementary and secondary schools do not in all respects meet the demands of a democratic people occupied with the conquest of a great agricultural country;

That the schools in their internal organization are planned less for the normal child than for the exceptional child, and offer slight opportunity for individual aptness and initiative;

That the system of examinations in use is a questionable norm of the average pupil's scholarship, ability, maturity and fitness for advancement;

That bodily health and hygenic conditions in the schools, so essential to effective study, have received little attention in the daily teaching and are largely disregarded in the physical equipment of the schools;

That the schools, while liberally maintained, must receive even larger support in order that commensurate returns may be obtained on the school investment.

References

Saskatchewan, *A Survey of Education in the Province of Saskatchewan*, 1918.

235 COMMISSION OF INQUIRY TO STUDY THE PUBLIC REVENUES TAX AND TO INQUIRE GENERALLY INTO THE MATTER OF EQUALIZATION OF ASSESSMENTS FOR PURPOSES OF PROVINCIAL TAXATION IN THE MUNICIPALITIES OF THE PROVINCE, URBAN AND RURAL (Related Commission)

Appointed   May 17, 1921

Reported   January 10, 1922

Commission   Five members; George Armstrong (Wildlands Tax Commissioner) chairman

Purpose   To study the Public Revenues Tax and to inquire generally into the matter of equalization of assessments for purposes of provincial taxation in the municipalities of the Province, urban and rural.

Conclusions/Recommendations

That, if land values are to be taken as a basis, the system fails because different systems of valuation are adopted in the different classes of municipalities, and in municipalities of the same class. If ability to pay is taken as a basis, the system fails because the rural dweller is paying on a larger proportion of his wealth than the urban dweller, and again the city dweller pays more than the inhabitant of the town, who in turn pays more than the inhabitant of a village. The system also fails on account of the large percentage of businesses and individuals who pay none or a very small percentage of the tax.

References

Saskatchewan, *Sessional Papers*, 1921-22, No. 19.

236 SELECT COMMITTEE TO INVESTIGATE THE ADVISABILITY OF ESTABLISHING THE RURAL MUNICIPALITY AS THE UNIT OF ADMINISTRATION FOR RURAL SCHOOLS (Legislative Committee)

Appointed   February 9, 1923

Reported   March 9, 1923

Committee   Twenty-seven members; Donald Finlayson (Member of Jack Fish Lake) chairman

Purpose   To investigate the advisability of establish-
           ing the rural municipality as the unit of
           administration for rural schools.

Conclusions/Recommendations

That, in view of the many difficulties with which the subject of administration of rural schools is surrounded,
further exhaustive consideration be given to this question.

References

Saskatchewan, *Journals,* 1923.

237 COMMITTEE ON SCHOOL FINANCE AND SCHOOL GRANTS
    (Departmental Committee)

    Appointed   April, 1932

    Reported   March 1, 1933

    Committee   Five members; N.L. Reid (Assistant Deputy
                Minister) chairman

    Purpose   To investigate school finance and school
                grants.

Conclusions/Recommendations

That, if education is a public responsibility, there is
something unsatisfactory and even unfair about a system
where, in the case of two adjoining districts providing
similar educational facilities, one district with inferior
taxable resources is called upon to levy a school rate four
or five times as high as its neighbor;

That a system of taxation and a basis for payment of
school grants be instituted that will make for equality of
educational opportunity and equality of costs as well.

References

Saskatchewan, *Report of the Committee on School Finance and*

School Grants, 1933.

238 DEBT SURVEY COMMITTEE
(Departmental Committee)

Appointed   August 23, 1934

Reported   February, 1935

Committee   Three members; J.W. Estey (King's Counsel)
              chairman

Purpose   To survey the debts of individuals, corpora-
              tions, and municipal and other public bodies
              within the province.

Conclusions/Recommendations

That of 4509 school districts, 2894 owe no teachers'
salaries, 203 could pay all salaries from cash on hand,
1389 could not pay salaries from cash on hand, 22 are not
in operation, and one has no return in for 1933.

References

Saskatchewan, 'Report of the Debt Survey Committee', 1935.

239 COMMISSION OF INQUIRY INTO PROVINCIAL AND MUNICIPAL
TAXATION
(Related Commission)

Appointed   August 21, 1936

Reported   December 19, 1936

Commission   Five members; Neil Herman Jacoby (Illinois
              Department of Finance) chairman

Purpose   To enquire into the whole subject of taxation
              within the Province of Saskatchewan.

Conclusions/Recommendations

That it is assumed that governmental services will be continued upon generally the same scale and with the same degree of completeness as at present;

That it is assumed that both the people of Saskatchewan and their provincial and local governments desire and intend to discharge past and present obligations in accordance with the terms of existing contracts or in accordance with terms voluntarily agreed upon by governmental or private creditors;

That it is assumed that the income of the people of the Province at large during the ensuing five years will be somewhat higher than the average income of the five-year period 1931-1935.

References

Saskatchewan, *Report of the Commission of Inquiry into Provincial and Municipal Taxation to the Government of the Province of Saskatchewan,* 1936.

240 COMMITTEE ON SCHOOL ADMINISTRATION
(Departmental Committee)

Appointed   July 12, 1938

Reported   December, 1939

Committee   Five members; William M. Martin (Court of
                Appeal Judge) chairman

Purpose   To inquire into and to report on the subject
                of school administration.

Conclusions/Recommendations

That, while the Committee is not prepared to recommend the formation and operation of experimental units without the approval of the ratepayers concerned, it is of the opinion that several areas of the Province should be selected and

the ratepayers resident therein given an opportunity to
decide whether or not the schools in the selected areas
are to be subjected to a larger unit administration.

References

Saskatchewan, *Report of the Committee on School Administration*, 1939.

241 SASKATCHEWAN RECONSTRUCTION COUNCIL
(Departmental Committee)

Appointed   October, 1943

Reported   August, 1944

Committee   Seven members; F.C. Cronkite (Dean of Law,
                University of Saskatchewan) chairman

Purpose   To study and investigate conditions and prob-
                lems likely to arise during or after the war
                and to consider, develop and recommend plans,
                policies and activities for the purpose of
                meeting such conditions and problems.

Conclusions/Recommendations

That education in Saskatchewan must develop on the following bases:

First, a sustained and increased attention to technical and
vocational education so that our youth may be fitted for a
part in a community and world of constantly changing
technology;
Second, an increased attention to social studies, which
seek an understanding of group relationships whether social,
political or economic;
Third, a sustained attention to the humanities, to literature, art, language and philosophy, with a view to developing a maximum range of human interests. Constant care
must be exercised that all studies are couched in terms of
current experience while sacrificing nothing of permanent
value;

and finally, constant care must be exercised to ensure that instruction, particularly in the field of social studies, shall not become indoctrination, and that the goal of teaching be development of the student's ability to make informed and reasoned judgements upon constantly emerging problems.

That the Council approves of the principle of larger units;

That the Department of Education should make a careful study of the problem of the larger administrative unit, and after such study, openly favour or oppose the establishment of these units and give guidance to districts, making known the advantages or disadvantages.

References

Saskatchewan, *Report of the Saskatchewan Reconstruction Council*, 1944.

242 COMMITTEE ON PROVINCIAL-MUNICIPAL RELATIONS
(Departmental Committee)

Appointed   1948

Reported   October 16, 1950

Committee   Three members; G.E. Britnell (Head of
                Economics and Political Science, University of
                Saskatchewan) chairman

Purpose   To make a complete examination of the finan-
                cial history of the province from the time of
                its formation in order to throw light on the
                common assumptions that real property is being
                over-taxed and that the municipalities are
                over-burdened with obligations in relation to
                their fiscal strength.

Conclusions/Recommendations

That in its desire to provide the children of the province
with an opportunity equal to those of other provinces the

provincial government has undoubtedly assumed a burden out of proportion to the resources at its disposal, and, in order that educational opportunity may be equalized as far as may be possible throughout the Dominion, some equalization plan based on differences in provincial resources should be undertaken by the Dominion government.

References

Saskatchewan, *Report of the Committee on Provincial-Municipal Relations,* 1950.

243 ROYAL COMMISSION ON AGRICULTURE AND RURAL LIFE
(Related Commission)

Appointed   October 31, 1952

Reported   Fourteen reports from March 18, 1955 to April 10, 1957

Commission   Six members; William Bernard Baker (School of Agriculture, University of Saskatchewan) chairman

Purpose   To study and make recommendations regarding:

(1) the problems involved in present day trends in agricultural production, land use and farm costs;

(2) the need for farm capital and credit;

(3) the further adaptation of social services and educational facilities to meet changing rural conditions; and

(4) the further development of rural transportation, communication and community services; and for these purposes to consult with all organizations and individuals interested and to accept for consideration, articles, submissions or other representations made by or on behalf of interested persons or

organizations, and to include in their considerations any questions which they may hold to
be relevant.

Conclusions/Recommendations

That, since education in rural Saskatchewan functions
within the rural social system, the basic characteristics
of agriculture and population have vital implications for
the provision of rural education;

That regrouping into larger units of school administration
be continued;

That balanced recourse to local, provincial, and federal
financial resources is imperative if there is to be maintenance and expansion of educational programmes;

That the problems of staffing rural schools with adequate
teaching personnel and of retaining students in schools be
faced;

That vocational education and continuing education be
expanded to meet the evergrowing demands of a technical
world and a complex society.

References

Saskatchewan, *Royal Commission on Agriculture and Rural
Life: The Scope and Character of the Investigation,* 1955.

Saskatchewan, *Royal Commission on Agriculture and Rural
Life: Rural Education,* 1956.

244 CONTINUING COMMITTEE ON LOCAL GOVERNMENT
(Departmental Committee)

Appointed   June 21, 1957

Reported   March 1, 1961

Committee   Fifteen members; John McAskill (Mayor of
              Saskatoon) chairman

Purpose   To study reorganization and boundaries and
               reallocation of finances and responsibilities.

Conclusions/Recommendations

That the provincial government undertake general reorganization of local government in Saskatchewan through the
following steps:

(a) Establish coterminous boundaries;

(b) As soon as practical, organize each coterminous area
    into a county or modified county, the choice between
    modified county or county to be made by a vote of the
    electors in each area;

(c) Reorganize school administration in each coterminous
    area as required by the selection made under (b).

References

Saskatchewan, *Local Government in Saskatchewan*, 1961.

245 COMMITTEE ON CONTINUING EDUCATION
    (Departmental Committee)

Appointed   September, 1962

Reported   January, 1963

Committee   Thirteen members; John H. Archer (Legislative
               Librarian and Provincial Archivist) chairman

Purpose   To delineate a policy of continuing education
               for Saskatchewan and to determine roles and
               responsibilities of formal agencies and
               voluntary organizations active in this field.

Conclusions/Recommendations

That because continuing education is so closely linked to
citizenship, government must treat it as a necessary part
of the educational provision of the province, and must also

achieve a sound balance between private and voluntary
efforts and public resources.

References

Saskatchewan, 'Report of Saskatchewan Commission on Continuing Education', [1963].

246 ROYAL COMMISSION ON TAXATION
    (Related Commission)

    Appointed   June 4, 1963

    Reported   May 1, 1965

    Commission   Three members; Thomas H. McLeod (Dean of
                   Commerce, University of Saskatchewan) chairman

    Purpose   To consider and report upon the systems of
                   taxation which comprise the total tax struc-
                   ture in effect in the Province.

    Conclusions/Recommendations

    That the idea of the foundation or basic programme in
    education reflects a social belief that all students
    should be guaranteed some adequate, uniform, minimum stan-
    dard of educational opportunities, regardless of where they
    live.

    References

    Saskatchewan, *Report of the Royal Commission on Taxation,*
    1965.

247 COMMITTEE ON INSTRUCTION IN LANGUAGES OTHER THAN ENGLISH
    (Departmental Committee)

    Appointed   August 11, 1965

    Reported   June 29, 1966

Committee	Five members; J.W. Tait (Director of Teacher Training, Department of Education) chairman
Purpose	To conduct a study of present programs of instruction in languages other than English in the provincial school system.

Conclusions/Recommendations

That English remain the language of instruction in the schools of Saskatchewan except as specifically recommended;

That *The School Act* which reads: 'English shall be the sole language of instruction in all schools, and no language other than English shall be taught during school hours.' be amended to read: 'Except as hereafter provided, English shall be taught during school hours.'

References

Saskatchewan, *Report of the Saskatchewan Committee on Instruction in Languages other than English*, 29 June 1966.

248 JOINT COMMITTEE ON HIGHER EDUCATION
(Special Committee)

Appointed	November 5, 1965
Reported	July 31, 1967
Committee	Sixteen members; J.W.T. Spinks (President, University of Saskatchewan) chairman
Purpose	To examine all aspects of post school education; to examine the feasibility of regional decentralization of post school education; and to examine and evaluate the articulation of all formal and informal educational programs in a community and, by so doing, to develop instruments and methods of enquiry with which other communities can carry out self evaluations.

Conclusions/Recommendations

That a number of educational regions be defined to provide
for development of effective 'middle-range' educational
services;

That these services be developed under a Commission for
Middle-Range Education, representative of the Government,
the University, the Saskatchewan School Trustees' Association, the Saskatchewan Teachers' Federation and the
regions;

That a Provincial Educational Advisory Council be established to act in an advisory capacity to the Minister of
Education with respect to the overall coordination and
articulation of provincial educational services.

References

Saskatchewan, *Second Interim Report: Joint Committee on
Higher Education,* July, 1967.

249 COMMITTEE ON TEACHERS' SALARY NEGOTIATION: LEGISLATION AND
PROCEDURES
(Departmental Committee)

Appointed   December 21, 1965

Reported   January 9, 1967

Committee   Three members; Benjamin Moore (Judge, Swift
             Current) chairman

Purpose   To inquire into the application of existing
             legislation to teachers' salary negotiation
             procedures.

Conclusions/Recommendations

That further study by a committee consisting of members of
the Department of Education, the Saskatchewan School
Trustees' Association and the Saskatchewan Teachers' Federation be made to determine the feasibility of a system of

compulsory area bargaining under the present system of
school administration;

That present legislation make provision for area bargaining on a voluntary basis;

That legislation provide a definite step by step time
table for negotiations, and that January 1 would be a
realistic anniversary date for agreements negotiated
between boards and their teachers;

That in the event of the parties failing to reach a voluntary agreement, or if jointly requested at an earlier date
by the board and its group of teachers, the Minister shall
appoint a Conciliation Officer from the Department of
Labour to mediate the dispute and assist the parties
thereto in reaching a voluntary agreement.

References

Saskatchewan, *Report to the Minister of Education of the
Committee on Teachers' Salary Negotiation: Legislation
and Procedures*, 1967.

250 ADVISORY COMMITTEE ON DIVISIONS THREE AND FOUR
    (Departmental Committee)

Appointed   December, 1967

Reported   August 15, 1969

Committee   Two members; L.S. Nicks (Past President,
             Saskatchewan School Trustees Association) and
             F.J. Gathercole (Director of Education,
             Saskatoon Public Schools and Collegiates) co-
             chairmen

Purpose   To inquire into the general efficacy and suit-
             ability of the division system as an educa-
             tional plan for the province of Saskatchewan.

Conclusions/Recommendations

Kindergarten Education, 1972.

253 ADVISORY COMMITTEE ON COMMUNITY COLLEGES
(Departmental Committee)

Appointed February 15, 1972

Reported August 15, 1972

Committee Ten members; Ron Faris (Senior Advisor on
Educational Community Development) chairman

Purpose To advise the Minister on the role of
community colleges in Saskatchewan's educational system and the educational process
throughout the province which would foster
understanding of the philosophy and potential
of community college development.

Conclusions/Recommendations

That the purpose of community colleges be to maximize
opportunities for continuing education through a decentralization of formal learning opportunities and the organization of programs at community and regional levels to
meet informal learning needs;

That colleges be developed on a regional basis with
priority in development given to rural areas;

That community college programs be organized to meet
identified needs and be disbanded when the need is met;

That community colleges grant no degree or diplomas, but
that formal programs be contracted as required from
existing educational institutions.

References

Saskatchewan, *Report of the Minister's Advisory Committee
on Community Colleges,* August, 1972.

254 ADVISORY COMMITTEE ON DENTAL CARE FOR CHILDREN
(Departmental Committee)

Appointed   November 30, 1972

Reported   March 31, 1973

Committee   Six members; K.J. Paynter (Dean of Dentistry,
              University of Saskatchewan) chairman

Purpose   To advise the Minister on proposals for a
              dental care program for children in Saskat-
              chewan.

Conclusions/Recommendations

That dental care benefits extend through the age of 17 for
all children;

That children younger than three years of age be included
in the plan on the basis of parental initiative;

That great care be taken in designing a system that will
ensure that treatment service does not gain dominance over
preventive service in terms of importance;

That in the interests of both dental health and economics,
water supplies in all communities with a central water
system be fluoridated and a constant promotional and
educational campaign be mounted to bring this about.

References

Saskatchewan, *Saskatchewan Advisory Committee on Dental
Care for Children Report,* 31 March 1973.

255 ADVISORY COMMITTEE ON PHYSICAL EDUCATION
(Departmental Committee)

Appointed   March 5, 1973

Reported   August, 1973

Committee   Eight members; John Campbell (Physical Educa-
             tion Consultant, Department of Education)
             chairman

Purpose   To make recommendations to the Minister with
             respect to Physical Education programs at the
             elementary and secondary level.

Conclusions/Recommendations

That a Saskatchewan Branch of Physical Education and
Recreation be created within the Department of Education;

That the Department of Education investigate the possibility of a Liaison Committee between the Departments of
Health, Culture & Youth and Education;

That a Physical Education Curriculum Steering Committee be
established on a permanent and rotating basis;

That Physical Education be a required daily subject for all
students from Kindergarten to 12;

That all students in Kindergarten through Grade 12 should
participate in Physical Education according to physiological development, ability, interests, and individual needs;

That Physical Education must be required for promotion from
all grades;

That certification standards for Physical Education
personnel be established;

That the first responsibility of the Physical Education
teacher is to the instructional programs, the second to
the inter-house activity program and the third to the
athletic program.

References

Saskatchewan, *Report of the Minister's Advisory Committee
on Physical Education,* August, 1973.

256 TASK FORCE ON THE STATUS OF WOMEN IN SASKATCHEWAN
(Departmental Committee)

Appointed   April 17, 1973

Reported   November, 1973 [to Minister responsible for
Status of Women Matters]

Committee   Two members; Arleen N. Hynd (Deputy Minister,
Department of Consumer Affairs) and Mary Rocan
(Women's Bureau, Department of Labour)

Purpose   To study the recommendations of the Report of
the Royal Commission on the Status of Women as
they affect the government of the Province of
Saskatchewan.

Conclusions/Recommendations

That consideration be given to promoting the production of
and obtaining textbooks which do portray men and women in
diversified roles;

That teacher training give greater emphasis to career
counselling;

That the Department of Education give consideration to
determining the adequacy of career counselling in
Saskatchewan schools;

That consideration be given to determining the degree to
which the Department of Education can exert pressure on
local school boards to have Family Life Education taught
in the schools; keeping in mind that the training of
teachers in Family Life Education is crucial to the success
of such a program;

That a study be made to determine whether or not girls have
an equal opportunity with boys to participate in sports
activities;

That the Department of Continuing Education ensure that the
post-secondary education institutions develop programs to
meet the special educational needs of women with family
responsibilities;

That consideration be given to extending the Saskatchewan Student Aid Fund to include part-time students;

That continued attention be paid to providing facilities and encouraging native peoples to take upgrading and training courses, and to encouraging native persons to become trained to teach their own people.

References

Saskatchewan, *Saskatchewan Women '73: Task Force Report on the Status of Women in Saskatchewan*, 1973.

257 ROYAL COMMISSION ON UNIVERSITY ORGANIZATION AND STRUCTURE (General Commission)

Appointed   May 3, 1973

Reported   December 22, 1973

Commission   Three members; Emmett Hall (former Supreme Court Justice) chairman

Purpose   To inquire into and report on university organization and structure in the Province of Saskatchewan.

Conclusions/Recommendations

That the campuses at Saskatoon and Regina be established as independent universities;

That there be a body to be known as The Saskatchewan Universities Commission which shall be comprised of nine part-time members, including the chairperson, all of whom shall be appointed by the Lieutenant Governor-in-Council;

That, under The Saskatchewan Universities Commission, there be a twenty-one member Universities Coordinating Committee, an eight member Capital Planning and Development Committee, and an eleven member Graduate Studies and Research Committee;

That a degree program in Engineering be re-established at
the University of Regina.

References

Saskatchewan, *Report of the Royal Commission on University
Organization and Structure,* 1973.

258 ADVISORY COMMITTEE ON THE EDUCATION OF THE DEAF
(Departmental Committee)

Appointed   October 19, 1973

Reported   July 8, 1974

Committee   Fifteen members; D.G. Drozda (Chief, Guidance
               and Special Education, Department of Education)
               chairman

Purpose   To study and make recommendations concerning
               communication and instructional policies at
               the Saskatchewan School for the Deaf, the
               development of community-based educational
               programs for the deaf, and the education of
               the deaf at the post-school level.

Conclusions/Recommendations

That preschool and kindergarten classes should follow an
oral program, and that provision should be made to assist
parents in learning Total Communication;

That Division 1 (Primary section) should provide two programs (oral and Total Communication) and that Divisions 2
and 3 should provide Total Communication;

That at all stages of the school program there should be
ready mobility from the School for the Deaf to community-
based classes and vice versa;

That the Education Act should be amended to provide for the
education of hearing impaired children from the age of
three up;

That the Saskatchewan Department of Education continue to
place greater dependence on Canadian based technical-
vocational and university program, rather than continuing
the traditional dependence on United States programs such
as those at St. Paul Technical Vocational Institute and
Gallaudet College in Washington.

References

Saskatchewan, *Kernel Report of the Minister's Advisory
Committee on the Education of the Deaf,* 1974.

259 ADVISORY COMMITTEE ON STUDENT EVALUATION
    (Departmental Committee)

   <u>Appointed</u>   November 27, 1973

   <u>Reported</u>   October 20, 1975

   <u>Committee</u>   Thirteen members; F. Nakonechny (Chief,
                 Student Evaluation, Department of Education)
                 chairman

   <u>Purpose</u>   To inquire into and make recommendations
                 regarding student evaluation.

Conclusions/Recommendations

That a major function of the preservice and inservice
education of teachers in student evaluation should be to
enhance the repertoire of evaluation strategies used by
teachers;

That a review of the teacher training programs be undertaken to ensure that teachers display an understanding of
the philosophy and procedures of student evaluation; that
they display competence in the selection, development,
application, and interpretation of a wide variety of
evaluation procedures; and that they be able to construct,
use and evaluate teacher-made tests.

That a provincial inservice education program in student
evaluation be undertaken by the Department of Education, in

collaboration with the Saskatchewan Teachers' Federation, the Saskatchewan School Trustees Association, and the two universities;

That teacher reports to parents be in terms of the intended learning outcomes of the courses of studies;

That parent-teacher interviews be encouraged as an appropriate and desirable reporting procedure to complement written reports on student progress;

That information kept by schools, school systems, and the Department of Education concerning student evaluation be such that it can be disclosed to students and their parents.

References

Saskatchewan, *Student Evaluation - Report of the Minister's Advisory Committee*, October, 1975.

260 ADVISORY COMMITTEE ON SCHOOL LAW
     (Departmental Committee)

Appointed   February 3, 1975

Reported   January 31, 1976

Committee   Five members; Clarence Amundrud (Chief,
                School Administration, Department of Education)
                chairman

Purpose   To study all existing statutes which have
                reference to and effect upon the K-XII educa-
                tional system of Saskatchewan, and to investi-
                gate and make recommendations regarding the
                consolidation and upgrading of existing
                statutes.

Conclusions/Recommendations

That fifteen separate statutes be consolidated and incorporated in a new statute, *The Education Act;*

That the existing high school districts be disorganized and their functions transferred to the school division in which they are incorporated;

That the role, powers and duties of boards of education be clearly defined in law;

That legislative provision be made for establishment of new school divisions, public and separate, in addition to those divisions which are created under this Act from existing administrative units;

That the basic rights of pupils be given specific definition in law;

That the duties and functions of teachers should be defined in general terms only;

That present provisions of *The Teacher Collective Bargaining Act,* 1973, be embodied in the new Education Act.

References

Saskatchewan, *Report of the School Law Review Committee,* January, 1976.

261 COLLEGE MATHIEU REVIEW COMMITTEE
(Departmental Committee)

Appointed   March, 1976

Reported   December 17, 1976

Committee   Ten members; L.M. Ready (Associate Deputy
               Minister of Education) chairman

Purpose   To review existing Department of Education
               policy with respect to the provision of
               French language opportunities in the elemen-
               tary and secondary schools of the province,
               and to assess the situation at College
               Mathieu.

Conclusions/Recommendations

That secondary bilingual education opportunities be
offered by fiscally-responsible school boards which have a
designated French elementary program, provided that certain
minimum requirements with respect to enrolments, time allot-
ments, qualifications of teachers and instructional
resource materials are met;

That the Department of Education establish a Designated
High School Committee to make recommendations concerning
provincial policy with respect to the provision of standards for secondary bilingual education;

That College Mathieu continue to offer a Roman Catholic
secondary education to Saskatchewan Francophones;

That designated secondary French programs should be
instituted in a location central to a region and financed
in a manner similar to the present financing of College
Mathieu.

References

Saskatchewan, *Report of the College Mathieu Review
Committee*, December, 1976.

262 COMMITTEE ON SERVICE FUNDING OF THE COLLEGE OF MEDICINE,
UNIVERSITY OF SASKATCHEWAN
(Departmental Committee)

Appointed   January, 1977

Reported   September 14, 1977 [to Minister of Health and
                Minister of Continuing Education]

Committee   Five members; N. Duane Adams (Assistant
                Deputy Minister of Health) chairman

Purpose   To review the funding of medical education and
                related service components and their relation-
                ship to cost-sharing agreements with the
                federal government.

Conclusions/Recommendations

That an Advisory Committee on Service Funding of the Saskatchewan Medical Education System be established;

That a Clinical Service Fund be established in the Department of Health;

That the financing of the University of Saskatchewan, College of Medicine Regina component be altered according to specific recommendations;

That the employment of part-time teachers by the College of Medicine be encouraged;

That the University of Saskatchewan review the education mandate assigned to the College of Medicine for the purpose of evaluating and monitoring the teaching load and ascertaining whether or not it is satisfied with the value received for education dollars.

References

Saskatchewan, *Report of the Committee on Service Funding of the College of Medicine, University of Saskatchewan,* September, 1977.

ALBERTA

263 COMMITTEE ON REVISION OF THE SCHOOL CURRICULUM FOR THE
PROVINCE
(Legislative Committee)

Appointed   1911 (?)

Reported   December 7, 1911

Committee

Purpose   To investigate the need for revision of the
               school curriculum for the Province.

Conclusions/Recommendations

References

Alberta, *Journals*, 1911.

264 COMMISSION OF INQUIRY TO CONSIDER THE GRANTING OF DEGREE-
CONFERRING POWERS TO CALGARY COLLEGE
(General Commission)

Appointed   May 22, 1914

Reported   February 25, 1915

Commission   Three members; Robert Alexander Falconer
               (President, University of Toronto) chairman

Purpose   To consider the granting of degree-conferring
                 powers to Calgary College.

Conclusions/Recommendations

That there be no departure from the historic policy of
Western Canada which was inaugurated by the Province of
Manitoba, adopted by the North West Territories, and re-
affirmed by the Province of Alberta, to establish one
university and one only, to be supported and controlled by
the Province for the purpose of giving instruction, granting degrees and controlling the requirements for admission
to the professions;

That an Institute of Technology and Art be established in
the City of Calgary to be supported and controlled jointly
by the City and the Province.

References

Alberta, *Report of the Commission Appointed to Consider the
Granting of Degree-conferring Powers to Calgary College,*
Sessional Paper No. 1, 1915.

265 GENERAL COMMITTEE ON THE REVISION OF THE ELEMENTARY SCHOOL
    CURRICULUM
    (Departmental Committee)

   Appointed   February, 1921

   Reported   [   ]

   Committee   Fifteen members; G. Fred McNally (Supervisor
                   of Schools) chairman

   Purpose   To consider and recommend the subjects which
                   are of most worth to Alberta boys and girls,
                   and to plan a new course which will be
                   flexible and easily adaptable to the varying
                   needs of the children of all parts of the
                   Province, but which will make any other than
                   thorough work and the development of habits
                   of industry impossible, no matter what subjects

have to be sacrificed.

Conclusions/Recommendations

References

Alberta, *Journals*, 1921.

Alberta, 'General Committee on the Revision of the Elementary School Curriculum', 1921.

266 ADVISORY COMMITTEE ON TAXATION
(Departmental Committee)

Appointed   April, 1926

Reported   February 14, 1928

Committee   Five members; H.M. Tory (President, University of Alberta) chairman

Purpose   To enquire into the following subjects:

A. The equalization of the burden of taxation.

B. Improved methods of collecting revenue.

C. Methods of collecting revenue from the natural resources of the Province, having regard to their possible transfer to the Province, paying particular attention to the taxation of mineral resources by provincial and municipal authorities.

D. The extent to which any tax may be reduced or modified, or one form of taxation substituted for another, having particular regard to the Supplementary Revenue Tax and the Wild Lands Tax.

E. The division of responsibility for revenue and expenditure as between the Government and

the municipalities, urban and rural, including the question of Mother's Allowance and the
care of indigents.

F. Adequacy of Sinking Fund and provision for the
retiral of provincial and local funded debts.

G. Systems of local government obtaining in the
Province of Alberta and elsewhere.

Conclusions/Recommendations

References

Alberta, *Report on Taxation by Advisory Committee on
Taxation,* 1928.

267 ALBERTA TAXATION INQUIRY BOARD ON PROVINCIAL AND MUNICIPAL
TAXATION
(Departmental Committee)

Appointed   December 1, 1933

Reported   November 30, 1935

Committee   Four members; J.F. Percival (Deputy Provincial
               Secretary) chairman

Purpose   To make a survey of the sources and incidence
               of taxation in the province.

Conclusions/Recommendations

That the burden of educational costs in the cities of the
Province has become so serious as to cause the gravest
concern;

That the raising of the necessary revenue solely by the
taxation of real property is discriminatory as between
classes composing the community, and that the burden so
placed cannot now be justified;

That the duty imposed by law upon the city to pay 100% of the demand of the School Board, whether it is collected or not, has a crippling effect on the finances of the city, and that the power now vested in School Boards to requisition large sums of money from the city irrespective of the latter's capacity to collect taxes, should be restricted;

That the Provincial Government is primarily responsible for education, and that its delegation of the financial burden to the Municipality to the extent of over 90% is an inequitable division of that burden;

That the Provincial Government, possessing as it does far wider powers of taxation than those enjoyed by the municipalities, should assume a much greater share of cost of education;

That due to the increasing cost of various social services which real property is now compelled to bear, land is being forfeited to the cities to an alarming extent, and the physical structure upon which the cities depend so largely for their revenue is steadily shrinking both as to area and revenue-producing capacity;

That the Federal Government should contribute substantially to the cost of technical education.

References

Alberta, *Report of the Alberta Taxation Inquiry Board on Provincial and Municipal Taxation,* 1935.

268 COMMISSION OF INQUIRY INTO REHABILITATION OF THE METIS (Related Commission)

Appointed   December 12, 1933

Reported   February 15, 1936

Commission   Three members; Albert Freeman Ewing (Supreme Court Judge) chairman

Purpose   To inquire into the problems of health,

education and the general welfare of the half-
breed population of the Province.

Conclusions/Recommendations

That a farm colony plan of settlement be established that
would keep groups of Metis families together for at least
parts of the year. Schools could be built and the wives
and families encouraged to remain in the colony. In any
case, all the children could be able to attend during
some portion of the year. The children should be taught
reading and writing and elementary arithmetic. In addition,
the boys should be taught stock raising and farming, while
the girls should be taught the elements of sanitation,
cleanliness, sewing, and knitting. The cost would not be
great and the Province would be saved the stigma which
attaches to any civilized country that permits a large
number of children to grow up within its boundaries without the slightest elementary education.

References

Alberta, *Journals*, 1933.

Alberta, 'Royal Commission on Rehabilitation of the Metis',
1936.

269 LEGISLATIVE COMMITTEE APPOINTED TO MAKE A COMPREHENSIVE
SURVEY AND STUDY OF EDUCATION IN THE RURAL DISTRICTS OF
ALBERTA
(Legislative Committee)

Appointed   April 3, 1934

Reported   April 12, 1935

Committee   Ten members; Perren E. Baker (Member for
               Cypress) chairman

Purpose   To make a comprehensive survey and study of
               education in the rural districts of Alberta.

Conclusions/Recommendations

That residential schools be established for families on the fringe of settlement;

That secondary education in rural areas be provided;

That school library facilities be expanded;

That scholarships be available for deserving students;

That radio school broadcasts be provided;

That a Library Commission be instituted and adult education be encouraged;

That Grade 12 be required for normal school entrance, or a two-year training course for all teachers be instituted;

That refresher courses be provided for those returning to teaching;

That the curriculum for smaller schools be enriched;

That more supervision be provided for rural schools;

That equalization of educational costs and opportunities be sought;

That the larger unit of administration be given careful study.

References

Alberta, 'Report of the Legislative Committee Appointed to Make a Comprehensive Survey and Study of Education in the Rural Districts of Alberta', 1935.

270 UNIVERSITY OF ALBERTA SURVEY COMMITTEE
(Departmental Committee)

Appointed   August 7, 1941

Reported   February 25, 1942

Committee   Six members; H.H. Parlee (Chairman, Board of
                   Governors, University of Alberta) chairman

Purpose   To conduct a survey of the affairs of the
                   University in order to determine (a) the place
                   of the university in the educational system of
                   the Province, (b) whether the University can
                   be made to serve more completely the cultural
                   needs of all the people of the Province, and
                   (c) whether it is possible to have the Univer-
                   sity function more effectively in the develop-
                   ment of the agricultural and industrial
                   resources of the Province.

Conclusions/Recommendations

That the College of Education be given faculty status;

That greater use be made of the existing University plant
by extending the time it is in full operation;

That a more systematic effort be made to inspire students
with loyalty and a sense of responsibility towards the
University, as a basis for Alumni interest and support;

That the work of the University Department of Extension be
expanded by at least one-third;

That junior college work be expanded;

That a small annual grant be earmarked for the encouragement of research;

That the Board of Governors be the controlling body in all
University affairs;

That the Senate be reduced in size; that it be representative of the various elements of provincial society including students and alumni, and that it have the important
function of acting as a bridge between the University and
the life and activities of the Province;

That the General Faculty Council take over most of the
purely academic functions presently discharged by the
Senate;

That there be a long-term financial policy ensuring steady growth; and that new responsibilities not be accepted until capacity to finance has been fully explored;

That a satisfactory salary schedule be implemented;

That the Administration review frequently the aptitudes, progress, and teaching loads of the staff.

References

Alberta, Order in Council 1117/41, August 7, 1941.

Alberta, *University of Alberta Survey Committee Interim Report*, 1942.

271 SUBCOMMITTEE ON EDUCATION AND VOCATIONAL TRAINING (Departmental Committee)

Appointed   1943 (Part of the Post-War Reconstruction Committee)

Reported   December 18, 1944

Committee   Five members; Robert Newton (President, University of Alberta) chairman

Purpose   To enquire into the functions, organization, and machinery of education and vocational training in the Province, and of recommending such measures as seem to be required to adapt, improve, or expand the system in whole or part, to meet the expected needs of the post-war period.

Conclusions/Recommendations

That in the interests of education the public be enlightened with respect to the highly unsatisfactory conditions surrounding the teaching profession;

That the Province expand its programme of educational reform, in order to promote improvements in teachers' salaries, training, legal status, pension provisions, and rural living conditions, in order that the profession may attract and hold the high calibre of personnel which its vital importance warrants;

That a minimum salary schedule be established, based on $1200 for the first year after certification, and recognizing the cost and professional value of successive years of training, also the value of increasing experience and the assumption of successive degrees of responsibility;

That the possibility of recruiting teacher material from returned men and women be explored;

That all teacher-training in Alberta be integrated;

(Other recommendations dealt with scholarships, school buildings and equipment, transportation, community schools and vocational institutes, home and school associations, adult education, and school finance.)

References

Alberta, *Report of the Subcommittee on Education,* 1944.

272 ROYAL COMMISSION ON TAXATION
(Related Commission)

Appointed   July 22, 1947

Reported   February 12, 1948

Commission   One member; J.W. Judge (Deputy Minister of
              Municipal Affairs)

Purpose   To inquire into the taxation imposed by the
              Province and by Municipalities, urban and
              rural.

Conclusions/Recommendations

That there is a place for inter-provincial equalization of educational opportunity. This would mean the creation by

the Dominion Government of an inter-provincial equalization
fund to be distributed among the Provinces according to
need for the purpose of providing equal educational opportunity to all the children of all the people of all the
Provinces;

That, in the opinion of the Commission, there is no legal
hindrance to the Dominion in establishing such a fund, and
further the Commission believes that no infringement of the
rights of the Province need take place in the administration of such fund.

References

Alberta, *Report of the Royal Commission on Taxation,*
Sessional Papers, No. 71, 1948.

273 ROYAL COMMISSION ON THE METROPOLITAN DEVELOPMENT OF CALGARY AND EDMONTON
(Related Commission)

Appointed   July 19, 1954

Reported   January 31, 1956

Commission   Five members; George Frederick McNally
                (former Chancellor, University of Alberta)
                chairman

Purpose   To enquire into the administration and finan-
                cing of schools and municipal services in the
                City of Edmonton and surrounding areas, and
                the City of Calgary and surrounding areas.

Conclusions/Recommendations

That Edmonton and Calgary are especially liable to rising
future costs because of their rapid growth and high proportion of children; and because a larger proportion of
pupils tend to stay on in high school, special instruction
for the handicapped increases, courses tend to proliferate,
teachers' qualifications tend to rise and so forth;

That the need for the planning of capital and operational budgets to prepare for the expected rising costs is obvious, and has been to a great extent taken in hand by province and the city school boards.

References

Alberta, *Report of the Royal Commission on the Metropolitan Development of Calgary and Edmonton,* 1956.

274 ROYAL COMMISSION ON TEACHERS' SALARIES
(General Commission)

Appointed   July 9, 1957

Reported   January 31, 1958

Commission   Three members; Gilbert McNeil Blackstock
              (Queen's Counsel) chairman

Purpose   To consider:

(a) the feasibility of establishing a scale or scales of salaries for teachers in the Province;

(b) the form or forms which such salary scales might take;

(c) the manner by which such salary scales might be arrived at and altered from time to time;

(d) the effects of the establishment of teacher salary scales upon
    (i) the financing of education both in the Province generally and in particular areas within the Province, and
    (ii) the supply of teachers and upon the quality and morale of the teaching profession generally.

Conclusions/Recommendations

That, in the judgement of the Commission, the establishment of salary scales on a Provincial basis can have no other effect than to increase the supply of teachers available for service in Alberta's schools;

That, in view of these considerations, the Commission is convinced that the establishment of Provincial salary scales would improve the quality and morale of the teaching profession generally.

References

Alberta, *Report of the Royal Commission on the Feasibility of Establishing a Scale or Scales of Salaries for Teachers in the Province of Alberta and Allied Matters*, 1958.

275 ROYAL COMMISSION ON EDUCATION
    (General Commission)

Appointed	December 31, 1957
Reported	November 9, 1959 (A minority report was included)
Commission	Six members; Donald Cameron (Senator) chairman
Purpose	To study and consider the aims and objectives essential to maintain a proper and adequate educational program for pupils of the elementary and secondary schools of the Province; and to inquire into the various aspects of elementary and secondary education, having special regard to the curricular programs of the several school levels, the attainment of school pupils and the procedures governing their classification and promotion, the extent to which various special services are desirable and necessary, types of school organization, physical facilities, the quality and supply of teachers, the relationship of the educational system to the requirements of industry and the modern community, and the economics of education insofar as finance is a

factor.

Conclusions/Recommendations

(The 280 separate recommendations included the following:)

That a plan of accreditation for qualifying school systems be implemented;

That departmental examinations be continued at the Grade IX and Grade XII levels;

That course offerings be broadened; for example to include vocational areas;

That community colleges be developed;

That the curriculum be changed to permit more time and more depth in studies;

That entrance requirements to the Faculty of Education be raised;

That a Bachelor of Education degree or its equivalent be required for permanent certification of elementary and secondary teachers;

That working conditions for teachers be improved.

References

Alberta, *Report of the Royal Commission on Education,* 1959.

276 HUTTERITE INVESTIGATION COMMITTEE
(Departmental Committee)

Appointed   September 8, 1958

Reported   September, 1959

Committee   Three members; W.E. Frame (Chief Superintendent of Schools) chairman
[Upon the death of Mr. Frame, C.P. Hayes

assumed the chairmanship]

Purpose   To inquire into and report on certain matters in connection with the acquisition of lands by members of the Hutterian Brethren Church and the establishment of Hutterite colonies and to determine whether or not the existing educational facilities established for Hutterite colonies are satisfactory, especially in the matter of instruction in the responsibilities of Canadian Citizenship.

Conclusions/Recommendations

That the extraordinary mental health and freedom from mental conflicts and tensions can be attributed to the lack of contradiction between religious beliefs and social-political economic practice developed in individuals from early childhood;

That the problem, as it appears to the Hutterites, is that if their children are compelled to attend public schools they will be subject to indoctrination of values of the world outside the colony, which they regard as sinful.

References

Alberta, *Report of the Hutterite Investigation Committee*, 1959, App. A.

277 COMMITTEE ON ALBERTA SCHOOL BUS OPERATIONS
(Departmental Committee)

Appointed   November 30, 1960

Reported   April 1, 1961

Committee   Three members; Paul Lawrence (   )
chairman

Purpose   To inquire into and report all phases of school bus operations in the Province of Alberta, including the fatal accident

involving a school bus which occurred at a
level crossing at or near Lamont in the
Province of Alberta on the 29th day of
November, 1960.

Conclusions/Recommendations

That school boards recognize the fact of their responsibility for the safe transportation of children to and from
school and for the qualifications of bus drivers, even
though they may delegate by contract specific duties in
connection with the students' transportation;

That wherever possible school bus systems be operated as
publicly or privately owned fleets of buses;

That school boards prepare and promulgate policies
respecting bus discipline;

That an officer or member of each school board examine each
bus driver's licence and report thereon to the Highway
Traffic Board.

References

Alberta, *Report of the Committee on Alberta School Bus
Operations,* 1961.

278 SURVEY COMMITTEE ON HIGHER EDUCATION IN ALBERTA
(Departmental Committee)

Appointed   1961

Reported   (Four interim reports to 1966)

Committee   Seven members; E.W. Hinman (Provincial
              Treasurer) chairman

Purpose   To inquire into and report on all those prob-
              lems and possibilities which bear on the
              future growth and development of the programs
              of higher education in Alberta with particular
              emphasis on the development of the best

possible policies consistent with the greatest economy of operation.

Conclusions/Recommendations

That Junior College Programs be encouraged;

That, provided they can meet the standards approved by the University, private schools be permitted, and encouraged, to offer first and second year courses in University work;

That the semester system be adopted at the earliest possible time, and studies be made of year round use and the trimester system;

That planning for the future of higher education be continued by both the Provincial Government and the University;

That every step be taken to make as efficient and economic use as possible of the resources available to higher education;

That formulae be devised to be used as a basis for determining future Provincial Government grants to the University;

That a study be made of adult education programs in Alberta to determine where expansion, consolidation, and coordination is necessary and feasible.

References

Alberta, 'Survey Committee on Higher Education: Second Interim Report', [1963].

279 SPECIAL COMMITTEE ON COLLECTIVE BARGAINING BETWEEN SCHOOL TRUSTEES AND TEACHERS
(Legislative Committee)

Appointed   April 28, 1964

Reported   March 24, 1965

Committee   Five members; first R.H. McKinnon (Member for
            Strathcona West) and then A. Ludwig (Member
            for Calgary East) chairman

Purpose   To review procedures for collective bargaining
            between school trustees and teachers, includ-
            ing provisions of The School Act, The Alberta
            Labour Act, and The Teaching Profession Act.

Conclusions/Recommendations

That the Government enact no legislation which would deny
the teachers the right to strike;

That teachers' collective bargaining procedure be incorpor-
ated into a new Act with the suggested name of *Salary
Negotiation Act, to be administered by the Department of
Labour.

References

Alberta, *Report of the Special Committee on Collective
Bargaining between School Trustees and Teachers,* 1965.

280 SCHOOL CONSTRUCTION INQUIRY
    (Departmental Committee)

Appointed   July 20, 1964

Reported   January 26, 1965

Committee   One member; Walter R. Badun (Faculty of Com-
            merce, University of Alberta)

Purpose   To examine, inquire into and report upon the
            methods and procedures followed in the con-
            struction of school buildings in the Province
            of Alberta, north of the Saskatchewan River.

Conclusions/Recommendations

That, in order to give school boards guidance and to ensure
that future school buildings are able to provide for the

requirements of education, the Department of Education
provide leadership in addition to regulation; and that the
School Buildings Board be discontinued and a new committee
formed - a 'School Planning Committee'.

That, because of the condition of property, buildings and
equipment, a general maintenance program directed by the
Department of Education be undertaken.

References

Alberta, *Province of Alberta School Construction Inquiry*,
26 January 1965.

281 PUBLIC INQUIRY INTO THE APPOINTMENT BY THE MINISTER OF
EDUCATION OF AN OFFICIAL TRUSTEE FOR FORT VERMILION SCHOOL
DIVISION #52
(Judicial Commission)

Appointed   April 1, 1965

Reported   February, 1966

Commission   One member; Nelles V. Buchanan (Retired Chief
             Judge)

Purpose   To investigate and report upon the events and
             causes leading to the appointment of an
             Official Trustee for the Fort Vermilion
             School Division #52 and the consequent replace-
             ment of the School Division's elected Board
             of Trustees.

Conclusions/Recommendations

That the Minister, in appointing on November 20, 1964, an
Official Trustee for Fort Vermilion School Division No. 52
- thereby replacing the Division's elected Board of Trustees, was completely justified in so doing and that to have
delayed the appointment would have been detrimental to the
welfare of the Division and therefore unwarranted;

That thought be given as to whether the time has not now

arrived for the amendment of the Act making the Superintendent the appointee and employee of the Division rather than
of the Department, or in the alternative, to defining more
definitely the relationship between superintendent and
secretary-treasurer.

References

Alberta, *Public Inquiry into the appointment by the
Minister of Education of an Official Trustee for Vermilion
School District #52*, February 1966.

282 SPECIAL COMMITTEE ON CENTRALIZATION AND CONSOLIDATION OF SCHOOLS
(Legislative Committee)

Appointed   May 31, 1966

Reported   March 30, 1967

Committee   Five members; Romeo B. Lamothe (Member for
               Bonnyville) chairman

Purpose   To enquire into and make recommendations
               regarding the interest and concern of the
               public with respect to the centralization of
               schools; the educational opportunities pre-
               sently being offered in elementary and secon-
               dary schools; and the problem of centraliza-
               tion and consolidation in the rural areas and
               smaller cities with particular reference to
               vocational high schools.

Conclusions/Recommendations

That divisional and county officials make ratepayers aware
of the superiority of educational standards and facilities
available in large centralized schools;

That there be advance planning before centralization so
that adequate facilities may be provided;

That further centralization be carried out only with the

approval of the majority of ratepayers concerned, particularly at the elementary level;

That parents be made aware that modern, well supervised residences have nothing in common with the makeshift dormitories of the thirties and early forties;

That, to ensure the availability of teachers for small rural high schools, governments make loans available to local authorities, or make it possible for them to borrow to provide modern housing for teachers;

That additional funds be provided to compensate teachers for the higher work load in small rural high schools, and for the lack of amenities of small communities;

That legislation providing for government assistance to private schools be studied to determine its effect on high school instruction.

References

Alberta, *Report of the Special Committee on Centralization and Consolidation of Schools,* 1967.

283 ROYAL COMMISSION ON JUVENILE DELINQUENCY
(Related Commission)

Appointed   September 27, 1966

Reported   February 15, 1967

Commission   Three members; Francis Hugh Quigley (Calgary Magistrate) chairman

Purpose   To make an inquiry into the nature and scope of juvenile delinquency in Alberta, the basic causes, preventive measures, and steps that should be taken to aid in rehabilitation.

Conclusions/Recommendations

That inadequacy in school, and poor achievement, is often a

burden which many children find difficult to bear; that
they become psychological dropouts, present in body but not
in mind, early in their school life; and that later many
become truants, and later still seek expulsion or dropout
as a release from a situation of failure;

That the Department of Education, in co-operation with the
Alberta Teachers Association and the Alberta School
Trustees Association, devise a continuing academic course
for the teaching of morals, ethics, citizenship and law;

That readiness centres or pre-school classes be set up,
possibly through the Preventive Social Service Act in those
areas where children are having difficulty adjusting to
formal Grade 1 teaching;

That special training in child study at University level,
as well as in-service training, be required for elementary
grade teachers;

That counselling services be provided at junior and high
school levels by pupil personnel trained in this technique;

That Juvenile Squads of police departments in large centres
have an educational section to inform youth at the school
and community level of the positive function of police work
in the community and to seek the assistance of young persons in fostering recognition of the value of good law
enforcement.

References

Alberta, *Report of the Alberta Royal Commission on Juvenile
Delinquency*, 1967.

284 COMMISSION ON EDUCATIONAL PLANNING
(General Commission)

Appointed   June, 1967

Reported   June 16, 1972

Commission   Nine members; Walter H. Worth (former Vice-

President, University of Alberta) chairman

Purpose   To enquire into current social and economic
trends within the Province to determine the
nature of Alberta society during the next two
decades; to examine the needs of individuals
within that society; to study the total educational organization inclusive of elementary
and secondary schools, colleges, technical
institutes, universities and adult educational
programs to decide the necessary adaptations
of these institutions to the trends and needs;
to establish bases for the priority judgements
of Government with respect to the course of
public education in Alberta for the next
decade; and to give consideration to financing.

Conclusions/Recommendations

That there be:

- provision of universal opportunity and selective experience in early education;
- abolition of Grade XII departmental examinations;
- inauguration of the Alberta Academy, Early Ed and the
  supporting ACCESS network;
- extension of opportunities in further education;
- modification in certification requirements for teachers
  in early and basic education;
- reorganization of the Department of Education and Department of Advanced Education;
- revision of funding arrangements for all levels of recur-
  rent education, including provisions for life experience
  and student assistance;
- modification of the school year and of procedures for the
  transfer of credits;
- reduction in the length of all general and most professional first-degree programs in universities;
- preparation of an integrated Provincial Development Plan.

References

Alberta, *Report of the Commission on Educational Planning*,
1972.

285 SPECIAL COMMITTEE ON ASSESSMENT AND TAXATION
(Special Committee)

Appointed	May 7, 1969
Reported	March, 1970
Committee	Nine members; Ralph Brown (President, Alberta Association of Municipal Districts and Counties) chairman
Purpose	To study and make recommendations regarding real property assessment and taxation, and assessment equalization practices and procedures for the purpose of requisitions upon municipalities for school foundation and hospital levies.

Conclusions/Recommendations

That all dwellings including detached and multiple residences, and farm residences, should be treated alike: dormitories should be exempt only when used in the primary and secondary school systems and nurses' training institutes but not for colleges and universities;

That the power of a municipal council to classify property and provide a special portion of fair actual value for assessments be replaced with a power to classify properties and provide a special *exemption from taxation*, relating to the municipal rates, or the school or hospital requisitions, or provincial requisitions, or any combination of them.

References

Alberta, *Report of the Special Committee Appointed by the Government of Alberta to Study Assessment and Taxation*, March, 1970.

286 TASK FORCE ON INTERCULTURAL EDUCATION
(Departmental Committee)

Appointed   1971

Reported   June, 1972

Committee   Eight members; C.D. Ledgerwood (Coordinator,
                 Athabasca Regional Office of Education)
                 chairman

Purpose   To collect and summarize data to be used by
                 the government as a basis for establishing
                 policies and practices that will serve the
                 educational wants and needs of cultural
                 minorities.

Conclusions/Recommendations

That the Alberta Government encourage and support a revital-
ization of Native cultures;

That Natives and Whites join forces in cooperatively designing programs to fulfill the educational wants and needs of
Alberta's Native peoples;

That one objective of the cooperative effort be to generate
educational alternatives from which Native peoples can
choose;

That, since Metis receive no special considerations by the
Federal Government, the interests of Metis people be of
particular concern to the Government of Alberta;

That education that is representative of both Indian and
White culture be provided for Native people;

That there be more selective preparation and screening of
teachers for Native students;

That grants and bursaries be made available for Native
peoples wanting to train as teachers and teacher aides.

References

Alberta, *Native Education in the Province of Alberta,* June,
1972.

287 RED DEER COLLEGE INQUIRY
   (Judicial Commission)

   Appointed   March 21, 1972

   Reported   May 11, 1972

   Commission   One member; T.C. Byrne (President, Athabasca
                 University)

   Purpose   To inquire into the administration, organiza-
                 tion and operation of Red Deer College; the
                 relationships between the Colleges Commission,
                 the College Board, staff, Faculty, students
                 and the community, and the range of programs
                 offered or planned by the college.

Conclusions/Recommendations

That, for at least a year, the affairs of the College be
placed in the hands of an Administrator;

That the Administrator act as President of the College as
well during his term of office making the present position
of president redundant;

That legislation be enacted to facilitate the establishment
of different governing structures for Red Deer College if
these are deemed desirable;

That the Administrator shortly after his appointment establish a search and selection committee for a president to
assume office with the restoration of college self-
government.

References

Alberta, *Report of The Red Deer College Inquiry*, May, 1972.

288 INQUIRY INTO SCHOOL AFFAIRS: BONNYVILLE AREA
   (Departmental Committee)

   Appointed   September 8, 1972

Reported   January, 1973

Committee   One member; W.H. Swift (former Deputy Minister
                  of Education)

Purpose   To inquire into and report upon school matters
                  in respect of the Bonnyville Centralized High
                  School.

Conclusions/Recommendations

That the most salient fact, and the genesis of a number of
school problems that have arisen over the years, is that
although the population of the area is heterogeneous in
respect to ethnic origins, religions and other factors,
there is one fact that predominates; namely, the presence
of a very considerable cohesive population of French
ancestry who maintain a strong allegiance towards their
mother tongue and towards the Roman Catholic religion;

That despite the problems arising from the nature of the
agreement which brought the high school into existence,
the internal operation of the high school was not, in
general, the subject of criticism;

That in addition to any other virtues the school may have
it is a strong force in the direction of understanding,
co-operation and mutual respect; and hence any solution to
the legal problem which surrounds it must be with intent to
maintain such excellence, pedagogical and sociological, as
it possesses.

References

Alberta, *Inquiry into School Affairs: Bonnyville Area,*
January, 1973.

?89 STUDY GROUP ON NORTHLAND SCHOOL DIVISION
    (Departmental Committee)

Appointed   August 9, 1974

Reported   July, 1975

Committee   Three members; W.H. Swift (former Deputy
                   Minister of Education) chairman

Purpose   To inquire into and report upon matters
                   related to the Northland School Division No.
                   61.

Conclusions/Recommendations

That Northland School Division prepare and adopt a statement of purposes and philosophy;

That the board of trustees consist of nine members, all
appointed by the Minister of Education;

That Treaty Indians resident in communities served by
Northland be eligible for appointment;

That the superintendent of schools be the chief executive
officer, and that he be a resident of Peace River;

That the development and use of materials in harmony with
the children's environments be encouraged;

That teachers and school programs adopt a positive attitude
towards the pupils antecedents.

References

Alberta, *Report of the Northland School Division Study
Group,* July, 1975.

290 ALBERTA SCHOOL DISCIPLINE STUDY
(Special Committee)

Appointed   1975

Reported   May 12, 1977

Committee   Eight members; S.C.T. Clarke (Director,
                   Special Sessions, University of Alberta)
                   chairman

Purpose   To study the current state of school discipline, what school discipline should be like,
and what assistance could be provided to
practitioners in the field.

Conclusions/Recommendations

That the responses of the participants were spread across
the spectrum of possible views on most matters of school
discipline;

That the reaction of the largest single group, a plurality
of 41% of all participants, was that school discipline as
it was in 1975-76 was just about right. Among the various
groups polled, parents especially endorsed this position;

That the next most commonly held view was that school
discipline was a bit too lenient. Trustees and teachers
especially endorsed this position;

That 32% of participants perceived discipline as being a
bit too lenient and 34% called for it to be stricter.

[No recommendations were presented as such.]

References

Alberta, *General Report of the Alberta Discipline Study
1975-76*, 1977.

[Sponsored by the Alberta Teachers' Association, the Alberta School Trustees Association, and the Department of
Education]

291 PROJECT NORTH TASK FORCE
    (Departmental Committee)

Appointed   February, 1975

Reported   November 30, 1976

Committee   One member; Fred J. Dumont (School Superintendent) chairman

Purpose   To do a comprehensive assessment of educa-
                     tional needs of Northern Albertans in order to
                     fulfill planning and research obligations
                     undertaken by the Department of Education
                     under the terms of the Canada-Alberta North
                     Agreement.

Conclusions/Recommendations

That a curriculum project be designed and operationalized
to stimulate a concerted effort by school authorities to
identify and collect pertinent curriculum materials;

That a sustained program of orientation of teachers to
Northern people and the development of community relations
skills be initiated;

That community commitment to schooling by direct, active
involvement be increased;

That the Department of Education undertake an intensive
analysis of the variables of remoteness, sparsity and
isolation with the view to establishing means of quanti-
fying them for translation into a grant support program;

That an in-depth study of the Northern Saskatchewan program be undertaken to determine whether or not the use of
Cree in early grades contributed positively to school
success, and that the Department of Education design a
project similar to the Northern Saskatchewan program.

References

Alberta, *Report of an Assessment of Educational Needs of
Northern Albertans,* November, 1976.

292 TASK FORCE ON THE EVALUATION OF STANDARDIZED ACHIEVEMENT
TESTS FOR ALBERTA SCHOOLS
(Departmental Committee)

Appointed   June, 1976

Reported   1977

Committee   Twenty-three members; T. Mott (Guidance and
                Counselling Supervisor, Special Education
                Branch) coordinator

Purpose   To evaluate commercial standardized achieve-
                ment tests in terms of their congruency with
                Alberta curricula and their technical adequacy.

Conclusions/Recommendations

That findings indicated that some tests contained items
that related well to specific strands of Alberta curriculum
content in particular subject areas; however, none of the
tests adequately covered the total spectrum of Alberta
curriculum content.

References

Alberta, *Report of the Task Force on Evaluation of Standardized Achievement Tests for Alberta Schools,* Spring
1977.

293 MINISTER'S ADVISORY COMMITTEE ON STUDENT ACHIEVEMENT
    (Departmental Committee)

Appointed   October, 1976

Reported   May, 1979

Committee   Nine members; James Hrabi (Associate Deputy
                Minister for Instructional Services) chairman

Purpose   To review the quality and achievement stan-
                dards of basic education in Alberta.

Conclusions/Recommendations

That MACOSA (Minister's Advisory Committee on Student
Achievement) type tests be administered periodically at
selected grade levels, but with sampling plans extended to
permit generalization of results to school system populations;

That the proposed assessment program test curricular objectives selected from all domains (knowledge, attitudes and skills) and thought levels, and not only from the most easily tested areas;

That the tests developed by MACOSA investigators be revised as required, and that those tests which have not been given be normed in order that they may be used in subsequent assessments of student achievement;

That at some appropriate time the MACOSA Reading, Writing, Listening and Speaking tests be used to investigate relationships among various aspects of the language arts in order to determine recommendations about instruction;

That mandatory grade 12 departmental examinations for the purpose of awarding final marks not be reinstituted;

That grade 12 departmental examinations continue to be made available in January and June for school systems that wish to use them.

References

Alberta, *Student Achievement in Alberta,* May, 1979.

294 SELECT COMMITTEE TO EXAMINE THE WORKINGS OF THE 1872 SCHOOL
ACT
(Legislative Committee)

Appointed   March 12, 1875

Reported   January 24, 1976

Committee   Six members; A. Rocke Robertson (Member for
               Esquimalt) chairman

Purpose   To examine the workings of the 1872 School Act.

Conclusions/Recommendations

That compulsory education be made general throughout
British Columbia, taking as a basis the compulsory clauses
of the Ontario School Act, which make it obligatory on all
children to attend some school, or be otherwise educated
for four months in each year, from the age of seven to
twelve years, inclusive;

That Clause 7 of the 'Public School Amendment Act, 1873,'
be so amended as to make it obligatory on the Trustees to
select and appoint their Teacher from among the duly
qualified Teachers, whose names shall be submitted to the
Trustees by the Board of Education;

That on complaint being made to the Board of Education, by
any person resident in a School District, as to the moral
conduct of the School Teacher in such District, the Board
of Education should have power to investigate such charge;

and, upon being satisfied of its truth, if they shall deem it sufficient, to disqualify such Teacher from holding his position, the Board of Education should have power to cancel the certificate of such Teacher, and thereupon it should be the duty of the Trustees to dismiss such Teacher;

That power be given to the Board of Education to close Schools where the attendance falls below ten, if, in their discretion, they shall think fit.

References

British Columbia, *Sessional Papers*, 1875.

295 REPORT OF SELECT COMMITTEE ON PUBLIC SCHOOLS CONCERNING THE CACHE CREEK BOARDING SCHOOL
(Legislative Committee)

Appointed   January 13, 1876

Reported   January 24, 1876

Committee   Six members; A.E.B. Davie (Member for Cariboo) chairman

Purpose   To overhaul the working of Public Schools, including the *Cache Creek* Boarding School.

Conclusions/Recommendations

That it is advisable that boys and girls not be educated in the same establishment;

That the boarding and lodging of the children, and the washing of their clothes, be provided by some person or persons employed by the Master, if practicable, the remuneration of such person or persons to be in proportion to the number of scholars, and tenders to be invited for the performance of such duties;

That children not be required to perform menial duties;

That the following persons only shall be allowed to visit

the School, namely: Parents or relatives of the children, Judges of the Supreme or County Courts, Ministers of any religious denomination, members of the Legislative Assembly, Justices of the Peace, Government Agents, and such other persons as may be introduced to the Master by any of the above functionaries;

That no balls or political meetings be allowed in the school building;

That the teacher superintend the conduct of the scholars out of school hours;

That the school for boys be presided over by a Master and Matron, being husband and wife;

That the school for girls be presided over by a Mistress and, if necessary, a Matron in addition;

That it is advisable that the appointment and dismissal of Teachers be vested in the Lieutenant-Governor in Council;

That a Deputy Superintendent be appointed for and to reside on the Mainland at some central point; the Provincial Secretary to act as Superintendent on the Island.

References

British Columbia, *Sessional Papers,* 1876.

296 COMMISSION OF INQUIRY INTO THE SOUTH PARK SCHOOL DRAWING BOOKS
(Judicial Commission)

Appointed   November 29, 1905

Reported   1906

Commission   One member; Peter S. Lampman (County Court Judge, Victoria)

Purpose   To inquire into all matters pertaining to the action of the Board of Examiners, the

Department of Education and the Principal of
the South Park School at Victoria, in connection with the drawing books submitted by the
pupils of the said South Park School at the
High School Entrance Examination held in the
month of June, 1905.

Conclusions/Recommendations

That it appears there was a great deal of ruling which in
the opinion of the Commissioner was ample to justify the
examiners and the Department in the course they took.

References

British Columbia, 'Report on South Park School Drawing
Books', 1906.

297 COMMISSION OF INQUIRY INTO CHARGES AGAINST THE DEPARTMENT
OF EDUCATION BY MISS GERTRUDE DONOVAN OF VICTORIA
(Judicial Commission)

Appointed   January 8, 1908

Reported   [   ]

Commission   One member; Harold Bruce Robertson (Victoria
                Barrister)

Purpose   To inquire into charges against the Department
                of Education by Miss Gertrude Donovan of
                Victoria.

Conclusions/Recommendations

References

British Columbia, Order in Council, January 8, 1908.

298 COMMISSION TO SELECT A SITE FOR THE UNIVERSITY OF BRITISH

COLUMBIA
(General Commission)

Appointed   February 25, 1910

Reported   June 28, 1910

Commission   Five members; R.C. Weldon (Dean of Law,
               Dalhousie) chairman

Purpose   To visit and make a careful examination of the
               several cities and rural districts in the Pro-
               vince suggested as suitable University sites,
               and to select as a location for the University
               that city or rural district best suited for
               University purposes, which selection when
               made to be final.

Conclusions/Recommendations

That the University not be placed on a site which may in
time be completely surrounded by a city;

That not less than 250 acres be set apart for the University campus and 700 acres for experimental purposes in
agriculture and forestry, exclusive of a forest reserve
for forestry operations on a large scale;

That the most suitable site is at Point Grey, unless the
soil there and that of the delta land adjacent are found
to be unsuitable for the experimental work of the College
of Agriculture;

That should Point Grey prove impossible, the next choice is
a site along the shore west of North Vancouver, provided
the tunnel and bridge are constructed;

That the third choice is St. Mary's Hill overlooking the
Pitt, Fraser, and Coquitlam Rivers, provided residences
are erected for the students;

That Central Park, though conveniently located, will
probably be surrounded by the Cities of Vancouver and New
Westminster, and because of this and of the absence of
outstanding scenic advantages is undesirable.

References

British Columbia, *Statutes,* 10 Edw. VII, chap. 51.

British Columbia, *University Site Commission Report,* 1910.

299 COMMISSION OF INQUIRY INTO MUNICIPAL MATTERS OF THE CORPOR-
ATION OF THE DISTRICT OF SOUTH VANCOUVER
(Judicial Commission)

Appointed   May 16, 1912

Reported   May 16, 1913

Commission   One member; Matthew Joseph Crehan (Chartered
               Accountant)

Purpose   To enquire into all Municipal matters of the
               Corporation of the District of South Vancouver
               which relate to contracts and dealings of and
               with the Municipal Council of the said Cor-
               poration or any member thereof, and contract
               of and with the Board of School Trustees or
               any member thereof, since the 1st day of
               January, 1908.

Conclusions/Recommendations

That, although nothing very seriously wrong was found,
the Board should be more businesslike and should recognize
their responsibility in handling school affairs and in
disposing of the ratepayers' money;

That the purpose of supplies, construction of School buildings and works of a like character should be undertaken by
the proper Departments of the Municipality, as the Trustees
have not the machinery to carry out so much public work and
get full value for every dollar expended.

References

British Columbia, Order in Council 583/12, May 16, 1912.

British Columbia, 'Report on South Vancouver Investigation,'
1913.

300 COMMISSION OF INQUIRY INTO MATTERS RELATING TO THE SECT OF
DOUKHOBORS IN THE PROVINCE OF BRITISH COLUMBIA
(Related Commission)

Appointed	August 15, 1912
Reported	December 21, 1912
Commission	One member; William Blakemore (Mining Engineer)
Purpose	To inquire into matters relating to the Sect of Doukhobors in the Province of British Columbia.

Conclusions/Recommendations

That with reference to schools, the Doukhobors take the
ground that education unfits the young for the pursuits of
the peasant, and that this has become a problem already in
nearly all countries;

That they believe their children are being educated in the
best sense of the word, in their homes and on the soil, by
being held down to the simple beliefs and traditions of
their forefathers;

That they also fear that education will inoculate their
children with the ideas of their educators, which they
claim are alien to the Doukhobor belief.

References

British Columbia, *Report of Royal Commission on Matters
Relating to the Sect of Doukhobors in the Province of
British Columbia,* 1912.

301 COMMISSION OF INQUIRY INTO THE AFFAIRS OF THE PRESENT BOARD

AND PAST BOARDS OF SCHOOL TRUSTEES OF THE CITY OF VANCOUVER
(Judicial Commission)

Appointed   February 11, 1913

Reported   May, 1914

Commission   One member; Henry Osborne Alexander (Vancouver
                 Barrister)

Purpose   To inquire into the affairs of the present
                 Board and past Boards of School Trustees of
                 the City of Vancouver, such inquiry to include
                 the purchase and sale of school sites and
                 school property, the purchase of furniture
                 and other supplies, and generally all matters
                 coming under the jurisdiction of the Vancouver
                 School Board.

Conclusions/Recommendations

That some system of auditing be adopted by the Department
of Education;

That a standard set of books be instituted for the use of
school boards throughout the Province.

References

British Columbia, Order in Council 194/13, February 11,
1913.

Marjorie C. Holmes, *Royal Commissions and Commissions of
Inquiry under the 'Public Inquiries Act' in British
Columbia: 1872-1942*, [1950]

302 COMMISSION OF INQUIRY INTO THE AFFAIRS OF THE PRESENT BOARD
AND PAST BOARDS OF SCHOOL TRUSTEES OF THE CITY OF NELSON
AND COMPLAINTS REGARDING THE PRINCIPAL OF NELSON PUBLIC
SCHOOL
(Judicial Commission)

Appointed   February 19, 1913

Reported   March 12, 1913

Commission   One member; P.S. Lampman (Victoria Judge)

Purpose   To inquire into the affairs of the present
             board and past boards of school trustees of
             the City of Nelson and complaints regarding
             the principal of Nelson Public School.

Conclusions/Recommendations

That the principal's certificate be suspended.

References

British Columbia, Order in Council 232/13, February 13,
1913.

British Columbia, 'Report on Board of School Trustees of
the City of Nelson', 1913.

303 SURVEY OF THE SCHOOL SYSTEM
    (Departmental Committee)

Appointed   1924

Reported   May 30, 1925

Committee   Two members; J. Harold Putman (Senior Inspec-
             tor of Schools, Ottawa) and George M. Weir
             (Professor of Education, University of British
             Columbia)

Purpose   To enquire into all matters pertaining to
             state education.

Conclusions/Recommendations

That a central Canadian research bureau be established to
make possible educational development in accordance with
scientifically determined educational objectives;

That school boards not have the option of charging fees

except for non-resident pupils;

That the public school system provide for elementary schools from six to twelve years of age, middle schools from twelve to fifteen, and high schools beyond that;

That high school streams lead to a graduation diploma, normal school entrance, commercial specialization, or university matriculation;

That teacher training institutions include more on the psychology of the various subjects and on the use of tests and measurements;

That student teachers have a rich experience of observation and practice-teaching, and all schools of the province be available when required;

That the grade eight formal examination be done away with and a gradual introduction of the accrediting system be accomplished;

That the City of Vancouver be granted considerable educational autonomy, by statute if necessary;

That consolidation of assisted schools be carried out wherever it seems educationally or financially desirable, with the approval of local boards if possible, but in face of their disapproval if necessary.

References

British Columbia, *Survey to the School Systems,* 1925.

304 SPECIAL COMMISSION TO INQUIRE INTO THE SALE OF GOVERNMENT LANDS IN THE UNIVERSITY SUBDIVISION (Departmental Committee)

Appointed   May, 1929

Reported   February 25, 1930

Committee   One member; A.N. Daykin (Vancouver Barrister)

Purpose   To inquire into the sale of Government lands
in the University subdivision.

Conclusions/Recommendations

References

British Columbia, Order in Council 749/29, May 20, 1929.

305 SPECIAL INQUIRY INTO THE AFFAIRS OF THE UNIVERSITY
(Special Committee)

Appointed   April, 1932

Reported   [   ]

Committee   One member; Peter S. Lampman (Victoria Judge)

Purpose   To inquire into the affairs of the university.

Conclusions/Recommendations

References

British Columbia, (*Victoria Daily Times*, April 30, 1932).

306 COMMITTEE APPOINTED BY THE GOVERNMENT TO INVESTIGATE THE
FINANCES OF BRITISH COLUMBIA
(Special Committee)

Appointed   April 15, 1932

Reported   July 12, 1932

Committee   Five members; George Kidd (President, B.C.
Electric) chairman

Purpose   To investigate the finances of British
Columbia.

Conclusions/Recommendations

That free education be provided up to a pupil's fourteenth birthday only; that to age sixteen he pay 50 per cent of the entire cost of his education, and that after age sixteen he pay 100 per cent of the entire cost;

That teachers salaries be reduced by 25 per cent;

That should it eventually be found that the financial resources of the University are so meagre as to impair its efficiency, the question will have to be considered whether it may not be in the best interests of higher education to close the University and rely on the proposal to establish scholarships to furnish the means of attending a University elsewhere in the Dominion.

References

British Columbia, *Report of the Committee Appointed by the Government to Investigate the Finances of British Columbia*, 1932.

307 COMMISSION ON SCHOOL FINANCE IN BRITISH COLUMBIA
    (Departmental Committee)

    Appointed   June, 1934

    Reported   March 22, 1935

    Committee   Report written by 'Technical Advisor' H.B.
                  King (Principal, Kitsilano High School) and
                  presented to the two 'Commissioners', George
                  Weir (Minister of Education) and John Hart
                  (Minister of Finance)

    Purpose   To survey the whole field of educational
                  financing.

Conclusions/Recommendations

That the Provincial Government assume almost complete financial responsibility for education;

That there be a uniform Provincial tax upon real property of from 3 to 4 mills;

That equalization of assessments be put upon a scientific basis;

That administrative reorganization into large school units be carried out.

References

British Columbia, *School Finance in British Columbia*, 1935.

308 COMMISSION OF INQUIRY INTO THE ADMINISTRATION AND METHODS OF DISCIPLINE OF MOUNT VIEW HIGH SCHOOL (Judicial Commission)

Appointed   July 6, 1943

Reported   September 4, 1943

Commission   One member; John Owen Wilson (County Court Judge, Cariboo)

Purpose   To inquire into the administration and methods of discipline of Mount View High School.

Conclusions/Recommendations

That, in the opinion of the Commissioner, no person administering a unit the size of Mount View should be expected to teach for more than a very small portion of his working hours, if at all; and that he should be free to devote most, if not all of his time, to study, administration and supervision.

References

British Columbia, *Report of John Owen Wilson, Commissioner re Mount View High School*, 1943.

309 COMMISSION OF INQUIRY INTO EDUCATIONAL FINANCE
(General Commission)

Appointed   November 27, 1944

Reported   October, 1945

Commission   One member; Maxwell A. Cameron (Faculty of
                 Education, University of British Columbia)

Purpose   To inquire into the existing distribution of
                 powers and responsibilities between the
                 Provincial Government and the school districts
                 and to appraise the present fiscal position of
                 the school districts in British Columbia.

Conclusions/Recommendations

That consolidation discussion be encouraged, but that
implementation should proceed without seeking local
approval;

That there be equalization of standards and equalization of
assessments;

That the basic or Provincial programme be supported by
basic grants consisting of a Provincial salary schedule, an
allowance for posts of responsibility, a bonus for teachers
in especially remote schools, and an allowance for current
expenditures other than teachers' salaries, transportation,
and debt charges.

References

British Columbia, *Report of the Commission of Inquiry into
Educational Finance,* 1945.

310 COMMISSION ON PROVINCIAL-MUNICIPAL RELATIONS IN BRITISH
COLUMBIA
(Related Commission)

Appointed   February 16, 1946

Reported   January 20, 1947

Commission   One member; Carl Goldenberg (Montreal Barrister)

Purpose   To investigate provincial-municipal relations.

Conclusions/Recommendations

That the principle of equalization recommended by the Cameron Report is sound and the Government is to be commended for accepting it and implementing the recommendations so promptly;

That the system will, however, lose some of its effectiveness if the grants are not reviewed from time to time and adjusted to meet changing conditions.

References

British Columbia, *Provincial-Municipal Relations in British Columbia,* 1947.

311 COMMISSION ON SCHOOL TAXATION
    (General Commission)

Appointed   August 9, 1947

Reported   1948

Commission   Six members; H. Alan Maclean (Assistant Deputy Attorney General) chairman

Purpose   To inquire into and report upon the following matters.

1. The performance of assessment functions for school taxation purposes within the Province, and particularly in the unorganized and organized areas of large municipal school districts.

2. The degree to which land and improvements are

being assessed in accordance with the definitions thereof in the 'Public Schools Act' for school taxation purposes in the unorganized and organized areas of certain large municipal school districts.

3. The applicability and suitability of the definitions of 'land' and 'improvements' in the 'Municipal Act', the 'Village Municipalities Act', 'Public Schools Act' and the 'Taxation Act'.

4. The general incidence of taxation under the 'Public Schools Act'.

5. All matters relevant to the present system of school cost sharing.

Conclusions/Recommendations

That an authority be established which might be called an Assessment Commission, to bring about a provincial wide equalization of assessments.

References

British Columbia, 'Report of the Commission on School Taxation,' 1948.

312 ROYAL COMMISSION ON DOUKHOBOR AFFAIRS
(Related Commission)

Appointed   September 12, 1947

Reported   January 10, 1948

Commission   One member; Harry J. Sullivan (New Westminster Judge)

Purpose   To inquire into and concerning the recent disturbances in the Doukhobor settlements in British Columbia, to hear representatives from the factions concerned and to recommend possible remedial action.

Conclusions/Recommendations

That a new plan for the education of Doukhobor children be worked out immediately for School Districts 7, 8, 9, 12 and 13 comprising the Grand Forks and Kootenay areas; and that much permanent benefit would result from a consolidation of schools in these Districts;

That the only real and permanent solution of the Doukhobor problem lies in education and assimilation;

That opportunity must be provided the Doukhobor children to participate in all the educational, cultural and recreational activities which the larger schools afford.

References

British Columbia, Order in Council 2309/47, September 12, 1947.

313 SPECIAL COMMITTEE ON DOUKHOBOR AFFAIRS
(Special Committee)

Appointed   1950

Reported   March 29, 1952

Committee   Thirteen members; Harry B. Hawthorn (Department of Anthropology, University of British Columbia) chairman

Purpose   To inquire into the problems besetting the Doukhobors.

Conclusions/Recommendations

That the opposition to schooling is composed in part of objections to education in any form, and in part of objections to the Canadianizing influence of public schools.

References

British Columbia, *Report of the Doukhobor Research Committee*, 1952.

314 ROYAL COMMISSION ON EDUCATION
   (General Commission)

   Appointed   January 17, 1958

   Reported   December 29, 1960

   Commission   Three members; S.N.F. Chant (Dean of Arts &
                Science, University of British Columbia)
                chairman

   Purpose   To enquire into the various phases of the
                provincial educational system with particular
                attention to programmes of study and pupil
                achievement.

Conclusions/Recommendations

(Included in the 158 formal recommendations were the
following:)

That religious instruction in the schools not be extended
beyond the present provisions;

That Grade VII be returned to the elementary school level;

That the six-three-three grade sequence be replaced by a
seven-three-two (or three) sequence;

That the holding power of the rural schools be improved;

That instruction in the elementary schools be intensified
and the secondary school day be lengthened;

That the school year be lengthened to a minimum of 200
days;

That elementary schools planned in future not exceed 600

pupils, and schools of any other type not exceed 1,200 pupils;

That more attention be given to school libraries;

That kindergartens be established at the discretion of local boards;

That pupil/teacher ratios be studied;

That persistent efforts to recruit young people of high ability be continued and intensified;

That teacher certification be upgraded;

That the commencing salaries of fully qualified teachers continue to be set at a level that is comparable to those paid in other professions that require equivalent qualifications;

That a one-year period of internship be introduced between the second and third years of the elementary teacher training programme;

That objective examinations be used more sparingly, and more essay-type questions be used in subjects that stress the understanding of knowledge rather than the recall of items of information;

That the spiral of learning principle be abandoned, and more emphasis be placed upon mastery of the courses of instruction at each grade level;

That the use of instructional time for extra-curriculum activities be kept to a minimum;

That the possibility of procuring more Canadian and British text-books be thoroughly canvassed;

That pupils be required to devote more time to their school work out of school-hours;

That counselling services be improved;

That boards be explicitly empowered to impose regulations

regarding school clothing or the adoption of a school
uniform;

That community organizations and groups be encouraged to
make greater use of school facilities;

That the primary or general aim of the educational system
of British Columbia be that of promoting the intellectual
development of the pupils, and that this should be the
major emphasis throughout the whole school programme.

References

British Columbia, *Report of the Royal Commission on
Education,* 1960.

315 SURVEY OF HIGHER EDUCATION IN BRITISH COLUMBIA AND A PLAN
FOR THE FUTURE
(Special Committee)

Appointed   [not an official inquiry]

Reported   1962

Committee   One member; John B. Macdonald (President,
               University of British Columbia)

Purpose   To survey higher education in British Columbia
               and provide a plan for the future.

Conclusions/Recommendations

That three types of institutions be provided for higher
education: universities able to concentrate on the expen-
sive areas of graduate studies, research, and special
professional preparation, as well as undergraduate preparation; four-year degree granting colleges; and two-year
regional colleges;

That, for the present, the University of British Columbia
be *the university.*

That Victoria College have the privilege of deciding to

become an independent degree-granting college;

That a four-year degree-granting college be established in the western Lower Fraser Valley;

That the school districts of the Okanagan Valley co-operate in establishing a two-year regional college with the expectation of its becoming a four-year degree-granting college by 1970;

That a two-year regional college be established in the vicinity of Castlegar to serve the school districts from Trail to Nelson;

That a two-year regional college be established in metropolitan Vancouver;

That, in addition, two-year regional colleges be planned for operation by 1971 in the following regions: Central Vancouver Island Region; Kamloops and South Cariboo Region; Central Interior (Prince George); Eastern Lower Fraser Valley.

References

John B. Macdonald, *Higher Education in British Columbia and a Plan for the Future,* 1962.

316 SURVEY COMMITTEE ON SCHOOL LIBRARIES
   (Departmental Committee)

   Appointed   1963

   Reported   November 1, 1964

   Committee   Six members; Franklin P. Levirs (Assistant
                Superintendent of Education, Instructional
                Services) chairman

   Purpose   To survey school libraries in British Columbia
                and to make recommendations.

Conclusions/Recommendations

That except in the smallest schools of one or two teachers, classroom collections should be used only to supplement the central library of the school;

That the basic responsibility for the development of the library in any school must rest with the school librarian under the general supervision of the principal;

That although full use of external library services available should be made, a school district should undertake the development of its own school library service as a primary function.

References

British Columbia, *Survey of British Columbia School Libraries*, 1964.

317 BCTF COMMISSION ON EDUCATION
(Special Committee)

Appointed   July, 1967

Reported   September, 1968

Committee   Four members; D.B. MacKenzie (former Vancouver Assistant Superintendent) chairman

Purpose   To stimulate and provoke a study and debate within the teaching profession in British Columbia of major educational issues in the hope that out of such study and debate will emerge guidelines for the future design of education; and in particular to identify for study and debate issues related to: purposes and objectives in education, the need for change in the existing school system, directions for change that seem likely to produce quality education, and implications for the teaching profession as related to teacher preparation, continuing education of teachers, and deployment of teachers.

Conclusions/Recommendations

[The Report included 189 recommendations on a very wide range of educational issues; beginning with, 'Top priority should be given to the elementary schools in terms of educational planning and financial assistance.']

References

Involvement: The Key to Better Schools: The Report of the Commission on Education of the British Columbia Teachers' Federation, 1968.

[Sponsored by the British Columbia Teachers' Federation]

318 COMMITTEE ON SCHOOL UTILIZATION
(Departmental Committee)

Appointed   January 19, 1968

Reported   October, 1969

Committee   Four members; J.L. Canty (Superintendent, Administrative Services) chairman

Purpose   To investigate the extent to which public school facilities are utilized within the present framework of organization, the possible alternative organizational patterns which might increase the utilization, and the implications of such alternatives.

Conclusions/Recommendations

That an extended day of operation in the senior secondary school be adopted;

That there be developed a semester system of organization throughout the secondary school, with an extension of the summer organization as an introductory step;

That positive steps be taken to integrate planning of school and other community developments by those communities not already doing so.

References

British Columbia, *Report of the Committee on School Utilization,* 1969.

319 SELECT STANDING COMMITTEE ON SOCIAL WELFARE AND EDUCATION
(Legislative Committee)

Appointed   February 2, 1968

Reported   April 3, 1968

Committee   Fourteen members; J.D. Tisdalle (Member for
               Saanich) chairman

Purpose   To survey the extent to which marijuana, LSD,
               and other lysergic drugs are available to our
               young people, and to study the cause and
               effect of such drugs. [Motion of February 15]

Conclusions/Recommendations

That research be conducted to determine the individual,
social, and physiological reasons for persons misusing
drugs and how this misuse can be contained and reversed;

That a department of Government establish a bibliography of
acceptable and accredited research materials;

That suitable materials be drawn from such bibliographies
and included in travelling libraries of videotapes, films,
and filmstrips to be circulated to School Boards and used
at the discretion of the Boards in relation to their local
needs and in conjunction with local schools and individual
teachers;

That the Department of Education circulate with the
material a list of Provincial resource people available to
assist in dissemination or elaboration of such materials;

That each School Board be encouraged to make full use of

their own community resource people.

References

British Columbia, *Journals*, 1968.

320 ADVISORY COMMITTEE ON INTER-UNIVERSITY RELATIONS
    (Departmental Committee)

    Appointed   May 23, 1968

    Reported   March 7, 1969

    Committee   Five members; G. Neil Perry (Deputy Minister
                        of Education) chairman

    Purpose   To investigate inter-university relations and
                        those issues which have frequently appeared to
                        be a cause of friction between the Universi-
                        ties or between the Universities and the
                        Provincial Government.

    Conclusions/Recommendations

    That the Provincial Government consider the replacement of
    the existing Academic and Advisory Boards by a new inter-
    mediary body;

    That this intermediary body be given the task of developing
    a capital budget for the university system.

    References

    British Columbia, *Report of the Advisory Committee on
    Inter-University Relations*, 1969.

321 SELECT STANDING COMMITTEE ON SOCIAL WELFARE AND EDUCATION
    (Legislative Committee)

    Appointed   February 1, 1971

Reported   March 24, 1971

Committee   Eleven members; J.D. Tisdalle (Member for
             Saanich) chairman

Purpose   To examine the provisions and practices relat-
             ing to the security of tenure for teachers in
             the public schools of British Columbia [Motion
             of February 9]

Conclusions/Recommendations

That the function of tenure provisions is to indicate those
conditions under which a teacher may be assured of continuing employment by a school district; that it is desirable
that there be such provisions; but that it is essential
that these provisions apply only to those teachers who have
proven themselves capable of performing their duties satis-
factorily, and who continue to perform them at that level;

That there be some form of review provided in cases of
dismissal;

That a teacher be notified immediately whenever performance
of his duties is evaluated as unsatisfactory; that he be
notified of improvements considered necessary; that if,
after a reasonable period of time, he did not effect these
improvements, he be subject to dismissal on the grounds of
inefficiency.

[Specific recommendations for changes to the *Public Schools
Act* were given.]

References

British Columbia, *Journals,* 1971.

322 SELECT STANDING COMMITTEE ON SOCIAL WELFARE AND EDUCATION
    (Legislative Committee)

    Appointed   February 1, 1972

    Reported   March 23, 1972

Committee   Sixteen members; J.D. Tisdalle (Member for
               Saanich) chairman

Purpose   To report on the definition of the tenure of
               office of the members of the teaching staffs
               in the universities and on procedures followed
               by the universities relating to this matter,
               and to make recommendations. [Motion of
               February 11]

Conclusions/Recommendations

That the practice followed by universities in granting
'appointments without term' be continued;

That the three public universities of the Province work
together to agree on a common definition of 'appointment
without term';

That there be no discrimination, in terms of race, religion, sex, or politics.

References

British Columbia, *Journals,* 1972.

323 COMMITTEE ON TEACHER EDUCATION
    (Departmental Committee)

Appointed   1973

Reported   June 27, 1974

Committee   Thirty-three members; John Bremer (Commis-
               sioner of Education) chairman

Purpose   To conduct an inquiry into the state of
               teacher education in British Columbia.

Conclusions/Recommendations

That changes be made in the procedures followed by the
membership of such teacher education policy-making bodies

as currently exist, so as to provide for more consultation
with legitimate groups, including students, whose point of
view they should reflect;

That immediate constitution and funding of a continuing
representative advisory committee on teacher education be
made, to include three members from each of the following
groups: Trustees, Public, Parents, Universities (Faculties
of Education), Teachers, Students, and the Provincial
Department of Education;

That representation to the Advisory Committee from
community colleges be included when it becomes appropriate;

That two members from the Teacher Education Advisory
Committee serve on the Joint Board of Teacher Education
(one student and one public).

References

British Columbia, *Teacher Education in British Columbia:
Final Report,* 1974.

324 COMMITTEE TO EXAMINE SERVICES FOR THE COMMUNICATIVELY
IMPAIRED OF BRITISH COLUMBIA
(Departmental Committee)

Appointed   February, 1973

Reported   October, 1973 [to Minister of Health]

Committee   Twelve members; J.H.V. Gilbert (Faculty of
              Medicine, University of B.C.) chairman

Purpose   To examine, report and make recommendations on
              service for the prevention and amelioration of
              communication disorders in British Columbia.

Conclusions/Recommendations

That individuals with communication impairments be assured
access to the necessary educational, social and rehabilita-
tive supports to enable them to function and participate

as equals in the formal and informal institutions of our society and that this be achieved by means of integration into, rather than segregation from, social, educational and work institutions within his or her community.

References

British Columbia, *Recommendations on Services for the Communicatively Impaired in British Columbia,* 1973.

325 SELECT STANDING COMMITTEE ON SOCIAL WELFARE AND EDUCATION
(Legislative Committee)

Appointed   February 7, 1973

Reported   April 18, 1973

Committee   Fourteen members; Rosemary Brown (Member for
             Vancouver-Burrard) chairman

Purpose   To inquire into the question of the advertis-
             ing of alcohol and tobacco products in the
             Province and legislation and regulations with
             respect thereto, and the effects of such
             advertising on the consumption of alcohol and
             tobacco products. [Motion of February 19]

Conclusions/Recommendations

That the Committee was more concerned by the growth in the
number of young people who were beginning to drink and
smoke than it was by the veteran smokers and drinkers
cognizant of the fact that the young people were more
vulnerable and susceptible to the wiles of advertising
than were the veterans;

That representation be made to the Federal Government
immediately, asking that it implement its ban on the
advertising of these products, and work towards supporting
a national and international advertising ban.

References

British Columbia, *Journals*, 1973.

326 ROYAL COMMISSION ON POST SECONDARY EDUCATION IN THE
    KOOTENAY REGION
    (General Commission)

Appointed   April 25, 1973

Reported   February 13, 1974

Commission   Seven members; Ian McTaggert-Cowan (Dean of
                Graduate Studies, University of B.C.) chairman

Purpose   To examine post-secondary educational needs in
                the Kootenay region of the Province, to
                examine the respective roles and opportunities
                of Selkirk College and Notre Dame University
                in meeting these needs, and to attempt to
                identify within the Province unique educa-
                tional needs which might effectively be met in
                the Kootenay region.

Conclusions/Recommendations

That an institution to be known as the Kootenay Institute
for Post Secondary Studies be created in the Kootenay
region of British Columbia and that it provide courses and,
as may be appropriate, diploma, certificate and degree
programs in the fields of vocational education, technologi-
cal education, academic education, community service and
cultural activities;

That the Governing Council provide, forthwith, post
secondary educational services for the East Kootenay Region;

That Notre Dame University of Nelson be replaced by a four-
year College concerned with liberal studies within the
Kootenay Institute for Post Secondary Studies;

That Selkirk College become a College within the Kootenay
Institute;

That the Government of the Province undertake a review of

vocational training and particularly apprenticeship training within the Province.

References

British Columbia, *Report of the Royal Commission on Post
Secondary Education in the Kootenay Region,* 1974.

327 COMMITTEE ON UNIVERSITY GOVERNMENT
(Departmental Committee)

Appointed   August, 1973

Reported   May 2, 1974

Committee   Five members; first John Bremer (B.C. Commis-
             sioner of Education) and then Walter Young
             (Political Science Department, University of
             Victoria) chairman

Purpose   To consider the internal and external forms of
             university governance, with particular refer-
             ence to the relationship between the Universi-
             ties and the Provincial Government, and to
             make recommendations to the Minister of
             Education for appropriate changes in the
             Universities Act.

Conclusions/Recommendations

That the size of the Boards of Governors be increased to
fifteen members;

That the membership be as follows: the Chancellor, the
President, six appointed by the Lieutenant-Governor in
Council, three members of faculty elected by and from the
faculty at large, two students elected by and from the Alma
Mater Society or its equivalent, two members of the Alumni
Association elected by and from the Alumni Association;

That the present bi-cameral Senate/Board structure be
retained;

That the Act specify those powers of Board and Senate that are exclusive and those that are joint;

That a basic structure be established for the composition of Senate, but that beyond this, that the membership of Senate for each university be modified appropriately;

That the basic structure include: (a) the President, Academic Vice President, Chancellor, Deans of Faculties, Librarian, Director of Continuing Education (or equivalent), one representative of the Community Colleges; (b) a number of faculty twice the number in 'a'; and (c) a number of students equal to the number in 'a';

That the University Council consist of eleven members appointed by the Lieutenant-Governor in Council, and that the following be excluded from membership; Members of Parliament, Members of the Legislative Assembly, Presidents, members of the Board of Governors, Faculty members and students of any of the provincial universities, and employees of the Department of Education.

References

British Columbia, *Report of the University Government Committee,* 1974.

328 TASK FORCE ON THE COMMUNITY COLLEGE
(Departmental Committee)

Appointed   November, 1973

Reported   March, 1974

Committee   Thirteen members; Hazel l'Estrange (Douglas
              College Council) chairman

Purpose   To examine college-government relationships,
              college-university relations, the problems of
              college financing, the role of community
              colleges in British Columbia, and to recommend
              changes in legislation leading to the creation
              of a Community College Act.

Conclusions/Recommendations

That every area of the province be included in a college region;

That 100% funding by the provincial treasury of capital costs be continued;

That colleges be granted corporate status;

That the college councils be charged with the responsibility of establishing a democratic system of internal governance ensuring effective involvement by all elements of the internal college community in the decision-making process;

That a provincial continuing education advisory committee be established to advise the Department of Education on the needs for continuing education;

That all citizens 65 years of age and older and all those who qualify for mincome may enrol in any college programme tuition free;

That admission policies be standardized for all colleges;

That the department of education initiate a feasibility study of worker study-leave for British Columbia;

That priority be given to the employment of Canadian citizens within the college system;

That a concerted effort be made to establish policies to increase the number of women hired by colleges so that the sex ratio of college personnel at all levels will better reflect the balance between men and women in the labour force.

References

British Columbia, *Towards the Learning Community: Working Paper on the Community College in British Columbia,* 1974.

329 STUDY COMMITTEE ON THE SMALL SENIOR SECONDARY SCHOOL
   (Departmental Committee)

   Appointed   November, 1973

   Reported   August 27, 1974

   Committee   Six members; William D. Reid (Superintendent,
                  Field Personnel) chairman

   Purpose   To study and report upon the small senior
                  secondary school in British Columbia.

Conclusions/Recommendations

That correspondence courses be placed more directly under
individual school control;

That counselling services for small secondary schools be
improved;

That itinerant specialists be made available to small
secondary schools to provide instruction, clinics, and
workshops in highly specialized activities;

That special education services be provided for small
secondary schools on the basis of need rather than numbers;

That immediate provision be made for a professional development workshop for principals of small secondary schools;

That immediate provision be made for a professional development program for teachers currently working in small
secondary schools and also for teachers who will be
working in this type of school;

That special consideration, in financial terms, be given to
small secondary schools by the Department of Education.

References

British Columbia, *Interim Report of the Small Senior Secondary School Study Committee,* 1974.

330 JERICHO HILL SCHOOL INQUIRY
   (Departmental Committee)

   Appointed   June 18, 1974

   Reported   September 4, 1974 [to Provincial Secretary]

   Committee   One member; B. Chud (School of Social Work,
                  University of British Columbia)

   Purpose   To examine certain aspects of Jericho Hill
                  School.

Conclusions/Recommendations

That the Department of Education remove Jericho Hill School
and other activities related to the deaf and blind from the
office of Supportive and Integrated Services except as
specified;

That the Department of Education allocate the provincial
resources commensurate with the costs involved in providing the very best education for children suffering from
hearing or eye impairment;

That in other respects the Department of Education relate
to the educational needs of these children as it does to
other children living and studying in the school districts
of British Columbia;

That the Department of Health consider the creation of a
Registry for Children at Risk in the Province of British
Columbia;

That a British Columbia Board for the Education of Deaf and
Blind Children be established;

That the present transportation system be critically
reviewed;

That every effort be made to get away from institution-
alized living for these children.

References

British Columbia, *Report of Inquiry: Jericho Hill School*
[1974]

331 SURVEY COMMITTEE ON COMMUNITY COLLEGES IN THE LOWER MAIN-
LAND OF BRITISH COLUMBIA
(Departmental Committee)

Appointed   September, 1974

Reported   January, 1975

Committee   Three members; Leonard Marsh (Emeritus
              Professor of Education, UBC) chairman

Purpose   To study the total college system in the Lower
              Mainland, to assess the desirability of
              reorganization, and to make specific recommen-
              dations for the development of smaller and
              administratively simpler college structures
              to serve the people of the Lower Mainland.

Conclusions/Recommendations

That community colleges in the Lower Mainland not operate
exclusively within specific school district boundaries;

That vocational training be accorded equality of recognition and support with all other types of college instruction;

That social as well as instructional and study facilities
be considered an integral part of college development;

That the Department of Education initiate a detailed study
of the role, philosophy, organization and financing of
adult and continuing education in British Columbia;

[Several recommendations dealt with the role of present and
future colleges and institutions; namely Vancouver
Community College, 'Langara Community College', Vancouver
School of Art, 'Vancouver Vocational College', 'Burnaby
Vocational College', 'Richmond Vocational College',
Fraser Valley College, Capilano College, Douglas College,

Haney Correctional Institute, 'Green Timbers Community
College', and future community colleges in Delta and
Langley.]

References

British Columbia, *Report of the Survey Committee on Community Colleges in the Lower Mainland,* British Columbia, 1975.

332 STUDY OF RESEARCH AND DEVELOPMENT IN BRITISH COLUMBIA
(Departmental Committee)

Appointed   January 23, 1975

Reported   August 31, 1975

Committee   Five members; K. George Pedersen (Dean of
              Education, University of Victoria) chairman

Purpose   To conduct a survey of the current status of
              practice-oriented research and development
              divisions in various governmental and other
              agencies (with an obvious emphasis on educa-
              tion), to determine the perceptions of the
              various educational interest groups in British
              Columbia regarding research and development,
              and to consider the local feasibility of
              alternate approaches.

Conclusions/Recommendations

That a research and development competence be supported
within the B.C. Department of Education;

That the modest beginnings of a research and development
unit be focused on satisfying the internal service needs of
the Department of Education;

That a representative advisory committee to the Minister be
established for the purpose of assisting in the establishment of overall school system's goals and objectives;

That the Division of Communications with the Department of

Education assume responsibility for developing, in consultation with the various educational vested interest groups, an adequate dissemination consultative service, primarily for the use of the school systems of this province.

References

British Columbia, *A Study of Research and Development in British Columbia,* 1975.

333 SELECT STANDING COMMITTEE ON HEALTH, EDUCATION, AND HUMAN
RESOURCES
(Legislative Committee)

Appointed   March 13, 1975

Reported   April 30, 1975

Committee   Fourteen members; Rosemary Brown (Member for
               Vancouver-Burrard) chairman

Purpose   To examine into and study the subjects of
               school district organization and administra-
               tion and the system of teacher salary bargain-
               ing, including learning and working conditions
               contracts.
               [Motion of March 26]

Conclusions/Recommendations

That both trustees and teachers take advantage of the
opportunities which the Department of Labour intends to
provide in training personnel to be more effective in the
collective bargaining process;

That in the event the parties fail to establish an arbitration board, the Department of Labour appoint an arbitrator;

That the final resolution of disagreements in the bargaining process be through the form of arbitration after a full
process of negotiation and conciliation has been attempted.

References

British Columbia, *Journals*, 1975.

334 ROYAL COMMISSION OF INQUIRY ON PROPERTY ASSESSMENT AND
TAXATION
(Related Commission)

Appointed   April 24, 1975

Reported   July 30, 1976

Commission   Seven members; Robert A. McMath (former
              Richmond Alderman) chairman

Purpose   To inquire into all ramifications of the
              implementation of an assessment system based
              on actual value, and to review all aspects of
              real property taxation procedures.

Conclusions/Recommendations

That the Provincial Government should consider committing
itself publicly to paying 75 percent of the current and
capital cost of the public school system as a whole in
British Columbia within a period of five years, and that
equalization grants should continue;

That the Government require the universities to pay full
property taxes with respect to land and improvements used
for commercial purposes, and that the Government tax
university residences on the same basis as other residential property in the same local taxing jurisdictions;

That the Department of Municipal Affairs and the Department
of Education jointly study alternatives to taxing or continuing to exempt private schools.

References

British Columbia, *Commission of Inquiry on Property Assessment and Taxation: Preliminary Report*, 1976.

335 COMMISSION OF PUBLIC INQUIRY IN THE MATTER OF VANCOUVER
COMMUNITY COLLEGE
(Departmental Committee)

<u>Appointed</u>   May 15, 1975

<u>Reported</u>   July, 1975

<u>Committee</u>   Three members; George Suart (Vice-President of
Administration, Simon Fraser University)
chairman

<u>Purpose</u>   To examine the overall administrative, opera-
tional and financial processes utilized in
the operation of Vancouver Community College
Technical and Vocational Institute and the
impact of these processes on the delivery of
College service to the community.

Conclusions/Recommendations

That Vancouver Community College continue to develop
accounting procedures which will provide a workable
management information and control system;

That the Department of Education ensure that all procedures
developed for the control and funding of college programmes
are clearly understood by all parties;

That the Department of Education initiate plans for the
development of a long-range planning capability for
colleges so that preliminary budget forecasting can be
begun two to three years before a budget becomes operational;

That the College Council thoroughly study and unequivocally
decide what is to be the nature of Vancouver Community
College;

That the Vancouver School of Art be separated from Vancouver Community College and established as an institution in
its own right;

That the college principal and administration recognize the
need for a change in administrative style.

References

British Columbia, *Report of the Public Inquiry Commission Appointed to Examine Certain Aspects of Vancouver Community College,* 1975.

336 COMMISSION ON UNIVERSITY PROGRAMS IN NON-METROPOLITAN AREAS
(Departmental Committee)

Appointed   May 5, 1976

Reported   September 2, 1976

Committee   One member; William C. Winegard (former
President, University of Guelph) chairman

Purpose   To advise on all matters related to the
delivery of academic and professional programs outside of the Vancouver and Victoria
metropolitan areas, and academic transfer
programs and their articulation.

Conclusions/Recommendations

That a multi-campus university be established by 1990 to
serve the non-metropolitan areas of British Columbia;

That the new university begin as a separately funded
Division of Simon Fraser University charged with the
responsibility to provide a comprehensive outreach degree-
credit program;

That the Division be headquartered in Vernon and have four
small University Centres in Prince George, Kamloops,
Kelowna and Nelson;

That the Division offer upper level degree-completion programs in Arts, Science and Education;

That the new University College of Simon Fraser University
be funded by the Universities Council of British Columbia
separately from the main campus of Simon Fraser University;

That the University of British Columbia and the Association of Professional Foresters jointly assess the need for
Forestry courses in various parts of the Province;

That the University of British Columbia and the University
of Victoria cooperate in the delivery of degree-completion
programs in Nursing to the non-metropolitan areas.

References

British Columbia, *Report of the Commission on University
Programs in Non-Metropolitan Areas,* 1976.

337 COMMITTEE ON CONTINUING AND COMMUNITY EDUCATION IN BRITISH
COLUMBIA
(Departmental Committee)

Appointed   June, 1976

Reported   December, 1976

Committee   Twenty-three members; Ronald Farris (Superin-
              tendent of Communications) chairman

Purpose   To study continuing and community education in
              British Columbia, and to recommend future
              policy on funding, administration, and pro-
              gramming in this field.

Conclusions/Recommendations

That the concept of life-long learning be adopted as basic
to the planning of the total public educational system in
British Columbia;

That the government place in statute a statement of purposes and goals with respect to the development of adult
education in the province;

That a mechanism be established to provide more vigorous
provincial leadership and co-ordination for adult education;

That a provincial 'open college' be established to satisfy

a wide range of adult education needs, especially those in non-metropolitan areas;

That every citizen be given the opportunity, on a tuition-free basis, for educational upgrading, up to and including the grade 12 level or its equivalence.

References

British Columbia, *Report of the Committee on Continuing and Community Education in British Columbia*, 1976.

338 ADVISORY COMMISSION ON VOCATIONAL, TECHNICAL AND TRADES TRAINING IN BRITISH COLUMBIA
(Departmental Committee)

Appointed   July 14, 1976

Reported   January 31, 1977 [to Minister of Education and Minister of Labour]

Committee   Six members; Dean H. Goard (former Principal, B.C. Institute of Technology) chairman

Purpose   To study and report on vocational, technical, and trades training in British Columbia.

Conclusions/Recommendations

That an Occupational Training Council be established;

That the proposed new B.C. Occupational Training Council establish occupational counselling centres throughout the province, and that these centres provide information and guidance on vocational programs (selection procedures, entrance qualifications, and course prerequisites), as well as on the labour market (current or future demand for specific occupations);

That the new council provide qualified counselors to the secondary schools as requested by them;

That the new council be provided with the resources to do

research;

That vocational preparation programs, such as English-language training, employment orientation for women, programs on deafness, and trained community aids, be recognized as vocational and continue to receive funding and support;

That the Occupational Training Council ensure that federal participation in the field of adult vocational training be coordinated with and in controlled support of provincial efforts to guarantee that the interests of the students are best served, and that the provincial government affirm, both legislatively and administratively, its paramountcy in the educational and training fields.

References

British Columbia, *Report of the Commission on Vocational, Technical, and Trades Training in British Columbia,* 1977.

339 COMMITTEE ON THE EDUCATION AND TRAINING OF TEACHERS
(Departmental Committee)

Appointed   September 21, 1977

Reported   June 16, 1978

Committee   Five members; Malcolm F. McGregor (former
                 Professor of Classics, University of British
                 Columbia) chairman

Purpose   To conduct a thorough examination of the pro-
                 grams for the preparation of teachers.

Conclusions/Recommendations

That the Joint Board of Teacher-Education be eliminated and that a Council for the Education of Teachers be established;

That the Council be advisory to the Faculties of Education and that it serve as a co-ordinating authority for

Continuing Education throughout the Province;

That a Board of Certification be established;

That greater rigour than is now employed be applied to the granting of admission to the Faculties of Education; that completion of at least one academic year in an academic Faculty with an average of 70% be a prerequisite for admission to a Faculty of Education; that the student be required to submit a letter of application, stating his qualifications and aims; that each applicant be interviewed; and that each applicant be required to write a test in English usage;

That the Standard Certificate for elementary teachers be abolished, and that every teacher have a degree;

That during the last two years of training in the elementary program at least sixteen weeks be spent in the schools and that the final practicum comprise at least eight continuous weeks;

That the secondary programme require five years of study, of which four will be devoted to academic education and one to professional training; and that students prepare themselves in two Teaching Fields from the subjects taught in the secondary school;

That the secondary practica require a minimum total of twelve weeks, and the final practicum demand a minimum of eight continuous weeks.

References

British Columbia, *The Education and Training of Teachers in British Columbia*, 1978.

CANADA

340 ROYAL COMMISSION ON INDUSTRIAL TRAINING AND TECHNICAL
EDUCATION
(General Commission)

Appointed   June 22, 1910

Reported   March 28, 1911, and May 31, 1913

Commission   Seven members; James W. Robertson (Principal,
               Macdonald College) chairman

Purpose   To inquire into the needs and present equip-
               ment of the Dominion as respects industrial
               training and technical education, and into
               the systems and methods of technical instruc-
               tion obtaining in other countries.

Conclusions/Recommendations

That all children to the age of 14 years receive the
benefits of elementary general education, but after 12
years of age, for the children whose parents expect or
desire them to follow manual occupations, the content of
the courses, the methods of instruction and the experience
from work undertaken at school should have as close relation as practicable to the productive, constructive and
conserving occupations to be followed after the children
leave school;

That advanced vocational training and technical education
be provided at a higher level;

That interest and financial support be shared by individuals, corporations and associations, and by local, provincial, and federal governments;

That overall organization be carefully planned with development boards and administrative commissions at all levels;

That the sum of $3,000,000 be provided annually for a
period of ten years by the Parliament of Canada and paid
annually into a Dominion Development Fund.

References

Canada, *Sessional Papers*, 1913, vol. 28.

341 ROYAL COMMISSION ON RADIO BROADCASTING
(Related Commission)

Appointed   December 6, 1928

Reported   September 11, 1929

Commission   Three members; John Aird (President, Canadian
             Bank of Commerce) chairman

Purpose   To examine into the broadcasting situation in
             the Dominion of Canada and to make recommen-
             dations to the Government as to the future
             administration, management, control and
             financing thereof.

Conclusions/Recommendations

That broadcasting be placed on a basis of public service
and that the station providing a service of this kind be
owned and operated by one national company; and that provincial authorities have full control over the programs
of the station or stations in their respective areas;

That the company be known as the Canadian Radio Broadcasting Company; that it be vested with all the powers of
private enterprise and that its status and duties corres-
pond to those of a public utility;

That time be made available for firms or others desiring to
put on programs employing indirect advertising; that no
direct advertising be allowed; that specific time be made
available for educational work; that where religious
broadcasting is allowed, there be regulations prohibiting
statements of a controversial nature or one religion making
an attack upon the leaders or doctrine of another; that the
broadcasting of political matters be carefully restricted
under arrangements mutually agreed upon by all political
parties concerned; that competent and cultured announcers
only be employed.

References

Canada, *Report of the Royal Commission on Radio Broadcasting*, 1929.

342 ROYAL COMMISSION ON DOMINION-PROVINCIAL RELATIONS
(Related Commission)

Appointed   August 14, 1937

Reported   May 4, 1940

Commission   Five members; Newton W. Rowell (Chief Justice
                of Ontario [When Chief Justice Rowell resigned
                because of ill health, Joseph Sirois (Law
                Department, Laval University) replaced him as
                chairman]

Purpose   To re-examine the economic and financial basis
                of Confederation and of the distribution of
                legislative powers in the light of the
                economic and social developments of the last
                seventy years.

Conclusions & Recommendations

That the quality of education and welfare services is no
longer a matter of purely provincial and local concern;

That in Canada today, freedom of movement and equality of
opportunity are more important than ever before, and these

depend in part on the maintenance of at least minimum
national standards for education, public health, and care
of the indigent;

That the most economically-distressed areas are the ones
least capable of supporting these services, and yet are
also the ones in which the needs are likely to be greatest;

That not only national duty and decency, if Canada is to be
a nation at all, but equity and national self-interest
demand that the residents of these areas be given average
services and equal opportunities.

References

Canada, *Report of the Royal Commission on Dominion-
Provincial Relations,* 1940. Book I & II.

343 ROYAL COMMISSION ON NATIONAL DEVELOPMENT IN THE ARTS,
LETTERS AND SCIENCES
(Related Commission)

Appointed   April 8, 1949

Reported   May, 1951

Commission   Five members; Vincent Massey (Chancellor,
               University of Toronto) chairman

Purpose   To examine and make recommendations upon:

(a) the principles upon which the policy of Canada
    should be based, in the fields of radio and
    television broadcasting;
(b) such agencies and activities of the government
    of Canada as the National Film Board, the
    National Gallery, the National Museum, the
    National War Museum, the Public Archives and
    the care and custody of public records, the
    Library of Parliament; methods by which re-
    search is aided including grants for scholar-
    ships through various Federal Government

agencies; the eventual character and scope of
the National Library; the scope or activities
of these agencies, the manner in which they
should be conducted, financed and controlled,
and other matters relevant thereto;
(c) methods by which the relations of Canada with
the United Nations Educational, Scientific
and Cultural Organization and with other
organizations operating in this field should
be conducted;
(d) relations of the government of Canada and any
of its agencies with various national voluntary bodies operating in the field with which
this inquiry will be concerned.

Conclusions/Recommendations

That in addition to the help already being given for
research and other purposes the Federal Government make
annual contributions to support the work of the universities on the basis of the population of each of the provinces of Canada;

That these contributions be made after consultation with
the government and the universities of each province, to
be distributed to each university proportionately to the
student enrolment;

That these contributions be sufficient to ensure that the
work of the universities of Canada may be carried on in
accordance with the needs of the nation;

That all members of the National Conference of Canadian
Universities be eligible for the federal grants mentioned
above;

That scholarships in the natural sciences continue, and
machinery be set up to make advance scholarships available
in the humanities, the social sciences and in law.

References

Canada, *Report: Royal Commission on National Development
in the Arts, Letters and Sciences,* 1951.

344 SURVEY OF SOCIAL AND ECONOMIC CONDITIONS OF THE INDIANS OF
BRITISH COLUMBIA
(Departmental Committee)

Appointed   1954

Reported   1955

Committee   Three members; Harry B. Hawthorn (Department
               of Anthropology, University of British
               Columbia) chairman

Purpose   To survey the social and economic conditions
               of the Indians of British Columbia, and in
               particular to study community and family life,
               resources, employment, education, relations
               with the law, social welfare needs, and
               administration.

Conclusions/Recommendations

That teachers accept the continued existence of an Indian
life which is different, and understand that race does not
imply intellectual or moral attributes;

That teachers not try to remake the child beyond the
recognition and acceptance of his community;

That the school not be made the vehicle of postponed social
reform;

That community reform be undertaken at the adult level, and
to that end, teachers take part (in an informed and responsible manner) in community affairs and adult education;

That with the ultimate aim of giving every person the
possibility of integrating favourably into Canadian life,
the principle of joint education of Indian and White
children be followed wherever possible.

References

Canada, *The Indians of British Columbia: A Survey of Social
and Economic Conditions,* 1955.

345 SURVEY OF THE EDUCATIONAL FACILITIES AND REQUIREMENTS OF
THE INDIANS IN CANADA
(Departmental Committee)

Appointed   January, 1955

Reported   July 26, 1956

Committee   Three members; G.G. Brown (former Municipal
             Inspector of Schools) chairman

Purpose   To survey the Indian day schools and residen-
             tial schools in order to assess the present
             facilities and to ascertain the future needs
             and educational requirements of the Indian
             children and to establish, as far as possible,
             a priority rating indicating about when the
             respective requirements should be met.

Conclusions/Recommendations

That the overall aim of any really functional program is to
give the Indian children a second educational foundation
extending into secondary and higher education for increasing numbers, to develop good standards of health, social
and moral attitudes, and to equip them to adjust themselves
competently, on an equal footing with white youths, in
Canadian society as self-reliant and self-supporting
citizens.

References

Canada, *Survey of the Educational Facilities and Requirements of the Indians in Canada,* Part I, General Report,
1956.

346 ROYAL COMMISSION ON CANADA'S ECONOMIC PROSPECTS
(Related Commission)

Appointed   June 17, 1955

Reported   1957

Commission   Five members; Walter Lockhart Gordon (Chartered Accountant) chairman

Purpose   To inquire into and report upon the long-term
prospects of the Canadian economy, that is to
say, upon the probable economic development of
Canada and the problems to which such development appears likely to give rise, and without
limiting the generality of the foregoing, to
study and report upon:

(a) developments in the supply of raw materials
and energy sources;
(b) the growth to be expected in the population of
Canada and the changes in its distribution;
(c) prospects for growth and change in domestic
and external markets for Canadian productions;
(d) trends in productivity and standards of
living; and
(e) prospective requirements for industrial and
social capital.

Conclusions/Recommendations

That the functions of the universities touch every facet of
our society. Through the preservation of our heritage they
maintain our way of life, and through the interest they
generate in the arts, they enrich it. They enliven the
perception of social processes, and contribute to the
orderly development of social institutions and relations.
It is incredible that we would allow their services to
society in these ways to lapse or to lag;

That, in relation to the increase in the national productivity and wealth of the country, Canadian universities
occupy a key position. They are the source of the most
highly skilled workers, whose knowledge is essential in
all branches of industry, and, in addition, they make a
substantial contribution to research and in the training
of research scientists.

References

Canada, Order in Council P.C. 1955-909.

Canada, *Royal Commission on Canada's Economic Prospects,*
1957.

347 ROYAL COMMISSION ON BROADCASTING
(Related Commission)

Appointed   December 2, 1955

Reported   March 15, 1957

Commission   Three members; Robert MacLaren Fowler
                (Barrister; President, Canadian Pulp and
                Paper Association) chairman

Purpose   [Keeping in mind that the reconsideration of
                television should be based upon the principles
                that the grant of the exclusive use of certain
                frequencies or channels for broadcasting shall
                continue to be under the control of the
                Parliament of Canada, and that the broadcast-
                ing and distribution of Canadian programmes
                by a public agency shall continue to be the
                central feature of Canadian broadcasting
                policy] to examine television broadcasting
                and the aspects of sound radio broadcasting
                which are related to television broadcasting.

Conclusions/Recommendations

That in Canada there appear to be four principal functions
which we expect our broadcasters to discharge. These are,
first, to inform (news, public events, the reporting of
facts); secondly, to enlighten (interpretation of the news,
education, discussion, debate on the facts); thirdly, to
entertain (enjoyment, relaxation); and fourthly, to sell
goods (advertising, distribution of goods and services);

That concerning broadcasting generally, a surprising
amount of interest was shown in educational broadcasts.
Most witnesses recognized that radio, and more particularly
television, are tremendously influential instruments, and
many would like to see greater use made of these instruments in the realm of formal education. The value of the

present school broadcasts was stressed by many witnesses from all parts of Canada. The general view was that the Canadian Broadcasting Corporation could advantageously expand its activities in this field, without in any way impinging on provincial rights, simply by cooperating fully with, or by having educational programmes prepared entirely by, the various provincial ministries of education.

References

Canada, *Report: Royal Commission on Broadcasting,* March 1957.

348 JOINT COMMITTEE ON INDIAN AFFAIRS
(Legislative Committee)

Appointed	April 29, 1959 (House of Commons); May 5, 1959 (Senate)
Reported	July 8, 1961
Committee	Twelve Senators and twenty-four Members of Parliament: Senator James Gladstone (Senator) and Lucien Grenier (M.P. for Bonaventure) joint-chairmen
Purpose	To investigate and report upon Indian administration in general and, in particular, on the social and economic status of the Indians.

Conclusions/Recommendations

That education is the key to the full realization by Indians of self-determination and self-government;

That education of Indian children in schools under the jurisdiction of the provinces be continued and expanded;

That kindergarten facilities for Indian children be provided;

That the provincial authorities be approached to ensure that a more comprehensive and accurate account of the

Indian people is used and described in history courses and texts;

That agreements be entered into with provincial authorities to extend adult education facilities to Indians with the program expanded;

That travelling library facilities to Indian communities be expanded wherever possible;

That academic upgrading and social orientation courses to prepare young Indians for placement or specialized training be greatly expanded;

That full support and encouragement be given to formation of Home and School or Parent-Teacher Associations;

That the fullest possible encouragement and incentive be given to Indian children to go as far as they can in school;

That in addition to an intensive educational program, the economic opportunities and environment of the Indian people be developed;

That the Canadian Broadcasting Corporation and other agencies prepare factual presentations of the Indians' way of life and their contribution to the development of Canada.

References

Canada, *Joint Committee of the Senate and the House of Commons on Indian Affairs,* 1959.

349 COMMITTEE ON EDUCATION FOR THE YUKON TERRITORY
(Departmental Committee)

Appointed   April 14, 1960

Reported   August 26, 1960

Committee   Three members; G.G. Brown (former Municipal
              Inspector of Schools) chairman   [Upon the

death of Mr. Brown, J.C. Jonason (School
Inspector) assumed the chairmanship]

Purpose   To prepare recommendations relative to:

1. The School Ordinance, including the function
   and responsibility of the office of Commissioner and of Superintendent of Schools; the
   establishment of school districts; and the
   advisability of establishing separate schools
   for religious minorities.
2. School Facilities, Elementary and Secondary.
3. Curriculum.
4. Pupils.
5. Teachers.
6. Adult Education.
7. Advisability of Territorial supervision of
   Old Crow School and Mission Schools.
8. Advisability of having both Territorial and
   Mission schools.
9. Cost Analysis.
10. School Administration.

Conclusions/Recommendations

That in recent years there has been a growing interest by
Canadians in the problems of integrating Canadian Indians
with the life of Canadians in general;

That the traditional policy in Canada has been to regard
Indians as wards of the state, to maintain them on Indian
reserves and to see that they did not suffer unduly from
privation;

That undoubtedly there was a time when the building of
large residential schools or schools with hostels was
justified by circumstances, but the Committee questioned
the need for and the advisability of continuing the policy
of racial segregation by the maintenance of these large
establishments.

References

Canada, *Report of the Committee on Education for the Yukon
Territory*, 1960.

350 ROYAL COMMISSION ON PUBLICATIONS
(Related Commission)

Appointed   September 16, 1960

Reported   May, 1961

Commission   Three members; M. Grattan O'Leary (President,
                Ottawa Journal) chairman

Purpose   To inquire into and report upon the recent and
                present position of and prospects for Canadian
                magazines and other periodicals with special
                but not exclusive consideration being given to
                problems arising from competition with similar
                publications which are largely or entirely
                edited outside of Canada or are largely or
                entirely foreign in content.

Conclusions/Recommendations

That every nation must provide within itself the means of
maintaining stability. In North America today this function is largely directed and exercised through the communications media. No technique of social control could be
more reflective of our ideals of freedom and competition.
Here is no coercion. The teacher explains, the politician
proposes, the salesman displays, and society -- when it is
satisfied acts. It is a process of suggestion and of
persuasion, the very essence of democracy;

That in this role, communications are the thread which
binds together the fibres of a nation. They can protect
a nation's values and encourage their practice. They can
make democratic government possible and better government
probable. They can soften sectional asperities and bring
honorable compromises. They can inform and educate in the
arts, the sciences and commerce. They can help market a
nation's products and promote its material wealth;

That, while Canada and the United States may have the same
basic cultures, they each at the same time have domestic
and other tasks and problems -- political, social and
economic -- which differ widely. Canada's particular
responsibilities, her government, her constitutional

structure, her ideals and aspirations, her memories and milestones, even her discords, are facts in her existence which cannot be approached understandingly or usefully by communications media owned or controlled in another country, even though that country be friendly.

References

Canada, *Report: Royal Commission on Publications,* May, 1961.

351 ROYAL COMMISSION ON BILINGUALISM AND BICULTURALISM
(Related Commission)

Appointed   July 19, 1963

Reported   February 1, 1965 ('Preliminary Report') and
                October 8, 1967, May 23, 1968 ('Education'),
                September 19, 1969, October 23, 1969, February
                14, 1970

Commission   Ten members; Davidson Dunton (President,
                Carleton University) and Andre Laurendeau
                (Editor in Chief, Le Devoir) co-chairmen

Purpose   To inquire into and report upon the existing
                state of bilingualism and biculturalism in
                Canada and to recommend what steps should be
                taken to develop the Canadian Confederation on
                the basis of an equal partnership between the
                two founding races, taking into account the
                contribution made by the other ethnic groups
                to the cultural enrichment of Canada and the
                measures that should be taken to safeguard
                that contribution.

Conclusions/Recommendations

That it would appear from what is happening that the state of affairs established in 1867, and never since seriously challenged, is now for the first time being rejected by the French Canadians of Quebec;

That we are going to have to put our country's divisions on display, and we appreciate the dangers of doing so, but the feeling of the Commission is that at this point the danger of a clear and frank statement is less than the danger of silence;

That, above all, the Commissioners are convinced that they are demonstrating a supreme confidence in Canada; because to tell a people plainly, even bluntly, what you believe to be the truth, is to show your own conviction that it is strong enough to face the truth. It is in fact to say to the country that you have faith in it and in its future;

That, since language is the basic ingredient of culture, a major concern has been the opportunities for each of the two main linguistic groups in Canada to have access to an education which would allow the fullest expression and development of the mother tongue, and at the same time ensure an adequate communication between the two societies;

That it is the right of Canadian parents to have their children educated in the official language of their choice, and the opportunity to learn the second language;

That citizens of a country with two official languages should be provided with an education which allows them to participate in either society;

That the Commissioner's interpretation of bilingualism in Canada means that the major social and political institutions will function in the two languages, but that individual Canadians will not be required to know the second language;

That, in order to have a true opportunity of decision, all children must be given an introduction to the second language through the school system.

References

Canada, *A Preliminary Report of the Royal Commission on Bilingualism and Biculturalism,* 1965.

Canada, *Report of the Royal Commission on Bilingualism and Biculturalism,* vol. 2, 1968.

352 STUDY OF UNIVERSITY GOVERNMENT IN CANADA
(Special Committee)

Appointed   November, 1963

Reported   August, 1965

Committee   Two members; Sir James Mountford and Robert O.
               Berdahl (Political Science Department, San
               Francisco State College) [Sir James Duff
               (former Chancellor, University of Durham)
               replaced Sir James Mountford who resigned
               because of ill health.]

Purpose   To make a dispassionate examination and evalu-
               ation of the present structure and practices
               of the government of both the English- and
               French-language universities of Canada,
               including provincial, church-related and
               independent institutions.

Conclusions/Recommendations

That if tension levels are already high at many Canadian
universities, it seems likely that future developments will
only serve to heighten them;

That the rapid rate of expansion planned for higher education in most provinces points to increasing pressures on
the President to obtain rapid decisions at the very time
that the teaching faculties are asking for more and more
of a share in these decisions;

That the two-tier pattern of university government be
retained but with an almost fundamental alteration; that
is, in place of the assumed separation of powers between
Board and Senate, a system be introduced whereby they are
brought into much closer contact at many stages.

References

University Government of Canada, 1966.

[Sponsored by Canadian Association of University Teachers,
the Association of Universities and Colleges of Canada, and

the Ford Foundation]

353 COMMISSION ON FINANCING HIGHER EDUCATION IN CANADA
(Special Committee)

Appointed   1964

Reported   June 30, 1965

Committee   Four members; Vincent W. Bladen (Dean of Arts
              & Science, University of Toronto) chairman

Purpose   To study, and report and make recommendations
              on the financing of universities and colleges
              of Canada with particular reference to the
              decade ending in 1975.

Conclusions/Recommendations

That the Federal Government review annually with the Provincial Governments the adequacy of the federal contribution to the cost of higher education;

That such federal support be in a form which avoided any
invasion of the provincial right;

That a Minister of the Crown be given responsibility for
coordinating university assistance from all federal
agencies;

That there be an increase in the federal per capita grants
to $5 for the year 1965-66, and a further increase of $1
each year thereafter until appropriate revision has been
achieved;

That a Capital Grants Fund be established into which $5
per head of the Canadian population would be paid each year
and that federal grants for research be greatly increased;

That the Student Loans Plan be continued and expanded as
necessary;

That provincial governments adopt long-range planning for

higher education and that the essential role of university
research and good research libraries be recognized;

That for the next decade, popular pressure for the abolition of fees be resisted;

That universities coordinate and cooperate with other
universities for the sake of economy and efficiency;

That universities continue to pursue excellence without
extravagance;

That individual and corporate donors be aware that continued and indeed increasing private support is necessary.

References

*Financing Higher Education in Canada: being the Report of
a Commission to the Association of Universities and
Colleges of Canada,* 1965.
[Sponsored by the Canadian Universities Foundation and the
Ford Foundation]

354 COMMITTEE ON BROADCASTING
   (Departmental Committee)

   Appointed   May 25, 1964

   Reported   September 1, 1965 [to the Secretary of State
                   and Registrar General of Canada]

   Committee   Three members; Robert M. Fowler (Barrister;
                   President, Canadian Pulp and Paper Association)
                   chairman

   Purpose   To study, in the light of present and possible
                   future conditions, the purposes and provisions
                   of the Broadcasting Act and related statutes
                   and to recommend what amendments, if any,
                   should be made to the legislation.

Conclusions/Recommendations

That the federal government, although concerned neither
with curriculum nor directly with cost, has an undoubted
obligation, as the owner of the public sector of broadcasting and the controller of the private sector, to ensure
that the facilities of the entire broadcasting system are
placed at the disposal of the provincial educational
authorities to the greatest practical extent;

That the closed-circuit technique is better suited to
purely scholastic programming, because it affords greater
flexibility and adaptability to differing regional and
provincial requirements; and that for adult school courses
and at the university level, for which evening courses are
numerous and available space limited, broadcasting would
reach a larger number of students;

That the educator must try to understand the nature of
broadcasting, and the broadcaster must accept the
authority of the educator with respect to program content
and scholastic presentation;

That there is no justification for permitting television
broadcasts to start earlier than noon, except in very
special circumstances, and that the morning hours could be
put to more important national use in transmitting school
and university broadcasts.

References

Canada, *Report of the Committee of Broadcasting*, 1965.

355 ROYAL COMMISSION ON THE STATUS OF WOMEN IN CANADA
    (Related Commission)

    Appointed   February 16, 1967

    Reported   September 28, 1970

    Commission   Seven members; Florence Bird (Writer, Lecturer,
                   Broadcaster) chairman

    Purpose   To inquire into and report upon the status of
                   women in Canada, and to recommend what steps

might be taken by the Federal Government to
ensure for women equal opportunities with men
in all aspects of Canadian society, having
regard for the distribution of legislative
powers under the constitution of Canada,
particularly with reference to federal
statutes, regulations and policies that
concern or affect the rights and activities of
women.

Conclusions/Recommendations

That equal opportunity for education is fundamental; that
education opens the door to almost every life goal; and
that wherever women are denied equal access to education
they cannot be said to have equality;

That changes in education could bring dramatic improvements
in the social and economic position of women in an aston-
ishingly short time;

That federal Crown Corporations and agencies make clear to
educational institutions, and to the public, that career
opportunities within their organizations are open to women
and that they are encouraging women to prepare themselves
for such careers;

That the provinces and territories adopt textbooks that
portray women, as well as men, in diversified roles and
occupations;

That the federal government provide special funds for
young women and young men to acquire university education
leading to a degree in fields designated to be of special
interest for aid to developing areas;

That the provinces and territories provide co-educational
guidance programmes in elementary and secondary schools;

That the provinces and territories set up courses in co-
educational family life education, including sex education;

That the current educational needs and interests of women
in rural areas be studied;

That Eskimo and Indian women be encouraged to take training in adult education for work in the northern communities.

References

Canada, *Report of the Royal Commission on the Status of Women in Canada,* 1970.

356 SPECIAL SENATE COMMITTEE ON A SCIENCE POLICY FOR CANADA
    (Legislative Committee)

Appointed	November, 1967
Reported	December 17, 1970, December 17, 1971, September 11, 1973
Committee	Twenty-two members; Maurice Lamontagne (Senator) chairman
Purpose	To consider and report on the science policy of the Federal Government with the object of appraising its priorities, its budget and its efficiency in the light of the experience of other industrialized countries and of the requirements of the new scientific age.

Conclusions/Recommendations

That the university is where a man starts to become a scientist or technologist, and whether he then builds a university career or works outside the academic world, his university education will have been a significant influence on the whole country's relations with the world of science and technology;

That if Canada moves ahead in the international science and technology race, the universities will deserve much of the credit, and if we fall behind, or if the population comes to consider the scientist as an ivory-tower isolationist and science as a sinister force, the universities will have to accept much of the blame.

References

Canada, *A Science Policy for Canada: Report of the Senate Special Committee on Science Policy,* vol. 1, 1970.

357 COMMISSION ON THE RELATIONS BETWEEN UNIVERSITIES AND
GOVERNMENTS
(Special Committee)

Appointed   May, 1968

Reported   October, 1969

Committee   Two members; René Hurtubise (Faculty of Law,
              Université de Montreál) and Donald C. Rowat
              (Political Science Department, Carleton
              University) co-chairmen

Purpose   To consider the distinctive role of universi-
              ties in the changing Canadian society, parti-
              cularly with respect to their responsibilities
              for the development of this role at the
              various levels of society; community, provin-
              cial, regional, national and international; to
              determine the need, nature and extent of
              university autonomy and of government and
              public control of universities; and to recom-
              mend the appropriate instruments by which
              relations between universities and governments
              can be established that do justice to their
              responsibilities.

Conclusions/Recommendations

['Concluding Reflections' included the following:]

That the university, a many-sided reality in time and
space, should be envisaged as making a constant effort to
reach an equilibrium between the poles of socialization and
critical research;

That it is necessary to reach a basic consensus on the
functions and responsibilities appropriate to a university
with respect to: other levels of teaching; centres and

agencies of research; and the obligations which are incumbent on other social institutions;

That the university of the future will tend to democratize itself;

That the university of the future will be permanent;

That the university will be creative;

That the university will look to the future.

References

The University, Society and Government: The Report of the Commission on the Relations between Universities and Governments, University of Ottawa Press, 1970.

[Sponsored by the Canadian Association of University Teachers, the Association of Universities and Colleges of Canada, the Canadian Union of Students, and the Union générale des étudiants du Québec.]

358 SPECIAL SENATE COMMITTEE ON POVERTY
(Legislative Committee)

Appointed   November 26, 1968

Reported   November 10, 1971

Committee   Sixteen members; David A. Croll (Senator)
                chairman

Purpose   To investigate and report upon all aspects of
                poverty in Canada, whether urban, rural,
                regional, or otherwise, to define and eluci-
                date the problem of poverty in Canada, and to
                recommend appropriate action to ensure the
                establishment of a more effective structure of
                remedial measures.

Conclusions/Recommendations

That education is one of the keys to social and occupational mobility; and for the individual, education can mean
an escape from poverty, access to meaningful and steady
employment, and full participation in the social and
political life of the nation;

That without in any way interfering with or limiting or
denying the constitutional and traditional prerogatives of
the provinces in education, the Government of Canada establish a National Office of Education with the following
functions:
  a) to develop and articulate national educational goals;
  b) to co-ordinate the distribution of federal investments
     in education and training;
  c) to sponsor and support educational research at the
     national level;
  d) to provide a national centre for information and data
     on education throughout the country;
  e) to sponsor and support action-research programs;
  f) to support local communities and organizations, includ-
     ing those of Canada's native people, in achieving
     their participation in local educational systems.

References

Canada, *Poverty in Canada: Report of the Special Senate
Committee on Poverty*, 1971.

359 COMMITTEE ON YOUTH
    (Departmental Committee)

    Appointed   August, 1969

    Reported   December 18, 1970 [to Secretary of State]

    Committee   Three members; David Hunter (Parole Officer)
                 chairman

    Purpose   To undertake a study of the aspirations,
                 attitudes and needs of youth and the govern-
                 ment's present role in this area.

Conclusions/Recommendations

That traditionally, the involvement of Canadian governments in the field of youth has revolved primarily around the question of education;

That over the past 50 years, more and more aspects of a young person's life have become an institutional responsibility shared by federal, provincial and municipal governments, and private organizations;

That the federal government undertake a detailed appraisal and evaluation of its entire system of support to post-secondary institutions;

That the federal government undertake a thorough evaluation of its student aid program, and that the Canada Student Loans Plan be revised immediately;

That the federal government drastically revise and restructure its method of training and recruiting officers for the Canadian Armed Forces;

That the existing Youth Allowance program be thoroughly evaluated to determine its effectiveness in encouraging the 16-18 age group to stay in school;

That the program of Summer Language Courses include financial credit and be broadened to include more students and more universities;

That in cooperation with provincial governments the Occupational Training for Adults program be assessed, re-evaluated and reworked;

That the Canada Council expand its present program to include new emphasis on innovative and experimental cultural and artistic programming for young people.

References

Canada, *It's Your Turn: A Report to the Secretary of State by the Committee on Youth* (revised report dated July 26, 1971).

360 SURVEY OF EDUCATION IN THE NORTHWEST TERRITORIES
(Departmental Committee)

Appointed   1970

Reported   February 29, 1972

Committee   Professional staff of the Territorial Educa-
              tion System; B.C. Gillie (Director of Educa-
              tion, N.W.T.) chairman

Purpose   To examine the evolution of the present educa-
              tion system in the Northwest Territories; to
              obtain opinions and consider views of the
              staff impinging on the type of education
              offered; and to develop objectives for educa-
              tion which will reflect the stated wishes of
              the northern population served by the
              Territorial Department of Education.

Conclusions/Recommendations

That the Purpose of Education is to provide for all people
opportunity for maximum development of their aptitudes,
skills and competencies along with an understanding and
appreciation of the sum total of human experience; and
that such development should enable each individual to
choose freely between different courses of action in such
a manner that he can live a satisfying personal life while
discharging his responsibilities as a participating member
of a complex society.

[The 223 recommendations were apportioned as follows:]
  Purpose, Objectives and Goals of the Territorial Educa-
  tional Programme (Recommendation 1)
  Pre-School Education (2-11)
  Elementary Education (12-29)
  Secondary Education (30-43)
  Continuing and Special Education (44-92)
  Curriculum Development (93-100)
  Student Residence Programme (101-134)
  School Building-Construction, Management and Maintenance
  (135-141)
  Teaching Personnel and Staff Training (142-176)

Classroom Assistants Program (177-189)
Educational Resources (190-198)
Financial Resources and Administration (199-213)
Local Involvement in Education (214-219)
Territorial Schools Ordinance (220-223)

References

Canada, *Survey of Education: Northwest Territories,* 1972.

361 COMMITTEE ON EDUCATION FOR THE YUKON TERRITORY
(Departmental Committee)

Appointed   1972

Reported   September 22, 1972 [to Commissioner of the
               Yukon Territory]

Committee   Three members; Franklin P. Levirs (former
               Superintendent of Schools, Yukon) chairman

Purpose   To inquire into education in the Yukon Terri-
               tory and to make recommendations concerning
               the School Ordinance, with special reference
               to its revision; public participation in
               school administration and school affairs at
               the school level; the financing of education;
               the administration of the school system; the
               curriculum of the elementary and secondary
               schools; special needs of Yukon Indians;
               special education of handicapped children;
               vocational education; adult education; the
               future of post-secondary education; the
               employment and supervision of the teaching
               staff; and other related matters.

Conclusions/Recommendations

That the revised School Ordinance establish the general
powers and duties of all officers concerned in the school
systems, as well as the general policies under which the
system is to be operated;

That consideration be given as to whether it might be preferable in the Yukon to establish some sort of readiness test;

That the present local School Advisory Committee be reconstituted as Citizens' School Committees with definite powers and duties under the School Ordinance;

That each Indian village form an Education Committee of its own for purposes of encouraging an active interest and participation of Band members in school affairs;

That no school boards be established at this time;

That the Department of Education take whatever steps are necessary to establish at both the elementary and secondary levels appropriate studies on the history and culture of the Yukon including that of the native peoples.

References

Canada, *Report of the Committee on Education for the Yukon Territory*, 1972.

362 COMMISSION ON CANADIAN STUDIES
(Special Committee)

Appointed   June 28, 1972

Reported   October, 1975

Committee   One member; T.H.B. Symons (President of Trent University)

Purpose   To study, report, and make recommendations upon the state of teaching and research in various fields of study relating to Canada at Canadian universities.

Conclusions/Recommendations

That there be a major expansion in the attention given to Canadian studies in the university curriculum in many

academic areas at both the undergraduate and graduate
levels;

That a variety of approaches be followed in the development
of Canadian studies, depending upon the needs and circumstances of individual disciplines and institutes;

That Government departments and agencies, both federal and
provincial, adopt an open door policy to the fullest
extent possible to assist those engaged in research;

That each university in Canada engage in some teaching and
research about the area in which it is located;

That more attention be devoted, in all appropriate areas of
the university curriculum, to study of the cultural life of
Canada;

That a particular effort be made in teacher education to
ensure that future teachers in the elementary and secondary
schools of this country are given greater opportunity to
acquire a fuller knowledge of Canadian society, culture,
institutions and circumstances than is now provided in the
curriculum of teacher education programmes.

References

*To Know Ourselves: The Report of the Commission on
Canadian Studies*, Vol. I & II, 1975.

[Commissioned by the Association of Universities and
Colleges of Canada.]

363 STUDY OF NORTHERN PEOPLE AND HIGHER EDUCATION
(Special Committee)

Appointed   January, 1974

Reported   March, 1975

Committee   One member; Del M. Koenig (Institute for
               Northern Studies, University of Saskatchewan)

Purpose To analyze the teaching and research programmes sponsored by Canadian universities
in the North; to identify the main thrust of
Canadian universities in the North, to note
any gaps in their programmes, and to record
regional and provincial variations in teaching programmes and research projects; to
record the needs of northern people for
higher education and to note how these needs
are currently being met; and to recommend a
set of guidelines for universities research
projects to better fit the needs of northern
peoples.

Conclusions/Recommendations

That the Association of Universities and Colleges of Canada
facilitate the organization of a co-ordinating agency for
all universities and other post-secondary institutions
involved in northern activities;

That this proposed organization co-ordinate an on-going
programme evaluation, definition of goals of northern
involvement, and information exchange between member institutions;

That the government agencies involved in northern education
programming conduct in-depth assessments of their programmes in relation to the factors discussed in this
report;

That educators concentrate on listening to, and trying to
understand, what it is that parents and students see as
relevant northern content and try to adapt programmes to
fit these needs.

References

*Northern People and Higher Education: Realities and
Possibilities,* 1975.

[Sponsored by the Association of Universities and Colleges
of Canada. A previous volume, prepared by W.O. Kupsch and
taking the form of an inventory of existing programs, was
published by AUCC in 1973.]

364 COMMISSION ON GRADUATE STUDIES IN THE HUMANITIES AND SOCIAL
SCIENCES
(Special Committee)

Appointed   January, 1974

Reported   August, 1978

Committee   Three members; Dennis Healy (Principal,
               Bishop's University, Lennoxville, Que.)
               chairman

Purpose   To enquire into and report upon the nature,
               objectives and efficacy of Canadian graduate
               studies in the humanities and social sciences.

Conclusions/Recommendations

That the provinces initiate and administer a program to
support studies at the Master's level in small universities;

That within each province or, for the Maritimes, within the
region, committees be appointed to screen the Ph.D. candidates and to list the successful candidates in rank order;

That provincial governments meet a share of the costs of
doctoral training;

That fellowship recipients be allowed to enrol in the
doctoral program of their choice within the province;

That the Canada Council or its successor award a limited
number of fellowships in the humanities and social
sciences, tenable at any Canadian university and with a
grant to that university to cover the full costs of
tuition;

That such fellowships be tenable outside Canada only when
it can be shown that the student has sound academic reasons
for attending a foreign university;

That each university establish procedures to assess the
academic validity, the relationship to the university's
research objectives and the financial terms of all
research contracts involving university personnel;

That research grants awarded by the Canada Council or its
successor cover all indirect costs to the university and
also an amount equivalent to the salary of the principal
investigator;

That an additional 10 per cent be added to every federal
grant or contract to a French-language university.

References

Canada, *Report of the Commission on Graduate Studies in the
Humanities and Social Sciences,* August, 1978. [Appointed
by the Canada Council; Report received by the Social
Sciences and Research Council of Canada.]

365 THE MACKENZIE VALLEY PIPELINE INQUIRY
(Related Commission)

Appointed   March 21, 1974

Reported   April 15, 1977

Commission   One member; Thomas R. Berger (British
              Columbia Supreme Court Judge)

Purpose   To inquire into and report upon the terms and
              conditions that should be imposed in respect
              of any right-of-way that might be granted
              across Crown lands for the purposes of the
              proposed Mackenzie Valley Pipeline having
              regard to the social environmental and
              economic impact regionally, of the construc-
              tion, operation and subsequent abandonment of
              the proposed pipeline in the Yukon and the
              Northwest Territories.

Conclusions/Recommendations

That one of a society's purposes in requiring formal education for its children is to preserve and transmit to the
next generation its history, language, religion and
philosophy -- to ensure a continuity of the beliefs and
knowledge that a people holds in common. But the purpose

of the education provided to northern native people was to
erase their collective memory -- their history, language,
religion and philosophy -- and to replace it with that of
the white man;

That it is particularly important to understand the impact
of the present education system on the native languages.
When young men and women cannot understand their parents
and grandparents, they learn little about their own people
and their own past; nor do they acquire the confidence
that comes with adult understanding;

That the Dene and the Inuit today are seeking to reclaim
what they say is rightfully theirs. At the core of this
claim, and basic to their idea of self-determination, is
their right to educate their children -- the right to pass
on to them their values, their languages, their knowledge
and their history.

References

Canada, *Northern Frontier, Northern Homeland: The Report
of the Mackenzie Valley Pipeline Inquiry*, 1977.

366 COMMITTEE OF INQUIRY INTO THE NATIONAL BROADCASTING SERVICE
(Departmental Committee)

Appointed   March 14, 1977

Reported   July 20, 1977 [to the Prime Minister]

Committee   Seven members; Harry J. Boyle (Chairman of
               Canadian Radio-television and Telecommunica-
               tions Commission) chairman

Purpose   To inquire into the manner in which the CBC is
               fulfilling its mandate, particularly with
               respect to public affairs, news, and informa-
               tion programming.

Conclusions/Recommendations

That in those huge areas of Canada which are sparsely populated, the CBC remains the major source of information and entertainment, and it is also the primary source of information and entertainment for minority English and French language groups in all parts of Canada;

That the effort needed to keep Canada together is at least as great as it was in 1867, and the communications media have a grave responsibility to keep Canadians fully informed in subjects on which they have to make fateful decisions. If we did not have the CBC, we should have to invent it;

That, as presented by the media, Canada is in a state of deep schizophrenia: if English and French Canada were on different planets there could hardly be a greater contrast of views and information;

That when the present issues in Canada are clarified, when the CBC has had a chance to show what it can do on its own initiative, when some firmer trends become apparent in technology, when Parliament has reconsidered its relations to the CBC and other cultural and communication agencies, a fuller inquiry will then be needed to provide a proper basis for future legislation.

References

Canada, *Report: Committee of Inquiry into the National Broadcasting Service,* July, 1977.

[Established by the CRTC]

367 TASK FORCE ON CANADIAN UNITY
(Related Commission)

Appointed   July 5, 1977

Reported   January, 1979

Commission   Eight members; Jean-Luc Pepin (former Chairman
              of the Anti-Inflation Board) and John P.

Robarts (former Premier of Ontario) co-chairmen

Purpose   To enquire into questions relating to Canadian unity.

Conclusions/Recommendations

That the principle of the equality of status, rights and privileges of the English and French languages for all purposes declared by the Parliament of Canada, within its sphere of jurisdiction, be entrenched in the constitution;

That each provincial legislature have the right to determine an official language or official languages for that province, within its sphere of jurisdiction;

That linguistic rights be expressed in provincial statutes, which could include the entitlement recognized in the statement of the provincial first ministers at Montreal in February, 1978: 'Each child of a French-speaking or English-speaking minority is entitled to an education in his or her language in the primary or secondary schools in each province, wherever numbers warrant;' and that this right also be accorded to children of either minority who change their province of residence;

That the provinces review existing methods and procedures for the teaching and learning of both French and English and make greater efforts to improve the availability and quality of instruction in these languages at all levels of education;

That both the central and provincial governments meet to settle their respective areas of constitutional responsibility in the provision of essential services in the fields of health, social welfare, housing and education to status and non-status Indians, to Inuit, and to Metis on reserves, Crown lands, rural centres and large cities.

References

Canada, *A Future Together: The Task Force on Canadian Unity*, 1979.

Appendix

ROYAL COMMISSION ON OXFORD
AND CAMBRIDGE UNIVERSITIES
(PREAMBLE)

GEORGE THE FIFTH, by the Grace of God, of the United
Kingdom of Great Britain and Ireland and of the British
Dominions beyond the Seas, King, Defender of the Faith, to

Our Right Trusty and Well-beloved Counsellors:

Herbert Henry Asquith
Rowland Edmund, Baron Ernle
Robert, Baron Chalmers, Knight Grand Cross of Our Most
    Honourable Order of the Bath, late Secretary to the
    Treasury
Gerald William Balfour
Sir John Allsebrook Simon, Knight Commander of the Royal
    Victorian Order; and
Arthur Henderson; and

Our Trusty and Well-beloved:

Edward Gerald Strutt, Esquire (commonly called the
    Honourable Edward Gerald Strutt)
Thomas Banks Strong, Knight Grand Cross of Our Most
    Excellent Order of the British Empire, Doctor in
    Divinity, Dean of Christ Church, Oxford
Sir Howard Frank, Knight Commander of Our Most
    Honourable Order of the Bath
Sir Walter Morley Fletcher, Knight Commander of Our Most
    Excellent Order of the British Empire, Fellow of the
    Royal Society
Sir Horace Darwin, Knight Commander of Our Most
    Excellent Order of the British Empire, Fellow of the
    Royal Society

Sir Henry Alexander Miers, Knight, Fellow of the Royal
    Society, Vice-Chancellor of the University of
    Manchester
Sir John Hubert Oakley, Knight, Past-President of the
    Surveyors' Institution
William Henry Bragg, Esquire, Commander of Our Most
    Excellent Order of the British Empire, Fellow of the
    Royal Society; Quain Professor of Physics in the
    University of London
George Macaulay Trevelyan, Esquire, Commander of Our Most
    Excellent Order of the British Empire
Emily Penrose, Spinster, Officer of Our Most Excellent
    Order of the British Empire, Principal of Somerville
    College, Oxford
William George Stewart Adams, Esquire, Gladstone
    Professor of Political Theory and Institutions, Oxford
Hugh Kerr Anderson, Esquire, Doctor of Medicine, Fellow
    of the Royal Society
Blanche Athena Clough, Spinster, Vice-Principal of Newnham
    College, Cambridge
Herbert Mansfield Cobb, Esquire, Fellow and Member of the
    Council of the Surveyors' Institution
Montague Rhodes James, Esquire, Doctor of Letters, Provost
    of Eton
Albert Mansbridge, Esquire; and
Arthur Schuster, Esquire, Fellow and late Secretary of the
    Royal Society, Honorary Professor of Physics of the
    University of Manchester.

Great Britain, *Report of Royal Commission on Oxford and
Cambridge Universities,* 1922. (The official appointment
was made on November 14, 1919.)

Newfoundland	'An Act respecting Inquiries concerning Public Matters', 1888, Chapter 18
Nova Scotia	'An Act respecting Inquiries concerning Public Matters', 1876, Chapter 19
Prince Edward Island	'Public Inquiries Act', 1879, Chapter 17
New Brunswick	'An Act to Authorize the Issue of Commissions under the Great Seal in certain cases and for certain purposes', 1886, Chapter 4
Quebec	'An Act respecting inquiries concerning public matters', 1869, Chapter 8
Ontario	'An Act ... to make provision for Inquiries concerning public matters and official notices', 1868, Chapter 6
Manitoba	'An Act to make provision for Inquiries concerning Public Matters', 1873, Chapter 21
Saskatchewan	'An ordinance Respecting Commissioners to Make Enquiries Concerning Public Matters', *Ordinances of*

	the North-West Territories, 1895, No. 2
Alberta	'An Ordinance Respecting Commissioners to Make Enquiries Concerning Public Matters', *Ordinances of the North-West Territories*, 1895, No. 2
British Columbia	'An Act to make provision for Inquiries concerning Public Matters', 1872, Chapter 12
Canada	'An Act respecting Inquiries concerning Public Matters', 1868, Chapter 38

CHRONOLOGICAL TABULATION OF
47 'GENERAL' ROYAL COMMISSIONS
IN CANADIAN EDUCATION

DATE	PROV.	SUBJECT
1854-55	N.B.	King's College
1861-62	Ont.	Affairs and financial conditions of Toronto University and University College
1882-83	Que.	School Trust in the City of Montreal
1893-93	N.B.	Charges relating to Bathurst schools
1895-95	Ont.	Discipline in the University of Toronto
1897-98	Ont.	Cost of text books
1901-03	Man.	Establishing an Agricultural College
1902-02	N.S.	Teaching English in French speaking districts
1905-06	Ont.	University of Toronto
1906-07	Ont.	Cost and prices of text books
1907-09	Man.	University of Manitoba
1908-10	P.E.I.	Education
1909-11	Que.	Creating a board of Roman Catholic school commissioners for the City of Montreal
1910-10	B.C.	Site for the University of British Columbia
1910-12	Man.	Industrial education
1910-13	Canada	Industrial training and technical education
1912-14	Sask.	Agricultural and industrial education, and other school matters
1914-15	Alta.	Degree-conferring powers to Calgary College
1919-20	N.B.	Salaries of teachers
1920-21	Ont.	University finance
1923-25	Man.	Education

1924-24	Que.	Powers of R.C. school commissioners of Montreal, education of Jewish children, financial situation of Protestant schools
1929-30	P.E.I.	Education
1931-32	N.B.	Education
1933-34	Nfld.	Curriculum of colleges and schools
1944-45	B.C.	Educational finance
1945-47	Man.	Adult education
1945-50	Ont.	Education
1947-48	B.C.	School taxation
1953-54	N.S.	Public school finance
1953-55	N.B.	Financing of schools
1956-56	Nfld.	School tax at Corner Brook
1957-58	N.S.	School construction
1957-58	Alta.	Teachers' salaries
1957-59	Man.	Education
1957-59	Alta.	Education
1958-60	B.C.	Education
1959-60	P.E.I.	Educational finance
1961-62	N.B.	Higher education
1961-66	Que.	Education
1963-64	N.S.	Safe transportation of school children
1964-65	P.E.I.	Higher education
1964-67	Nfld.	Education and youth
1967-72	Alta.	Educational planning
1971-74	N.S.	Education, public service, and provincial municipal relations
1973-73	Sask.	University organization and structure
1973-74	B.C.	Post secondary education

INDEX OF COMMISSIONS AND COMMITTEES

R1 - General Commissions   L - Legislative Committees
R2 - Related Commissions   D - Departmental Committees
R3 - Judicial Commissions   S - Special Committees

NEWFOUNDLAND

1	(L)	1890-91	Select Committee on the Present School System (Murray) / 3
2	(R2)	1933-33	British Royal Commission on the Future of Newfoundland (MacKenzie) / 4
3	(S)	1933-33	Report on Certain Aspects of the Educational System of Newfoundland (Richardson) / 5
4	(R1)	1933-34	Commission of Enquiry into the Present Curriculum of the Colleges and Schools in Newfoundland (Burke) / 6
5	(S)	1941-46	Supervisory Committee on Newfoundland Studies (Stuart) / 7
6	(D)	1946-46	National Convention Education Committee (Hollett) / 7
7	(R2)	1953-57	Royal Commission for the Preparation of the Case of the Government of Newfoundland for the Revision of the Financial Terms of Union (Lewis) / 8
8	(R1)	1956-56	Commission of Inquiry into the Questions Relating to the Imposition of the School Tax at Corner Brook (Abbott) / 9
9	(R2)	1957-58	Royal Commission on Newfoundland Finances Under the Terms of Union

			of Newfoundland with Canada (McNair) / 9
10	(R1)	1964–67	Royal Commission on Education and Youth (Warren) / 10
11	(R2)	1972–74	Royal Commission on Municipal Government in Newfoundland and Labrador (Whalen) / 11
12	(R2)	1972–74	Royal Commission on Labrador (Snowden) / 12
13	(R2)	1974–74	Commission of Enquiry into the St. John's Urban Region Study (Henley) / 14
14	(R3)	1974–75	Commission of Inquiry into the Closing of Upper Bullies School (Corbett) / 15
15	(D)	1977–78	Minister's Advisory Committee on Grade XII (Roebotham) / 16
16	(D)	1978–78	Task Force on Declining Enrolment in Education (Crocker/Riggs) / 16

NOVA SCOTIA

17	(L)	1825–25	Joint Committee of Council and Assembly on Education (Fairbanks) / 18
18	(L)	1848–48	Select Committee on Education (Young) / 19
19	(R1)	1902–02	Commission for the Purpose of Investigating the Best Methods of Teaching English in the Schools Situate in the French-speaking Districts of the Province (MacLellan) / 19
20	(S)	1921–22	Report on Education in the Maritime Provinces of Canada (Learned/Sills) / 20
21	(D)	1930–33	Committee on School Studies (Sexton) / 21
22	(D)	1938–39	Commission on the Larger School Unit (Munro) / 22
23	(R2)	1943–44	Royal Commission on Provincial Development and Rehabilitation (Dawson) / 22
24	(D)	–46	Commission to Investigate and Report

			on all Matters Affecting Teachers Salaries (MacGregor) / 23
25	(D)	1950-50	Commission on Teacher Education (Phillips) / 24
26	(S)	1952-54	Survey Project of the Joint Committee on Public Attitudes Towards Our Schools (Marshall) / 25
27	(R1)	1953-54	Royal Commission on Public School Finance in Nova Scotia (Pottier) / 25
28	(R1)	1957-58	Royal Commission on School Construction in Nova Scotia (Macnab) / 26
29	(S)	1963-64	Survey Report on Higher Education in Nova Scotia (MacKenzie) / 27
30	(R1)	1963-64	Royal Commission on the Safe Transportation of School Pupils (Rand) / 28
31	(D)	1969-69	Tribunal on Bilingual Higher Education in Nova Scotia (Munroe) / 28
32	(R3)	1969-69	Royal Commission on Section 3 of the Expired Collective Agreement between the Sydney School Board and the Nova Scotia Teachers' Union, Sydney Local (Moreira) / 29
33	(D)	1970-70	Survey of Digby School System (Keating) / 30
34	(D)	1970-71	Community College Planning Commission (Gaudet) / 31
35	(R1)	1971-74	Royal Commission on Education, Public Services and Provincial-Municipal Relations (Graham) / 32
36	(D)	1973-74	Committee on Pre-school Education and Social Development Programs (MacKenzie) / 33
37	(D)	1974-75	Federal-Provincial Study of Educational Technology in Nova Scotia (Duncan) / 34
38	(L)	1974-75	Select Committee on Education, Public Services and Provincial-Municipal Relations (Mooney) / 35
39	(L)	1974-75	Select Committee on the Nova Scotia Technical College Act (MacLean) / 36
40	(D)	1976-77	Cooperative Educational Survey (Walker) / 37

41 (R3) 1976-76 Royal Commission on the Board of
                   School Commissioners for the Town
                   of Mulgrave (Moseley) / 38

PRINCE EDWARD ISLAND

42 (L)   1834-34 Special Committee on Education
                   (Dalrymple) / 40
43 (L)   1839-40 Special Committee on Education (Rae)
                   / 41
44 (L)   1842-42 Joint Committee of Council and
                   Assembly on Education (MacDonald)
                   / 41
45 (L)   1851-52 Special Committee to Enquire into the
                   Expediency of Making Education Free
                   Throughout the Island (Coles) / 42
46 (R3) 1873-73 Commission to Investigate the Cases
                   of Teachers Whose Salaries were in
                   Dispute (Sinclair) / 43
47 (L)   1876-76 Special Legislative Committee to
                   Investigate the Workings of the
                   Education Law (Davies) / 43
48 (R1) 1908-10 Royal Commission on Education
                   (McLeod) / 44
49 (R1) 1929-29 Royal Commission on Education
                   (MacMillan) / 45
50 (R3) 1955-55 Commission on School Division No. 1
                   (Darby) / 46
51 (L)   1956-56 Select Standing Committee on Educa-
                   tion (MacKay) / 47
52 (L)   1957-57 Select Standing Committee on Educa-
                   tion (Large) / 48
53 (L)   1958-58 Select Standing Committee on Educa-
                   tion (Bell) / 49
54 (R1) 1959-60 Royal Commission on Educational
                   Finance and Related Problems in
                   Administration (LaZerte) / 49
55 (R1) 1964-65 Royal Commission on Higher Education
                   (Bonnell) / 50
56 (S)   1968-69 Province of Prince Edward Island:
                   Provincial-Municipal Fiscal Study
                   (Touche) / 51
57 (S)   1970-71 Committee on Teacher Education in
                   Prince Edward Island (Smitheram)

			/ 52
58	(D)	1973–74	Evaluation of Elementary and Secondary Education in Prince Edward Island (Smitheram) / 54

NEW BRUNSWICK

59	(L)	1837–37	Committee on Education (Street) / 55
60	(L)	1842–42	Committee on Education (Wilmot) / 55
61	(S)	1844–45	Governor Colebrook's Elaborate Inquiry into Education (Brown) / 56
62	(L)	1845–45	Select Committee on Education (Wilmot) / 57
63	(R1)	1854–54	Royal Commission on King's College (Gray) / 57
64	(R3)	1886–86	Commission of Inquiry into the Conduct and Management of the Institution for the Deaf and Dumb, Fredericton (Mitchell) / 58
65	(R1)	1893–93	Commission of Inquiry into Charges Relating to the Bathurst Schools and Other Schools in Gloucester County (Fraser) / 59
66	(R1)	1919–20	Commission in Respect to the Salaries of Teachers in the Public Schools of the Province (Carter) / 60
67	(R1)	1931–32	Royal Commission on Education (McFarland) / 61
68	(S)	1937–37	Educational Survey of King's County (Plenderleith) / 62
69	(D)	1937–	Committee on Curriculum and Text Books (Peacock) / 63
70	(R1)	1953–53	Royal Commission on the Financing of Schools in New Brunswick (MacKenzie) / 64
71	(R1)	1961–62	Royal Commission on Higher Education in New Brunswick (Deutsch) / 65
72	(R2)	1962–63	Royal Commission on Finance and Municipal Taxation (Byrne) / 66
73	(R2)	1962–63	Royal Commission on Metropolitan Saint John (Goldenberg) / 67
74	(D)	1966–67	Committee on the Financing of Higher Education in New Brunswick (Deutsch) / 68

75	(S)	1968-69	Study of Teacher Education and Train- ing (Duffie) / 69
76	(S)	1969-69	Study of High Education in the Atlantic Provinces for the 1970's (Crean/Ferguson/Somers) / 70
77	(D)	1970-71	Task Force on Social Development and Social Welfare (LeBlanc/Nutter) / 72
78	(D)	1971-72	Study Committee on Auxiliary Classes (MacLeod/Owens) / 73
79	(D)	1971-73	Committee on the Community Use of School Facilities (Ritchie) / 74
80	(S)	1972-73	Committee on Special Education (Kendall) / 75
81	(D)	1973-73	Committee to Examine Human Rights Education in New Brunswick (McNeilly) / 76
82	(D)	1973-73	Committee on Educational Planning (MacLeod/Pinet) / 78
83	(D)	1974-74	Task Force for Kindergarten Design (Smith/Roy) / 79
84	(S)	1974-75	Committee on Higher Education in the French Sector of New Brunswick (Lebel) / 80
85	(D)	1975-76	Task Force on School Food Service in New Brunswick (Johnston) / 81
86	(D)	1975-76	Task Force on Provincial Testing and Evaluation (Bruneau/Fontaine) / 82
87	(D)	1975-77	Task Force on School Libraries (Aiken) / 83
88	(D)	1976-76	Special Committee on Student Aid (Arsenault) / 84
89	(D)	1976-77	Task Force on School Year (Girouard/ Kingett) / 85

LOWER CANADA/QUEBEC

90	(L)	1787-90	Committee of the Council on the Subject of Promoting the Means of Education (Smith) / 87
91	(R2)	1835-36	Royal Commission for the Investigation of all Grievances Affecting His Majesty's Subjects of Lower Canada (Gosford) / 88

92	(R2)	1838–39	Royal Commission on the Affairs of British North America (Durham) / 89
93	(L)	1853–53	Select Committee of the Legislative Assembly, Appointed to Enquire into the State of Education and the Working of the School Laws in Lower Canada (Sicotte) / 90
94	(R1)	1882–83	Commission of Inquiry into the School Trust in the City of Montreal (Coursol) / 92
95	(R2)	1883–83	Commission of Inquiry in All Departments of the Government / 93
96	(D)	1891–91	Committee on Agricultural Education (Ouimet) / 93
97	(R1)	1909–11	Commission of Inquiry into the Possibility of Creating A Board of Roman Catholic School Commissioners for the City of Montreal and its *Banlieue* (Dandurand) / 94
98	(R1)	1924–24	Commission of Inquiry into the Extension of the Powers of the Board of Roman Catholic School Commissioners of Montreal, the Education of Jewish Children in Protestant Schools or in Others, and the Financial Situation of the Protestant Schools of Verdun (Gouin) / 94
99	(S)	1937–38	Quebec Protestant Education Survey (Hepburn) / 96
100	(D)	1951–53	Sous-comité de Coordination de l'Enseignment à ses Divers Dégrés au Comité Catholique du Conseil de l'Instruction Publique (Désaulniers) / 97
101	(R2)	1953–56	Royal Commission of Inquiry on Constitutional Matters (Tremblay) / 98
102	(D)	1960–61	Comité d'Etude sur l'Enseignment Agricole et Agronomique (Regis) / 99
103	(D)	1961–62	Comité d'Etude sur l'Enseignment Technique et Professionnel (Tremblay) / 100

104 (R1) 1961–63 Royal Commission of Inquiry on Education in the Province of Quebec
(Parent) / 101

105 (D) 1962–64 Comité d'Etude sur l'Education des
Adultes (Ryan) / 104

106 (D) 1962–64 Comité d'Etude sur les Loisirs,
l'Education Physique et les
Sports (Bélisle) / 104

107 (R2) 1966–68 Commission d'Enquête sur l'Enseignement des Arts au Québec (Rioux)
/ 105

108 (D) –67 Comité Interministériel sur
l'Enseignement des Langues aux
Néo-Canadiens (Gauthier) / 107

109 (D) 1967–68 Conseil de Restructuration Scolaire
de l'Ile de Montréal (Pagé) / 108

110 (R3) 1968–68 Commission d'Enquête sur le Differend
entre les Parties a la Negociation
... dans le Secteur Scolaire
(Simard) /109

111 (R2) 1968–72 Commission of Inquiry on the Position
of the French Language and on
Language Rights in Quebec
(Gendron) / 110

112 (D) 1970–71 Commission d'Etude de la Propagande
Politique dans l'Enseignement
(Dion) / 111

113 (D) 1972–73 Comité Interministériel pour
entreprendre L'Etude du Probleme
de la Distribution des Imprimès,
Périodiques et Livres de Poche
(Grandpré) / 112

114 (D) 1972–75 Commission d'Etude de la Tâche des
Enseignants de l'Elementaire et
du Secondaire (Faucher) / 112

115 (D) 1972–76 Comité Provincial de l'Enfance
Inadaptée (Baron) / 113

116 (D) 1973–75 Commission d'Etude sur la Classification des Enseignants (Laberge)
/ 114

117 (D) 1973–75 Conseil Supérieur de l'Education sur
l'Etat et les Besoins de
l'Enseignement Collégial
(Beauchemin) / 115

118 (D) 1974–74 Comité d'Etude sur la Recherche et

			l'Enseignement en Technologie du Bois (Poliquin) / 116
119	(D)	1974-74	Comité d'Etude sur la Création de l'Institut des Sports du Québec (Bouchard) / 117
120	(D)	1974-75	Groupe de Travail sur l'Education Physique et le Sport à l'Ecole (Beauregard) / 118
121	(D)	1975-75	Comité d'Etude sur la Réadaptation des Enfants et Adolescents Placés en Centre d'Accueil (Batshaw) / 119
122	(D)	1976-77	Groupe de Travail sur l'Institut d'Histoire et de Civilisation du Quebéc (Frégault) / 120
123	(D)	1976-77	Comité d'Etude sur la Situation des Enseignants Religieux (Monfette) / 121
124	(D)	1977-78	Commission d'Etude sur les Universités (Angers) / 122

UPPER CANADA/ONTARIO

125	(L)	1835-36	Committee on Education (Duncombe) / 124
126	(R2)	1839-40	Commission of Inquiry into the Public Departments of the Province (Sullivan/McCaul) / 125
127	(D)	1844-46	Ryersons' Report on a System of Public Elementary Instruction for Upper Canada (Ryerson) / 126
128	(S)	1848-51	Commission of Inquiry into the Affairs of King's College University and Upper Canada College (Workman) / 127
129	(R1)	1861-62	Royal Commission on Affairs and Financial Conditions of Toronto University and University College (Patton) / 128
130	(D)	1866-68	Special Report on Popular Education in Europe and the United States (Ryerson) / 129
131	(L)	1868-69	Select Committee to Enquire into the Management and Working of the

			Education Department (Cameron) / 130
132	(D)	1873-74	Provincial Farm Commission (Christie) / 130
133	(L)	1874-74	Legislative Committee to Enquire into the Management of the Agricultural College and Model Farm (Bethune) / 131
134	(R3)	1877-77	Commission of Inquiry into Charges Against the Central Committee of Examiners of the Education Department (Patterson) / 131
135	(D)	1881-82	Commission to Investigate Certain Charges Against Dr. Samuel May of the Education Department (Senkler) / 132
136	(R3)	1884-	Commission of Inquiry into an Incident at the Agricultural College (Winchester) / 133
137	(D)	1887-87	Special Inquiry into Conditions of the French Schools in the United Counties of Prescott and Russell (Dufort) / 133
138	(R3)	1888-	Commission of Inquiry into the Fire at the Government Farm (Blue/ Winchester) / 134
139	(D)	1888-89	Survey of Leading Schools of Technology in the United States (Ross) / 135
140	(D)	1889-89	Special Inquiry into the Schools in the Counties of Prescott, Russell, Essex, Kent, and Simcoe (Tilley) / 135
141	(D)	1893-93	Special Inquiry into the Schools in the Counties of Prescott, Russell, Essex, Kent, and Simcoe (Tilley) / 137
142	(R3)	1893-93	Commission of Inquiry as to the Ontario Agricultural College and Experimental Farm (Winchester) / 138
143	(D)	1895-96	Special Inquiry into the Separate Schools of Ottawa (Scott) / 138
144	(R1)	1895-95	Commission of Inquiry into the Discipline and Other Matters in the

			University of Toronto (Taylor) / 139
145	(R1)	1897–98	Commission of Inquiry into Cost of Text Books (Morgan) / 141
146	(R3)	1905–05	Commission of Inquiry into the Matters Referred to in a Resolution of the Senate of the University of Toronto (Meredith) / 141
147	(R1)	1905–06	Royal Commission on the University of Toronto (Flavelle) / 143
148	(R1)	1906–07	Commission of Inquiry into Cost and Prices of Text Books (Crothers) / 144
149	(R3)	1906–07	Commission of Inquiry to Investigate the Workings of the Blind Institute at Brantford, and the Deaf and Dumb Institute at Belleville (Snow) / 145
150	(D)	1909–	Survey of Technical Education in the United States and Europe (Seath) / 145
151	(D)	1910–12	Special Inquiry Into the English-French Schools, Public and Separate, in the Counties of Essex and Kent and Elsewhere in the Province (Merchant) / 146
152	(D)	1913–13	Survey of the Systems of Industrial and Technical Instruction in Europe (Merchant) / 147
153	(R2)	1915–17	Commission of Inquiry into Medical Education in Ontario (Hodgins) / 147
154	(R3)	1916–17	Commission of Inquiry into Certain Complaints Against the Internal Discipline and Management of the Ontario School for the Blind, Brantford (Gash) / 148
155	(R2)	1917–19	Commission of Inquiry into the Care and Control of the Mentally Defective and Feeble-Minded in Ontario (Hodgins) / 149
156	(R3)	1918–	Commission of Inquiry into the Building Department of the Board of Education of the City of Toronto (Lennox) / 150

157	(R3)	1920–21	Commission of Inquiry into the Administration, Management, Conduct, Discipline, Equipment, and Welfare of the Victoria Industrial School (Waugh) / 151
158	(R1)	1920–21	Royal Commission on University Finance (Cody) / 152
159	(R3)	1921–	Commission of Inquiry into Examination Irregularities (Putnam) / 153
160	(L)	1922–23	Special Committee to Investigate the Organization and Administration of the University of Toronto (Drury) / 153
161	(R3)	1924–	Commission of Inquiry into the Building Department of the Ottawa School Board (McDonald) / 154
162	(R3)	1925–	Commission of Inquiry into Affairs of the Oshawa Board of Education (Ruddy) / 155
163	(D)	1925–27	Special Inquiry into Those Schools in the Province Attended by Pupils Who Speak the French Language (Merchant) / 155
164	(R3)	1926–27	Commission of Inquiry into Ottawa Collegiate Conditions (Orde) / 156
165	(D)	1935–38	Committee to Investigate the Costs of Education in Ontario (McArthur) / 157
166	(R1)	1945–50	Royal Commission on Education (Hope) / 158
167	(D)	1961–62	Minister's Committee on the Training of Secondary School Teachers (Patten) / 160
168	(L)	1962–63	Select Committee on Manpower Training (Simonett) / 161
169	(R2)	1963–67	Ontario Committee on Taxation (Smith) / 162
170	(R2)	1963–65	Royal Commission on Metropolitan Toronto (Goldenberg) / 164
171	(D)	1964–64	Grade 13 Study Committee (Hamilton) / 165
172	(L)	1964–67	Select Committee on Youth (Apps) / 166
173	(D)	1964–66	Minister's Committee on the Training of Elementary School Teachers

			(MacLeod) / 167
174	(D)	1965-68	Committee on Aims and Objectives of Education (Hall/Dennis) / 169
175	(S)	1965-66	Commission to Study the Development of Graduate Programs in Ontario Universities (Spinks) / 172
176	(D)	1966-69	Minister's Committee on Religious Education (MacKay) / 173
177	(D)	1967-72	Task Force on School Health Services (Webb) / 175
178	(D)	1967-68	Committee on French Language Schools in Ontario (Bériault) / 176
179	(S)	1968-69	Commission on the Government of the University of Toronto (Lynch/ Webster) / 177
180	(D)	1969-72	Commission on Post-Secondary Education in Ontario (Wright/Davis) / 179
181	(D)	1969-70	Study Committee on Recreation Services in Ontario (Secord) / 180
182	(D)	1970-73	Task Force on Industrial Training (Dymond) / 181
183	(D)	1970-72	Committee of Inquiry into Negotiation Procedures concerning Elementary and Secondary Schools of Ontario (Reville) / 182
184	(R2)	1970-72	Royal Commission on Book Publishing (Rohmer) / 183
185	(D)	1971-72	Committee on Year-Round Use of Schools (Waldrum/Mannings) / 184
186	(D)	1971-72	Committee on the Costs of Education (McEwan) / 185
187	(D)	1971-72	Ministerial Commission on French Language Secondary Education (Symons) / 187
188	(D)	1971-73	Educational Resources Allocation System Task Force (Stephen) / 188
189	(L)	1971-73	Select Committee on Economic and Cultural Nationalism (Rowe) / 188
190	(L)	1971-73	Select Committee on the Utilization of Educational Facilities (McIlvene) / 190
191	(D)	1972-72	Task Force on the School Year (Fisher) / 191
192	(D)	1972-73	Study Team on the Sharing or

			Transferring of School Facilities (Christie/Marrese) / 192
193	(D)	1973–74	Ministerial Committee on the Teaching of French (Gillin) / 193
194	(D)	1973–74	Ministerial Commission on the Organization and Financing of the Public and Secondary School Systems in Metropolitan Toronto (Lowes) / 194
195	(R2)	1974–77	Royal Commission on Metropolitan Toronto (Robarts) / 195
196	(D)	1974–76	Task Force on the Educational Needs of Native Peoples of Ontario / 196
197	(D)	1975–77	Interim Committee on Financial Assistance for Students (Dupré/ Sisco) / 197
198	(D)	1975–75	Study of Women and Ontario Universities (McIntyre) / 198
199	(R2)	1975–77	Royal Commission on Violence in the Communications Industry (LaMarsh) / 199
200	(R3)	1976–76	Royal Commission of Inquiry on Algoma University College (White-side) / 200
201	(R2)	1976–77	Commission on the Reform of Property Taxation in Ontario (Blair) / 201
202	(D)	1976–77	Work Group on Evaluation and Reporting (Foisy-Moon) / 202
203	(D)	1977–78	Commission on Declining School Enrolments in Ontario (Jackson) / 203

MANITOBA

204	(R1)	1901–03	Commission of Inquiry into the Wisdom and Advisability of Establishing and Maintaining an Agricultural College (Patrick) / 205
205	(R1)	1907–09	Royal Commission on the University of Manitoba (Aikins) / 206
206	(R1)	1910–12	Commission of Inquiry into Aims and Methods in Industrial Education (Coldwell) / 207
207	(D)	1915–16	Special Report on Bilingual Schools

			in Manitoba (Newcombe) / 207
208	(R3)	1916–17	Commission of Inquiry into all Matters Pertaining to the Manitoba Agricultural College (Galt) / 208
209	(D)	1919–	Commission on Status and Salaries of Teachers (Hill) / 209
210	(S)	1923–23	Special Commission on the Possibility of Readjusting the Relations of the Higher Institutions of Learning (Learned) / 210
211	(R1)	1923–24	Royal Commission on Education (Murray) / 210
212	(R3)	1932–33	Commission of Inquiry into Impairment or Depletion of University of Manitoba Funds (Turgeon) / 211
213	(L)	1934–35	Select Committee to Enquire into the Administration and the Financing of the Public Educational System of the Province (Hoey) / 212
214	(S)	1937–38	Special Report on Education in Manitoba (Woods) / 213
215	(L)	1944–45	Special Select Committee on Education / (Schultz) / 214
216	(R1)	1945–47	Royal Commission on Adult Education (Trueman) / 216
217	(L)	1946–48	Select Special Committee Appointed to Study and Report on All Phases of the Pension Scheme for Teachers (Dryden) / 217
218	(R2)	1955–59	Greater Winnipeg Investigation Commission (Bodie) / 218
219	(D)	1956–56	Survey Covering Costs and Other Factors in Connection with the Establishment of a Dental College in the Province of Manitoba (Paynter) / 218
220	(D)	1957–58	Study Committee on Physical Education and Recreation (Kennedy) / 219
221	(R1)	1957–59	Royal Commission on Education (MacFarlane) / 220
222	(D)	1962–67	Survey of Reading (Sibley) / 221
223	(R2)	1963–64	Royal Commission on Local Government Organization and Finance (Michener) / 222

224	(S)	1963–65	Study of Education of Handicapped Children in Manitoba (Christianson) / 223
225	(D)	1966–70	Local Government Boundaries Commission (Smellie) / 224
226	(D)	1969–73	Core Committee on the Reorganization of the Secondary School (Bullock) / 225
227	(D)	1972–73	Task Force on Text Book Evaluation (Cramer) / 226
228	(D)	1972–73	Task Force on Post-Secondary Education in Manitoba (Oliver) / 227
229	(S)	1977–78	Task Force on Government Organization and Economy (Spivak/Riley) / 229

SASKATCHEWAN

230	(R2)	1906–07	Royal Commission on Municipal Organization (Smith/Ferguson) / 231
231	(R3)	1909–09	Commission of Inquiry into Morang Text Book Contract (Wetmore) / 231
232	(R1)	1912–13	Royal Commission on Agricultural and Industrial Education, Consolidation of Schools, Training and Supply of Teachers, Courses of Study, Physical and Moral Education (McColl) / 232
233	(S)	1917–17	General Survey and Investigation of the Incidence of Taxation in the Urban Municipalities of Saskatchewan (Haig) / 233
234	(S)	1917–18	Survey of Education in the Province of Saskatchewan (Foght) / 234
235	(R2)	1921–22	Commission of Inquiry to Study the Public Revenues Tax and to Inquire Generally into the Matter of Equalization of Assessments for Purposes of Provincial Taxation in the Municipalities of the Province, Urban and Rural (Armstrong) / 235
236	(L)	1923–23	Select Committee to Investigate the Advisability of Establishing the

257	(R1)	1973-73	Royal Commission on University Organization and Structure (Hall) / 255
258	(D)	1973-74	Advisory Committee on the Education of the Deaf (Drozda) / 256
259	(D)	1973-75	Advisory Committee on Student Evaluation (Nakonechny) / 257
260	(D)	1975-76	Advisory Committee on School Law (Amundrud) / 258
261	(D)	1976-76	College Mathieu Review Committee (Ready) / 259
262	(D)	1977-77	Committee on Service Funding of the College of Medicine, University of Saskatchewan (Adams) / 260

ALBERTA

263	(L)	1911-11	Committee on Revision of the School Curriculum for the Province / 262
264	(R1)	1914-15	Commission of Inquiry to Consider the Granting of Degree-Conferring Powers to Calgary College (Falconer) / 262
265	(D)	1921-	General Committee on the Revision of the Elementary School Curriculum (McNally) / 263
266	(D)	1926-28	Advisory Committee on Taxation (Tory) / 264
267	(D)	1933-35	Alberta Taxation Inquiry Board on Provincial and Municipal Taxation (Percival) / 265
268	(R2)	1933-36	Commission of Inquiry into Rehabilitation of the Metis (Ewing) / 266
269	(L)	1934-35	Legislative Committee Appointed to Make a Comprehensive Survey and Study of Education in the Rural Districts of Alberta (Baker) / 267
270	(D)	1941-42	University of Alberta Survey Committee (Parlee) / 268
271	(D)	1943-44	Subcommittee on Education and Vocational Training (Newton) / 270
272	(R2)	1947-48	Royal Commission on Taxation (Judge) / 271

273	(R2)	1954-56	Royal Commission on the Metropolitan Development of Calgary and Edmonton (McNally) / 272
274	(R1)	1957-58	Royal Commission on Teachers' Salaries (Blackstock) / 273
275	(R1)	1957-59	Royal Commission on Education (Cameron) / 274
276	(D)	1958-59	Hutterite Investigation Committee (Frame/Hayes) / 275
277	(D)	1960-61	Committee on Alberta School Bus Operations (Lawrence) / 276
278	(D)	1961-66	Survey Committee on Higher Education in Alberta (Hinman) / 277
279	(L)	1964-65	Special Committee on Collective Bargaining between School Trustees and Teachers (McKinnon/ Ludwig) / 278
280	(D)	1964-65	School Construction Inquiry (Badun) / 279
281	(R3)	1965-66	Public Inquiry into the Appointment by the Minister of Education of an Official Trustee for Fort Vermilion School Division #52 (Buchanan) / 280
282	(L)	1966-67	Special Committee on Centralization and Consolidation of Schools (Lamothe) / 281
283	(R2)	1966-67	Royal Commission on Juvenile Delinquency (Quigley) / 282
284	(R1)	1967-72	Commission on Educational Planning (Worth) / 283
285	(S)	1969-70	Special Committee on Assessment and Taxation (Brown) / 285
286	(D)	1971-72	Task Force on Intercultural Education (Ledgerwood) / 285
287	(R3)	1972-72	Red Deer College Inquiry (Byrne) / 287
288	(D)	1972-73	Inquiry into School Affairs: Bonnyville Area (Swift) / 287
289	(D)	1974-75	Study Group on Northland School Division (Swift) / 288
290	(S)	1975-77	Alberta School Discipline Study (Clarke) / 289
291	(D)	1975-76	Project North Task Force (Dumont) / 290

292 (D)   1976-77   Task Force on the Evaluation of
                       Standardized Achievement Tests
                       for Alberta Schools (Mott) / 291
293 (D)   1976-79   Minister's Advisory Committee on
                       Student Achievement (Hrabi) / 292

BRITISH COLUMBIA

294 (L)   1875-76   Select Committee to Examine the
                       Workings of the 1872 School Act
                       (Robertson) / 294
295 (L)   1876-76   Report of Select Committee on Public
                       Schools Concerning the Cache
                       Creek Boarding School (Davie)
                       / 295
296 (R3)   1905-06   Commission of Inquiry into the South
                       Park School Drawing Books (Lamp-
                       man) / 296
297 (R3)   1908-   Commission of Inquiry into Charges
                       Against the Department of Educa-
                       tion by Miss Gertrude Donovan of
                       Victoria (Robertson) / 297
298 (R1)   1910-10   Commission to Select a Site for the
                       University of British Columbia
                       (Weldon) / 297
299 (R3)   1912-13   Commission of Inquiry into Municipal
                       Matters of the Corporation of the
                       District of South Vancouver
                       (Crehan) / 299
300 (R2)   1912-12   Commission of Inquiry into Matters
                       Relating to the Sect of Doukho-
                       bors in the Province of British
                       Columbia (Blakemore) / 300
301 (R3)   1913-14   Commission of Inquiry into the
                       Affairs of the Present Board and
                       Past Boards of School Trustees of
                       the City of Vancouver (Alexander)
                       / 300
302 (R3)   1913-13   Commission of Inquiry into the
                       Affairs of the Present Board and
                       Past Boards of School Trustees of
                       the City of Nelson and Complaints
                       Regarding the Principal of Nelson
                       Public School (Lampman) / 301

303	(D)	1924–25	Survey of the School System (Putnam/Weir) / 302
304	(D)	1929–30	Special Commission to Inquire into the Sale of Government Lands in the University Subdivision (Daykin) / 303
305	(S)	1932–	Special Inquiry into the Affairs of the University (Lampman) / 304
306	(S)	1932–32	Committee Appointed by the Government to Investigate the Finances of British Columbia (Kidd) / 304
307	(D)	1934–35	Commission on School Finance in British Columbia (King) / 305
308	(R3)	1943–43	Commission of Inquiry into the Administration and Methods of Discipline of Mount View High School (Wilson) / 306
309	(R1)	1944–45	Commission of Inquiry into Educational Finance (Cameron) / 307
310	(R2)	1946–47	Commission on Provincial-Municipal Relations in British Columbia (Goldenberg) / 307
311	(R1)	1947–48	Commission on School Taxation (Maclean) / 308
312	(R2)	1947–48	Royal Commission on Doukhobor Affairs (Sullivan) / 309
313	(S)	1950–52	Special Committee on Doukhobor Affairs (Hawthorn) / 310
314	(R1)	1958–60	Royal Commission on Education (Chant) / 311
315	(S)	–62	Survey of Higher Education in British Columbia and a Plan for the Future (Macdonald) / 313
316	(D)	1963–64	Survey Committee on School Libraries (Levirs) / 314
317	(S)	1967–68	BCTF Commission on Education (MacKenzie) / 315
318	(D)	1968–69	Committee on School Utilization (Canty) / 316
319	(L)	1968–68	Select Standing Committee on Social Welfare and Education (Tisdalle) / 317
320	(D)	1968–69	Advisory Committee on Inter-University Relations (Perry) / 318

321	(L)	1971-71	Select Standing Committee on Social Welfare and Education (Tisdalle) / 318
322	(L)	1972-72	Select Standing Committee on Social Welfare and Education (Tisdalle) / 319
323	(D)	1973-74	Committee on Teacher Education (Bremer) / 320
324	(D)	1973-73	Committee to Examine Services for the Communicatively Impaired of British Columbia (Gilbert) / 321
325	(L)	1973-73	Select Standing Committee on Social Welfare and Education (Brown) / 322
326	(R1)	1973-74	Royal Commission on Post Secondary Education in the Kootenay Region (McTaggert-Cowan) / 323
327	(D)	1973-74	Committee on University Government (Bremer/Young) / 324
328	(D)	1973-74	Task Force on the Community College (L'Estrange) / 325
329	(D)	1973-74	Study Committee on the Small Senior Secondary School (Reid) / 327
330	(D)	1974-74	Jericho Hill School Inquiry (Chud) / 328
331	(D)	1974-75	Survey Committee on Community Colleges in the Lower Mainland of British Columbia (Marsh) / 329
332	(D)	1975-75	Study of Research and Development in British Columbia (Pedersen) / 330
333	(L)	1975-75	Select Standing Committee on Health, Education, and Human Resources (Brown) / 331
334	(R2)	1975-76	Royal Commission of Inquiry on Property Assessment and Taxation (McMath) / 332
335	(D)	1975-75	Commission of Public Inquiry in the Matter of Vancouver Community College (Suart) / 333
336	(D)	1976-76	Commission on University Programs in Non-Metropolitan Areas (Winegard) / 334
337	(D)	1976-76	Committee on Continuing and Community Education in British Columbia (Farris) / 335

338	(D)	1976-77	Advisory Commission on Vocational, Technical, and Trades Training in British Columbia (Goard) / 336
339	(D)	1977-78	Committee on the Education and Training of Teachers (McGregor) / 337

FEDERAL INQUIRIES

340	(R1)	1910-11	Royal Commission on Industrial Training and Technical Education (Robertson) / 339
341	(R2)	1928-29	Royal Commission on Radio Broadcasting (Aird) / 340
342	(R2)	1937-40	Royal Commission on Dominion-Provincial Relations (Rowell/Sirois) / 341
343	(R2)	1949-51	Royal Commission on National Development in the Arts, Letters and Sciences (Massey) / 342
344	(D)	1954-55	Survey of Social and Economic Conditions of the Indians of British Columbia (Hawthorn) / 344
345	(D)	1955-56	Survey of the Educational Facilities and Requirements of the Indians in Canada (Brown) / 345
346	(R2)	1955-57	Royal Commission on Canada's Economic Prospects (Gordon) / 345
347	(R2)	1955-57	Royal Commission on Broadcasting (Fowler) / 347
348	(L)	1959-61	Joint Committee on Indian Affairs (Gladstone/Grenier) / 348
349	(D)	1960-60	Committee on Education for the Yukon Territory (Brown/Jonason) / 349
350	(R2)	1960-61	Royal Commission on Publications (O'Leary) / 351
351	(R2)	1963-65	Royal Commission on Bilingualism and Biculturalism (Dunton/Laurendeau) / 352
352	(S)	1963-65	Study of University Government in Canada (Duff/Berdahl) / 354
353	(S)	1964-65	Commission on Financing Higher Education in Canada (Bladen) / 355
354	(D)	1964-65	Committee on Broadcasting (Fowler) / 356